IMAGES
of America

AROUND KEESEVILLE

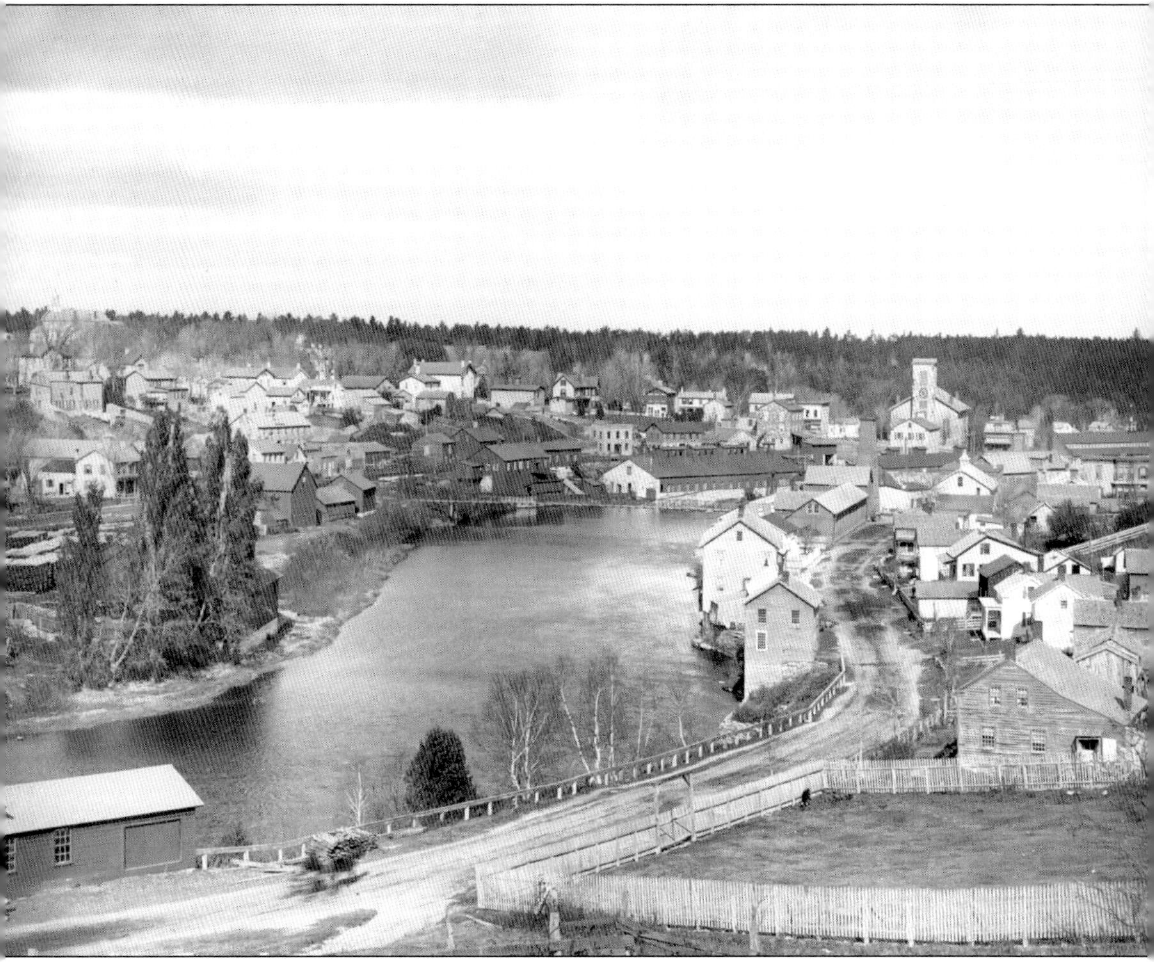

This photograph taken from a hilltop shows Keeseville, New York, as it appeared in 1890, in its industrial heyday. River Street is on the left, running alongside the Ausable River, and the suspension bridge in the center of the photograph. (Courtesy of Anderson Falls Heritage Society.)

ON THE COVER: A horse and cart are seen trotting down Front Street in Keeseville, New York, in this photograph dated between 1882 and 1899. In the left corner, the Methodist church is next to the row of businesses known as Kingsland's Block. While the buildings still exist today, the overhanging frames and awnings that were originally put up in 1866 were gone by 1949. (Courtesy Anderson Falls Heritage Society.)

IMAGES
of America

AROUND KEESEVILLE

Kyle M. Page
with the Anderson Falls Heritage Society

ARCADIA
PUBLISHING

ISBN 978-1-4671-2325-9

Published by Arcadia Publishing
Charleston, South Carolina

Printed in the United States of America

Library of Congress Control Number: 2014951591

For all general information, please contact Arcadia Publishing:
Telephone 843-853-2070
Fax 843-853-0044
E-mail sales@arcadiapublishing.com
For customer service and orders:
Toll-Free 1-888-313-2665

Visit us on the Internet at www.arcadiapublishing.com

To all those past, present, and future who preserve the history of this beautiful community and in the memory of Dennis Lewis, one of the finest historians I ever had the privilege of knowing, rest in peace my friend. Also, I dedicate this book to the memory of my father, Robert F. Page, and mother, Leona D. Page, who gave me the amazing gifts of a passion for words and history that have defined who I am today.

Contents

ACKNOWLEDGMENTS

No book is a completely solo project, and this book was certainly no exception. This book would not have been even remotely possible without the enormous support and resources of the Anderson Falls Heritage Society. In particular I wish to thank Sandi Connell, Betty Brelia, and Colin McDonough for their enthusiastic support, time, and tireless effort to help with this book.

I thank my editor at Arcadia Publishing, Sharon McAllister, for her belief in this project as well as her tremendous patience and advice. Heritage Printing in Plattsburgh, New York, was wonderful with its professional work in scanning the cover of this book.

Numerous historians before me inspired me and helped form my knowledge on the subject of Keeseville and surrounding areas. I spent an amazing year reading various works by these fantastic authors to build my knowledge of this wonderful area. I could not have written a word without their amazing knowledge, in particular George "Speedy" Arnold, Stephen Engelhart, Marjorie Lansing Porter, Dr. Gordon Pollard, Maurice Turner, and Virginia Westbrook.

Finally, I thank the love of my life, Darcy Hernandez, who was an amazing font of patience, support, assistance, joy, and love throughout this entire project. Unless otherwise noted, all photographs are the property of the Anderson Falls Heritage Society and are used with their kind permission.

INTRODUCTION

December 2014 marked the formal end the incorporation of Keeseville, New York, as the village dissolved into the townships of Ausable and Chesterfield. Certainly, it is an end, but it is also the beginning for a community that has often been beset by challenges, leaving behind a rich history to learn, follow, and treasure.

Originally, early explorers came up from downstate New York to chart and settle in the vast wilderness now known as the Adirondacks, an area of tremendous beauty rich in natural resources.

Robert Hoyle is considered the first settler, and he moved here around 1806, establishing a home and tavern. The center of the community was established by Capt. Jonathan Bigelow, who built a dam and sawmill. At this same time, Zephaniah Platt was settling in the area of Plattsburgh. One of his assistants, John Anderson, explored a little south, discovering the enormous breadth of natural resources in timber and iron ore, as well as the tremendous natural power of the Ausable River, its chasm, and falls. Ownership at first went to Hoyle and Anderson. Hoyle sold his rights to Anderson for a small raft and went on to Quebec, Canada, leaving Anderson the sole owner. He quickly named the area Anderson Falls. In 1817, John and Richard Keese from the nearby Quaker settlement went into business with Anderson, forming the Keese, Anderson, Keese firm. Soon business was booming with timber and iron. At this time, the town was forming, and Keeseville was born.

Keeseville flourished with the abundance of timber and iron. Factories and stores sprang up along both sides of the Ausable River. Over the decades, numerous stores would open and close. Ownership of the principle businesses would change hands. Names sprang up on building fronts from Keese to Prescott to Kingsland, each heralding a unique quality to the village.

Bridges were built and collapsed until the 1850s, and the three bridges built in the 1870s have withstood the elements and time. The stone Arch Bridge, iron truss bridge, and suspension bridge still stand in the Keeseville community and are designated as National Historic Civil Engineering Landmarks.

Today, Keeseville is home to numerous small businesses, a library, a few restaurants, and motels. Throughout its history, Keeseville has been home to an opera house, numerous large factories and mills, many businesses, and even a precursor of a mall with the Kingsland Square Block.

In the 1870s, businessmen pooled their resources and built a small-scale railroad, called the peanut railroad, to transport the heavy timber and finished iron products from the factories in Keeseville to the docks and nearby Canadian Pacific Railroad line at Port Kent, New York. Today, a few traces in backyards marking the former tracks, a rusted-out water tower standing above the 10th tee at Harmony Golf Course, and a Keesville restaurant in the building that used to be the station are all that remains of the railroad's former glory.

Villagers were beset by vicious North Country snowstorms and floods. Worse yet were devastating fires that destroyed bridges, factories, and buildings several times. Villagers were quick to rebuild and learn from their experiences. Keeseville was the home of one of the first volunteer fire departments in the United States.

What started as the naturally beautiful, wild region of the Adirondacks, with expanses of timber, hills plentiful with iron ore, and diverse bodies of water, became a booming industrial community before turning into the modern sleepy, quaint community it is today. Keeseville is a treasure trove of American history.

One

Village of Keeseville and Townships of Ausable and Chesterfield

The center point of Keeseville is the Ausable River, as the power provided by the rushing waters is what drew the explorers. The river creates an important border for the area. Keeseville lies on the edge of Clinton County to the north and Essex County to the south, with the river dividing the two. Keeseville was the village on both sides of the water, but the township of Ausable is on the west side of the river, while the township of Chesterfield is on the east side. While the region's predominant factories and stores grew on the banks of the Ausable River in Keeseville, numerous outlying areas grew to support the enterprises. Port Kent grew as a transportation point, as it abutted the shores of Lake Champlain and was a stop for the Canadian Pacific Railroad as it snaked from Montreal to New York City. Clintonville was the mining area for much of the iron ore that was turned into horse nails and other products at the mills in Keeseville. Harkness and Port Douglas grew as communities for settlers. Ausable Chasm and Poke-O-Moonshine were attractions with their natural beauty. In the middle of all this was the village of Keeseville and its rapid growth in the 1800s.

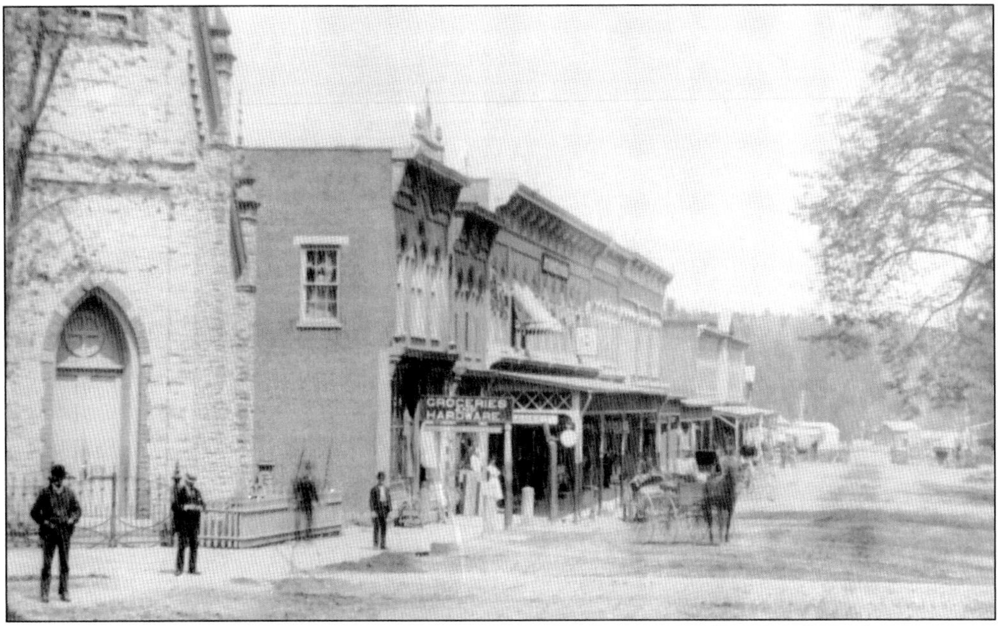

This photograph taken before the 1870s shows Front Street in Keeseville. Thanks to the invention of the horse nail machine by Daniel Dodge, Keeseville was in the midst of a second wind of its industrial age. Numerous businesses were opening and closing in the stretch of buildings known as Kingsland's Block, including active hotels and an opera house.

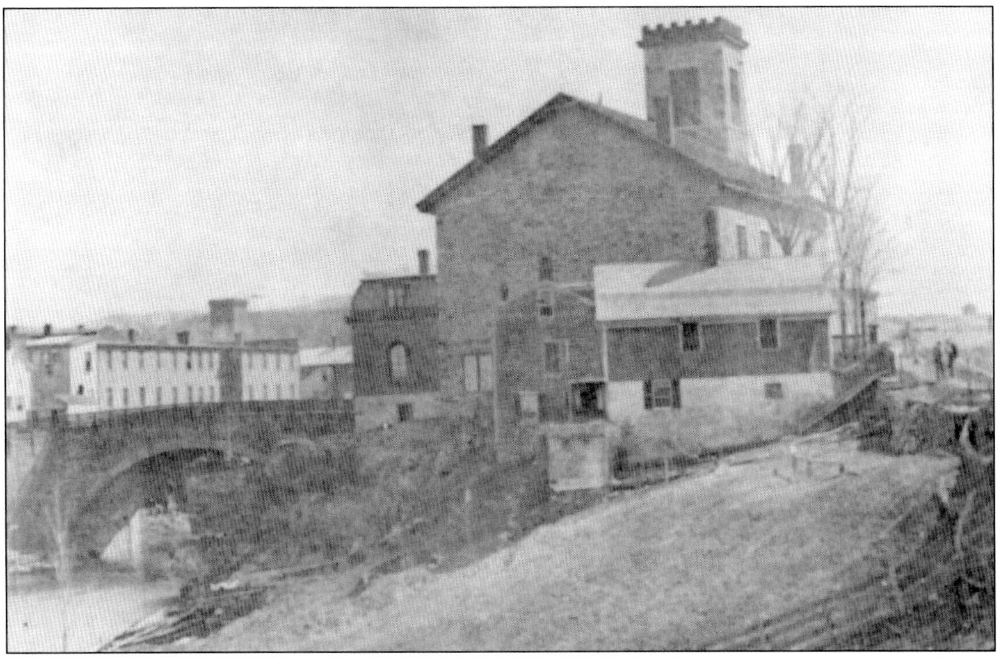

This photograph was taken at the Bigelow House, which was part of the Underground Railroad. Pictured here is the Keeseville National Bank standing immediately to the right of the Arch Bridge, with the Congregational Presbyterian church towering next to it. Behind the Arch Bridge, the backs of the Kingsland's Block buildings on Front Street can be seen. The dirt road in the foreground is now North Ausable Street.

On the opposite side of the street from the Congregational Presbyterian church and Keeseville National Bank is the entrance to the horse nail factory and the Grange Hall as seen in the mid-1870s. Of particular note is the eagle statue on the top of the horse nail factory. Originally installed in 1848, from wing to wing the wooden eagle spanned about six feet. It was taken down, repaired, and regilded in 1875, removed in 1923, and shipped to Massachusetts.

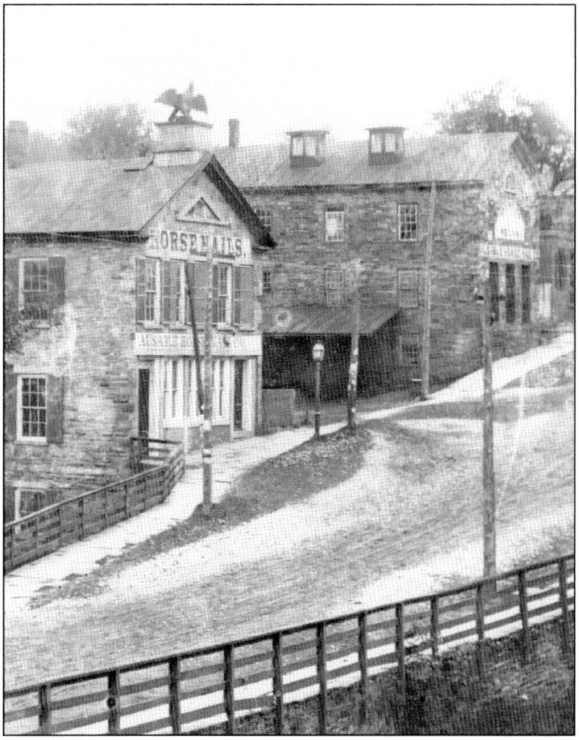

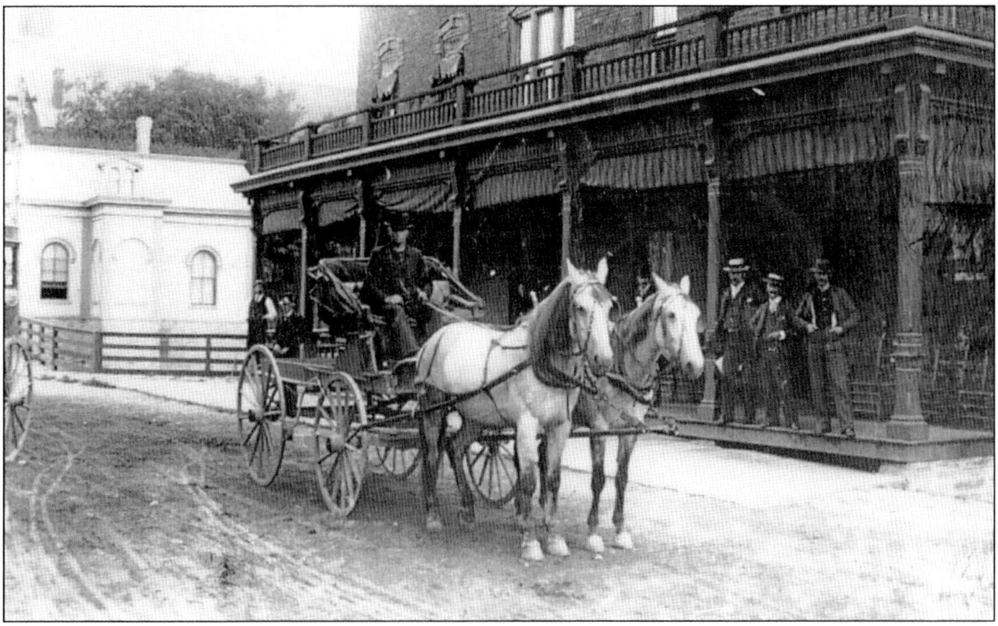

The Commercial Hotel was a popular hotel in downtown Keeseville conveniently located on Main Street. This photograph from the 1880s shows the hotel with a horse and buggy used for transporting guests and their luggage to and from the train station or ferry dock. The hotel was a total loss from a fire in the mid-1890s. In the background, the railing of the Arch Bridge and the bank behind that can be seen. The Congregational Presbyterian church is barely visible behind the bank.

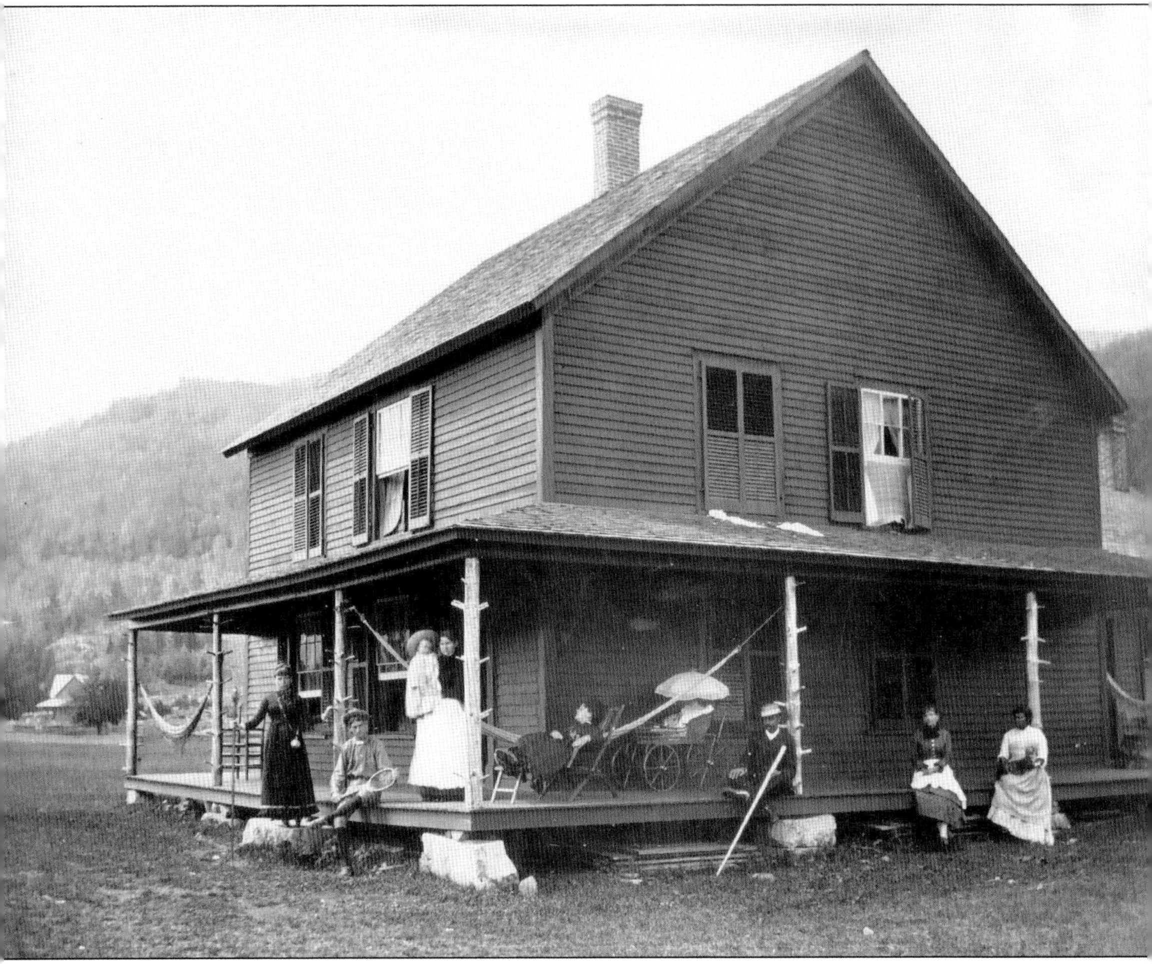

A nice-quality two-story Adirondack cottage was common among the higher-paid employees of the many factories in and around Keeseville. Keeseville was made up of two main streets: Front Street was home to businesses, and Main Street connected the two sides of the river and was home to more businesses and service buildings. Business owners such as the Keese family, Rufus Prescott, Willis Mould, and others built stately mansions immediately around these two streets, while their employees built smaller homes farther out as the community became more populated. While many of the outlying residences have been demolished and rebuilt, most of the stately manors still stand in the heart of the village of Keeseville and the townships of Ausable and Chesterfield.

With an active river flowing through the center of the village, bridges were an important part of the community. Several bridges were built, the earliest of which were wood. The first bridge was built in 1840, but it was washed away in 1856 by a flash flood that damaged many area bridges. The construction of a new bridge commenced within a year.

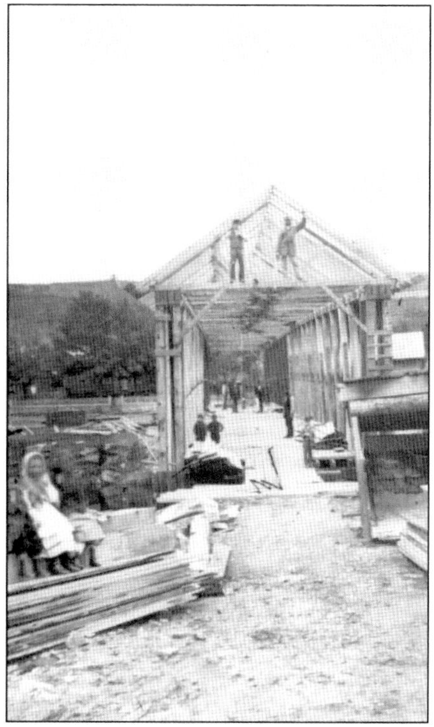

The second bridge was designed as a covered wooden bridge. In a single span, the bridge covered the 214-foot crossing. The design is similar to that of a bridge in nearby Jay, New York.

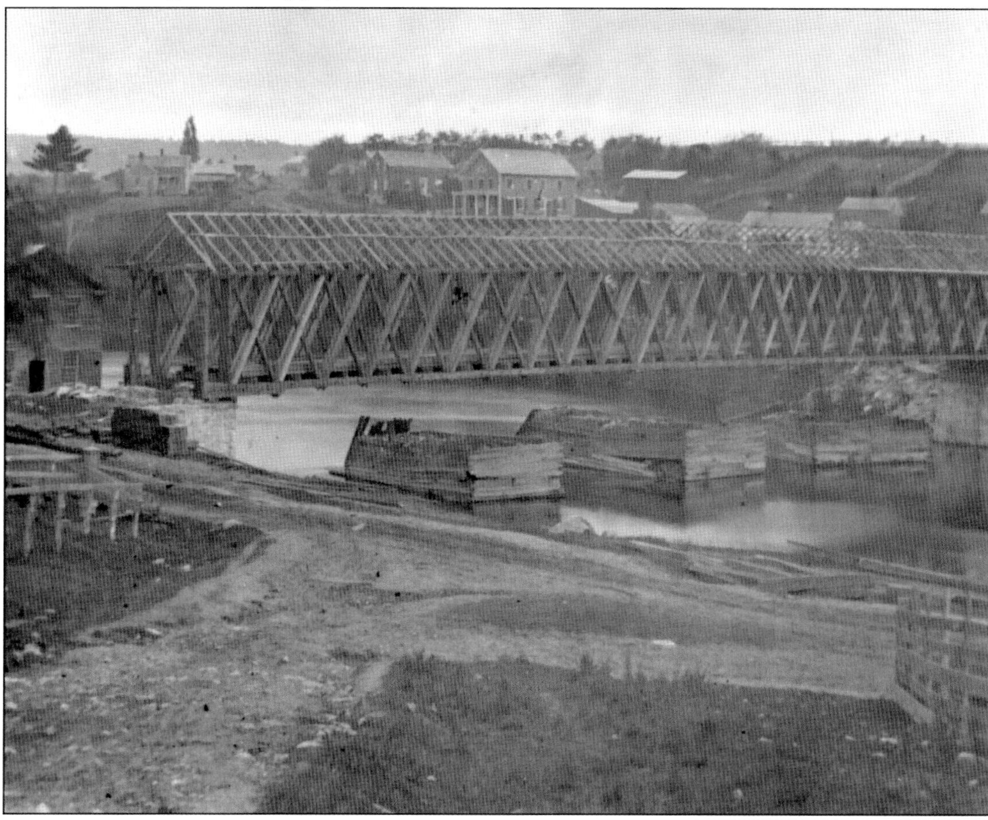

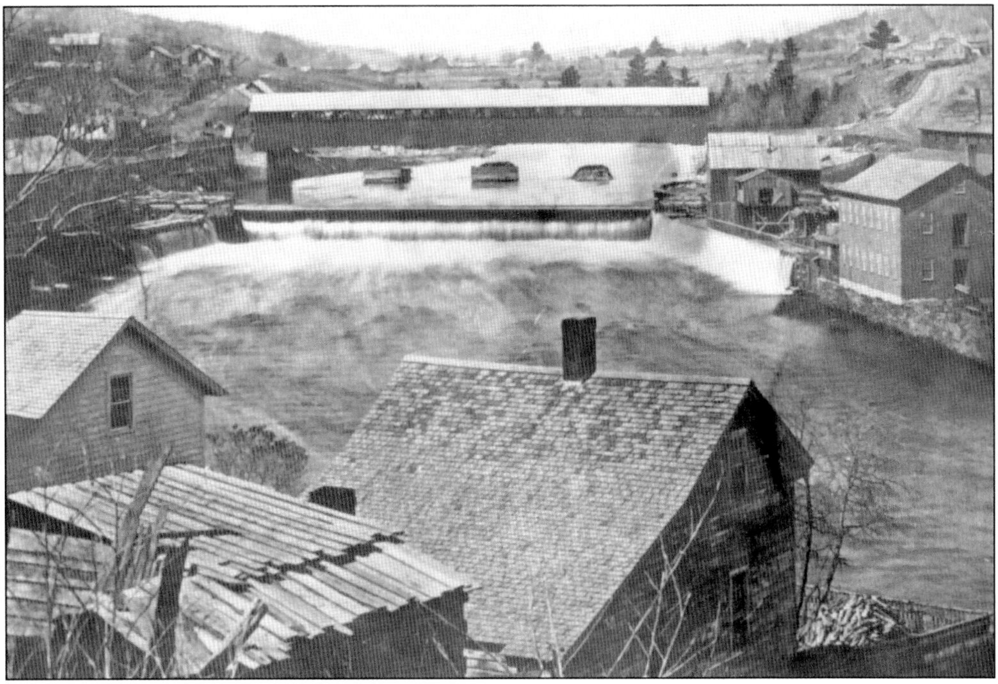

The wooden truss bridge was in service for 20 years. In the water directly beneath the bridge in the center of the photograph, the three original bases for the stone-filled timber cribs that supported the previous bridge can be seen.

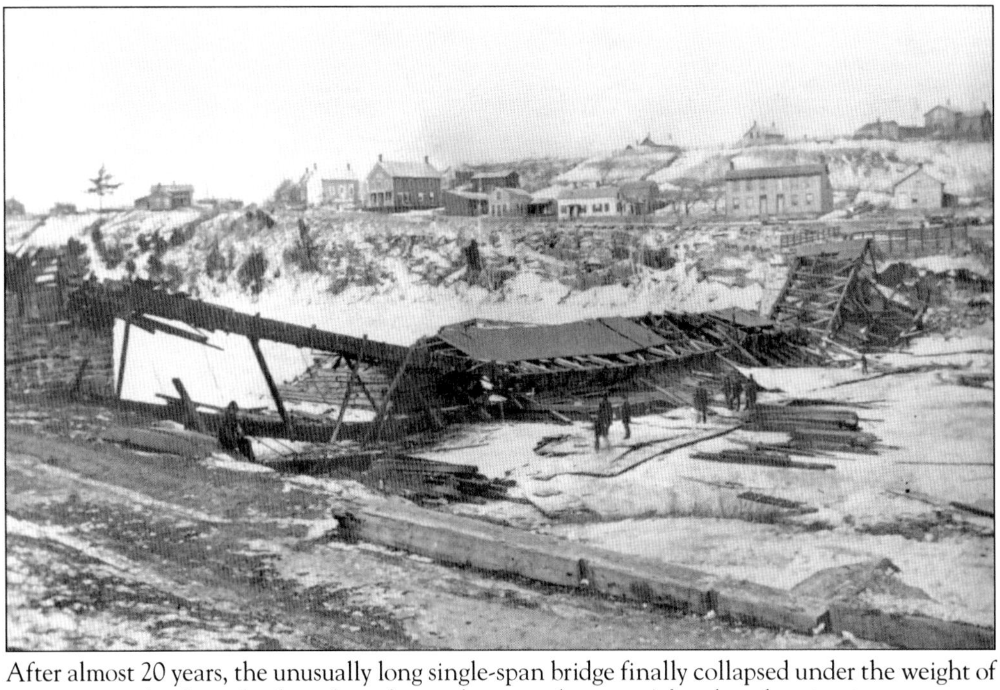

After almost 20 years, the unusually long single-span bridge finally collapsed under the weight of a snowstorm that brought three feet of snow down on the area. After this, the winning contractor Murray, Dougal & Company built the iron truss bridge that still stands since its construction in 1888.

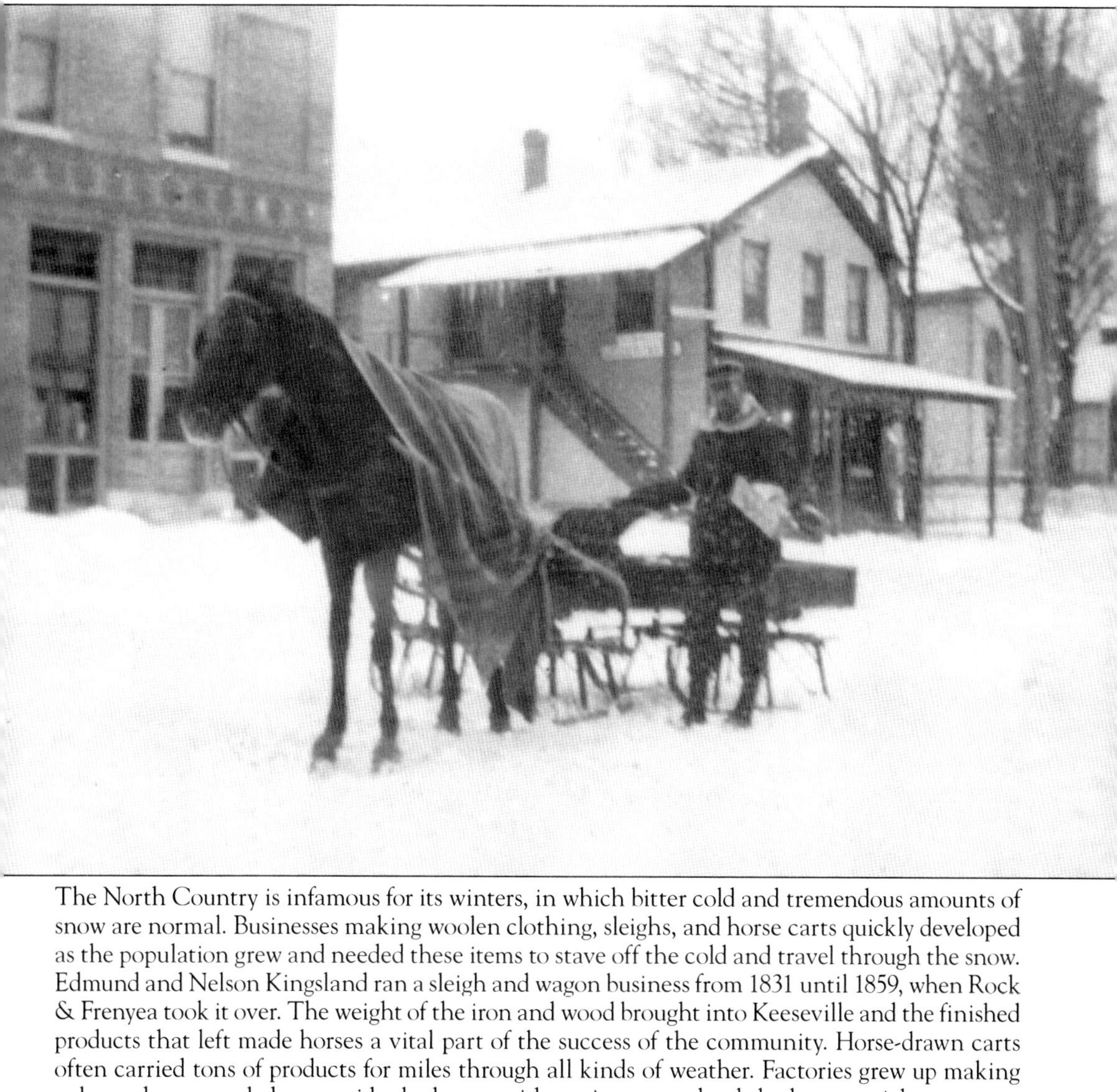

The North Country is infamous for its winters, in which bitter cold and tremendous amounts of snow are normal. Businesses making woolen clothing, sleighs, and horse carts quickly developed as the population grew and needed these items to stave off the cold and travel through the snow. Edmund and Nelson Kingsland ran a sleigh and wagon business from 1831 until 1859, when Rock & Frenyea took it over. The weight of the iron and wood brought into Keeseville and the finished products that left made horses a vital part of the success of the community. Horse-drawn carts often carried tons of products for miles through all kinds of weather. Factories grew up making axles and gear needed to provide the horses with equipment to haul the heavy weight.

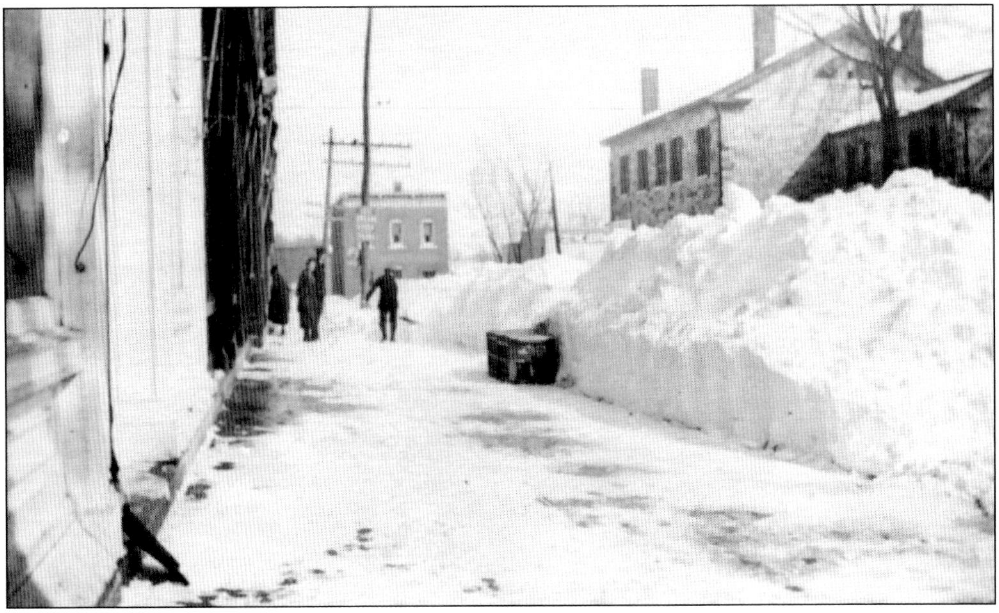

Snow removal was the task of everyone, young and old. By the mid-1800s, horse-drawn snow plows were being developed and put into use. This made clearing the busy dirt streets easier, leaving children and shop owners the tasks of clearing around homes and businesses.

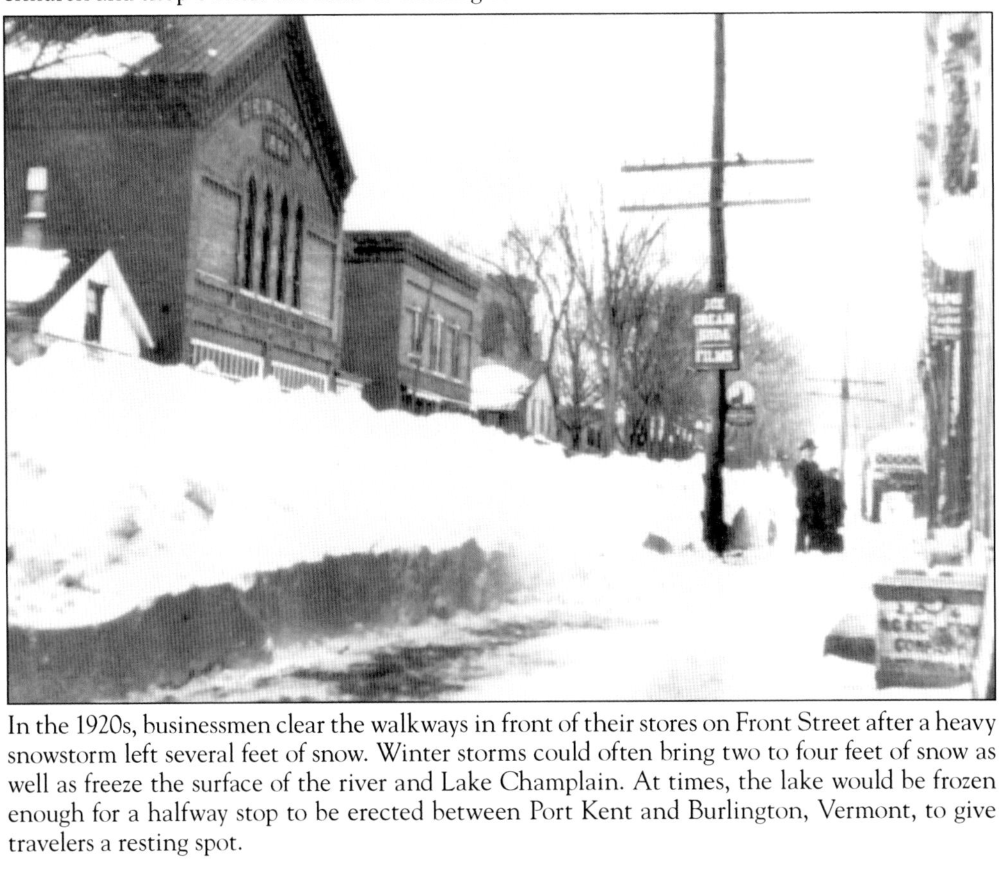

In the 1920s, businessmen clear the walkways in front of their stores on Front Street after a heavy snowstorm left several feet of snow. Winter storms could often bring two to four feet of snow as well as freeze the surface of the river and Lake Champlain. At times, the lake would be frozen enough for a halfway stop to be erected between Port Kent and Burlington, Vermont, to give travelers a resting spot.

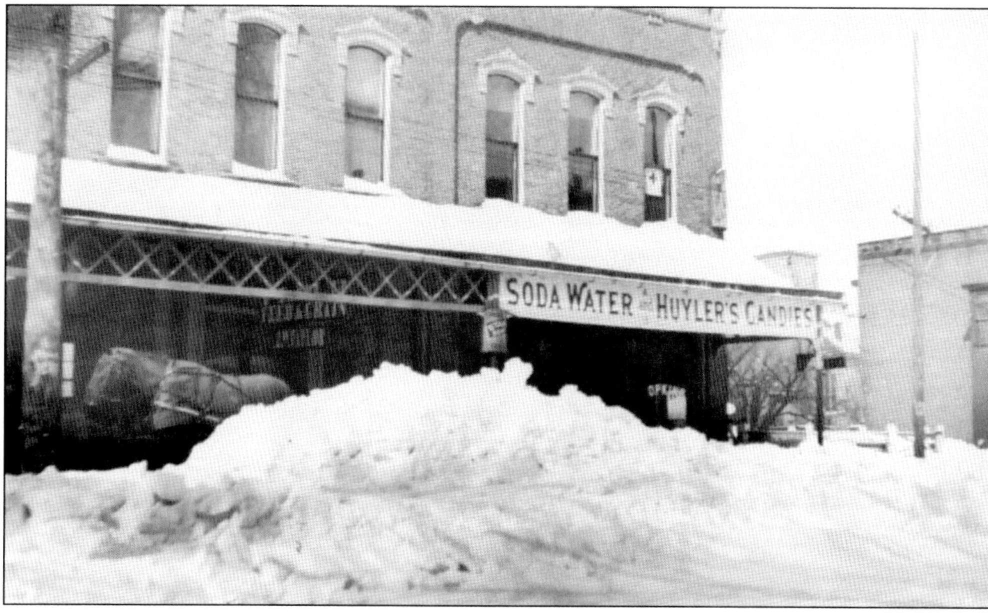

The horses in this undated photograph give a good gauge to the size of the snow bank cleared from Front Street. By 1846, sidewalks were laid with sandstone, and the first streetlights, kerosene lamps on posts, were erected around 1877.

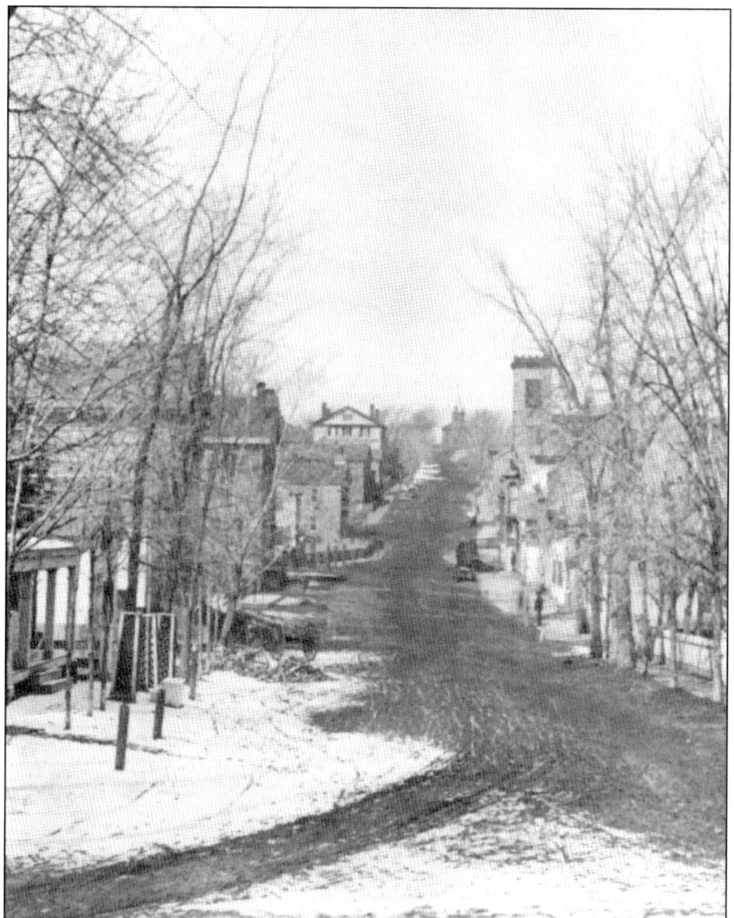

Main Street in Keeseville is seen with a light dusting of snow in this pre-1877 photograph. The streets are yet to be paved, and no utility poles cross Main Street.

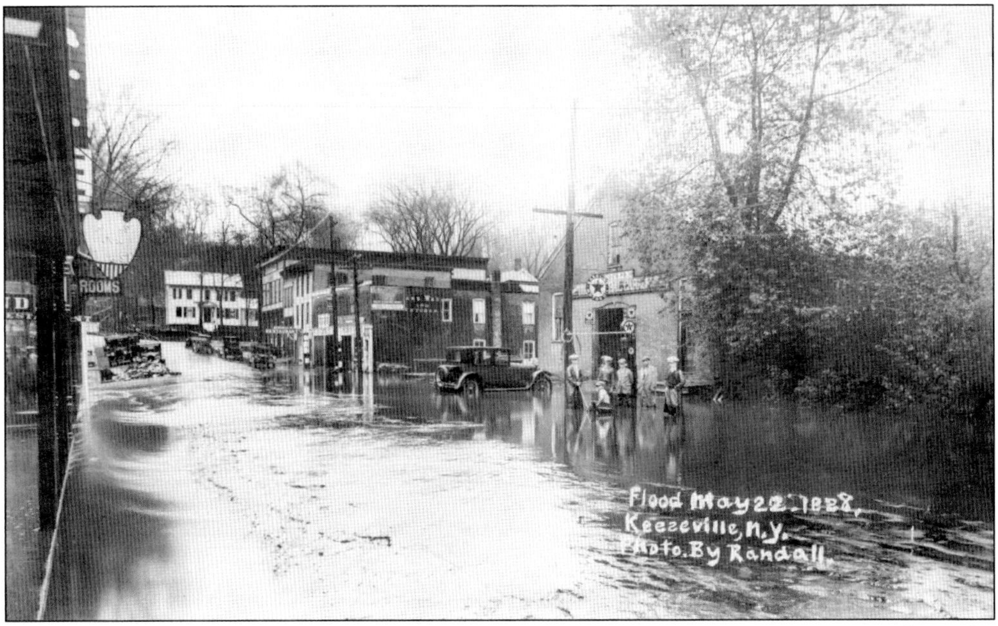

After the winter, spring comes with the constant peril of floods caused by runoff from the nearby Adirondack Mountains and ice jams on the river. This photograph from May 22, 1888, illustrates the flooding that can affect downtown Keeseville. The image was taken in front of the Adirondack Hotel looking east.

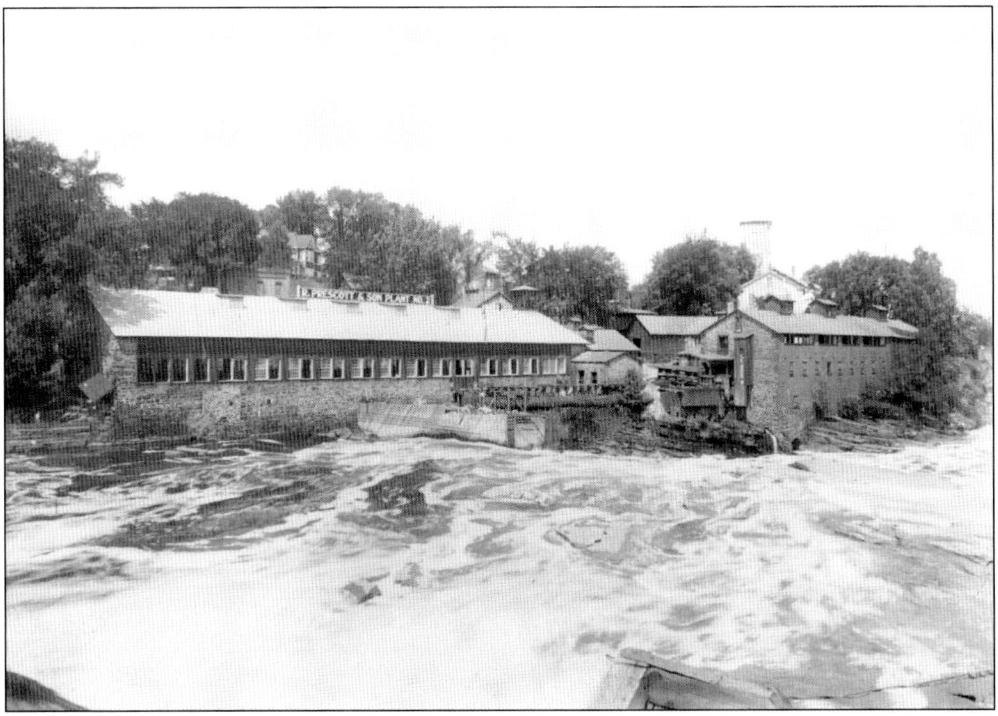

This undated photograph illustrates the enormous power of the Ausable River, which first drew settlers to the area. Pictured here are the R. Prescott and Sons Finishing Nail Plant No. Two (center) and the old nail factory next to it on the right.

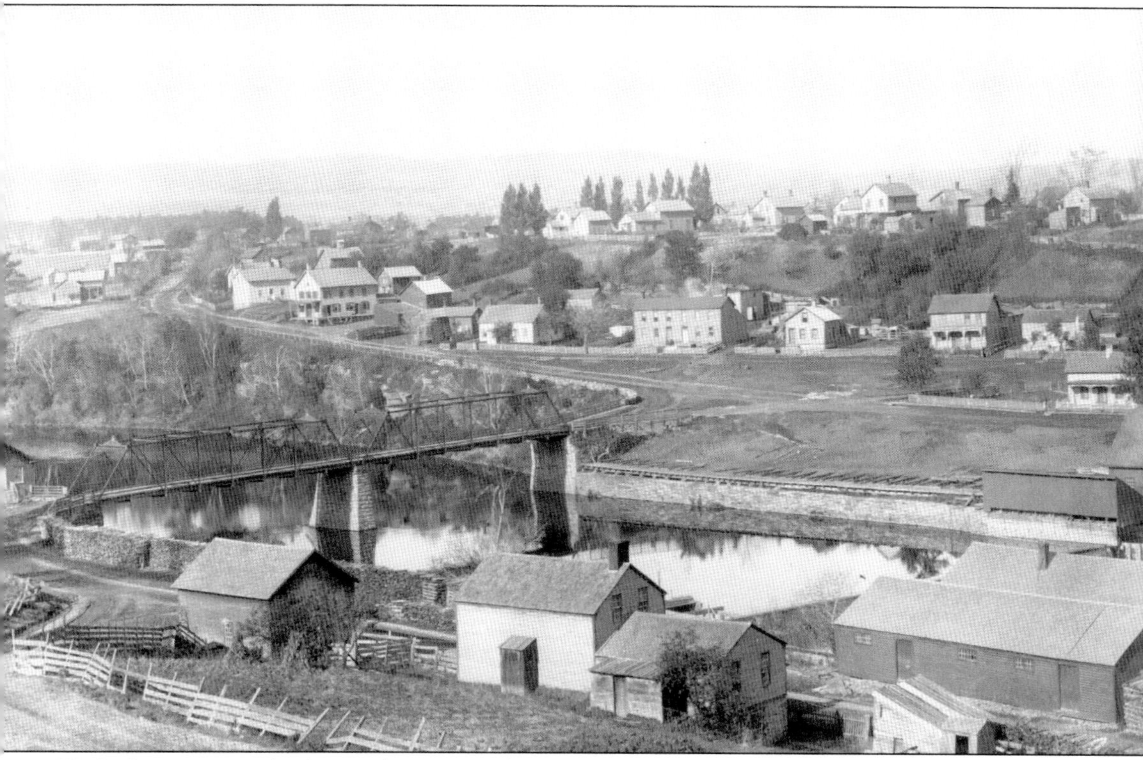

With the iron truss bridge in the center, this 1870 photograph shows the development on the Ausable side of the Ausable River, in the back of the photograph. Farms and factory-related buildings are seen foreground on the Chesterfield side of the river. From the late 1860s until the 1900s, the area stabilized in terms of major infrastructure growth. With the advent of the automobile in the early 20th century, building started up again, making the area shown here virtually unrecognizable today.

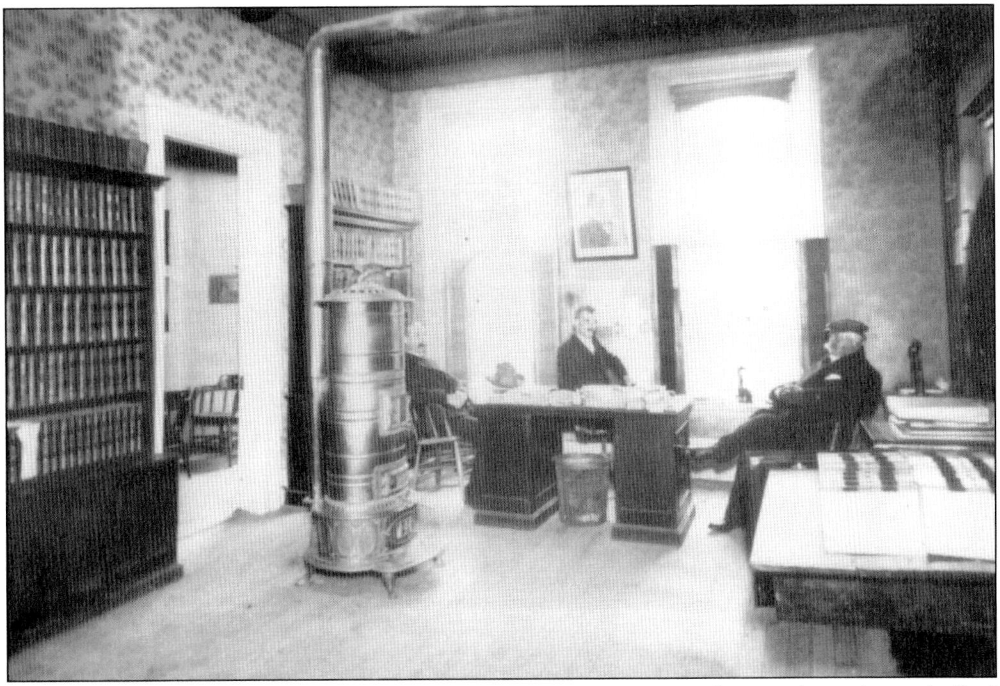

In 1878, Sidney Maders's law office on Front Street was spacious and warm from the potbellied stove in the center. At the time, several lawyers, including Martin Finch, were practicing in Keeseville. Keeseville's legal profession started with George Simmons in 1827.

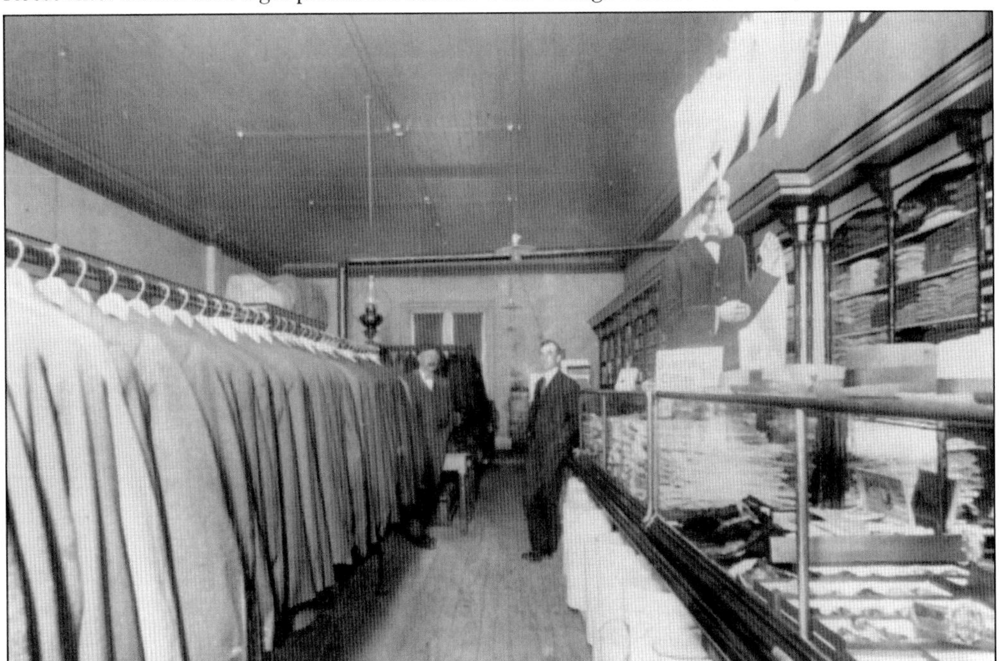

This photograph from 1876 shows the center aisle of the popular J.N. Atwood men's clothing store on Front Street in Keeseville. This was one of two clothing stores and four tailors that were in operation at the time.

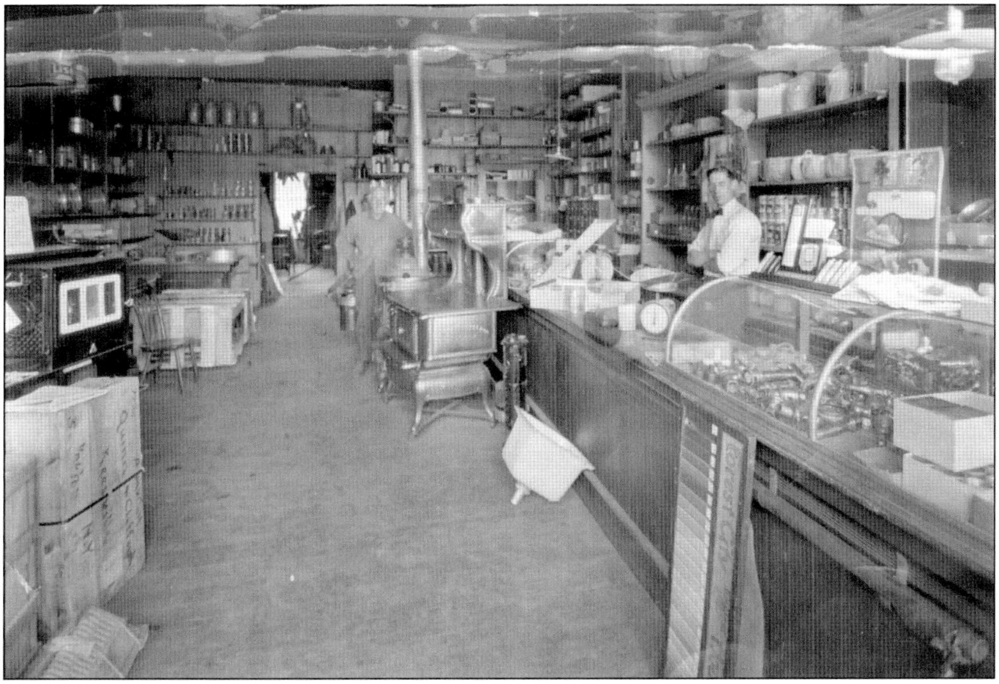

Tom Quinn is standing behind the counter of his store, T.R. Quinn & Company Tin Shop and Stove Store. In 1855, there were eight dry goods stores and 12 grocery stores among the retail businesses in Keeseville.

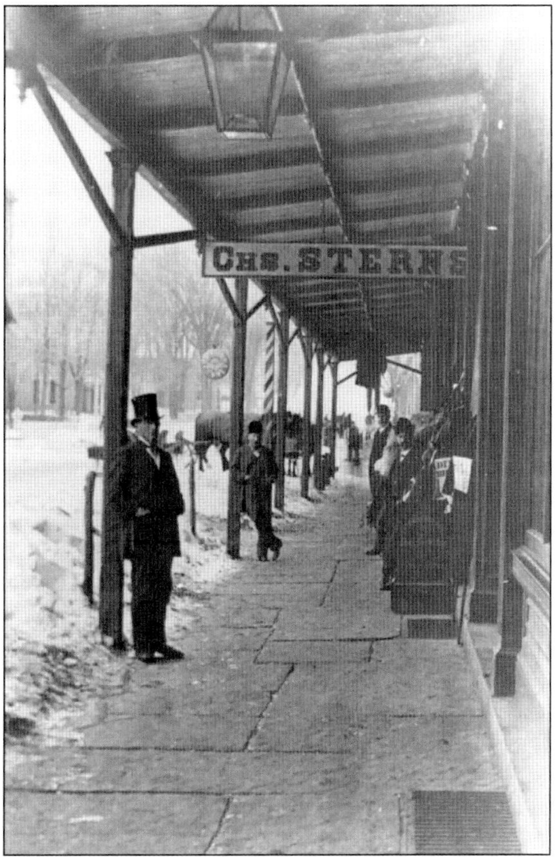

Men are standing under the awning sheltering the stores along Front Street in downtown Keeseville. Among the stores shown here is one of the barbershops, as evidenced by the striped pole. In 1883, local barbers teamed together for a pricing schedule, which included a shave for 10¢, hair cutting for 20¢, sea foam for 10¢, shave and a haircut at home for 25¢, and shaving the dead for $2. A current barbershop, Modern Traditions, has this notice framed on the wall.

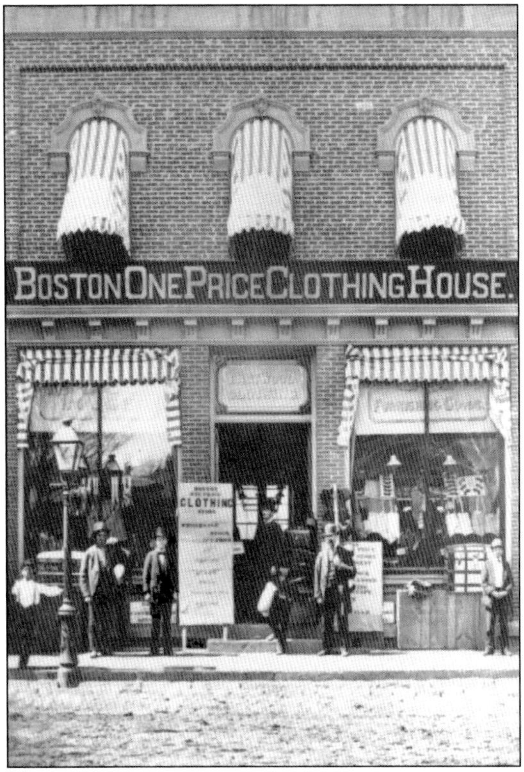

A series of three photographs taken in the 1870s shows the entrances to three of the businesses along Front Street. Pictured here is the Boston One Price Clothing Store, a popular chain throughout New England.

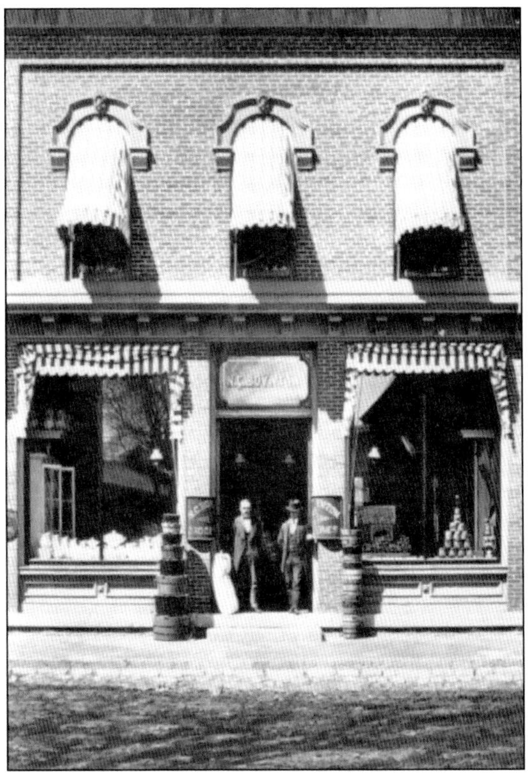

In the second of the three photographs, the grocery store run by N.C. Boynton is pictured. There were plenty of farms on the outskirts of Keeseville to provide fresh produce as well as trains and ferries to bring in goods from outside the region.

In the final image is Thomas and Coppins's General Store with its crowded display windows. The store carried notions and dry goods as well as fabrics and papers to decorate the walls of the local residences.

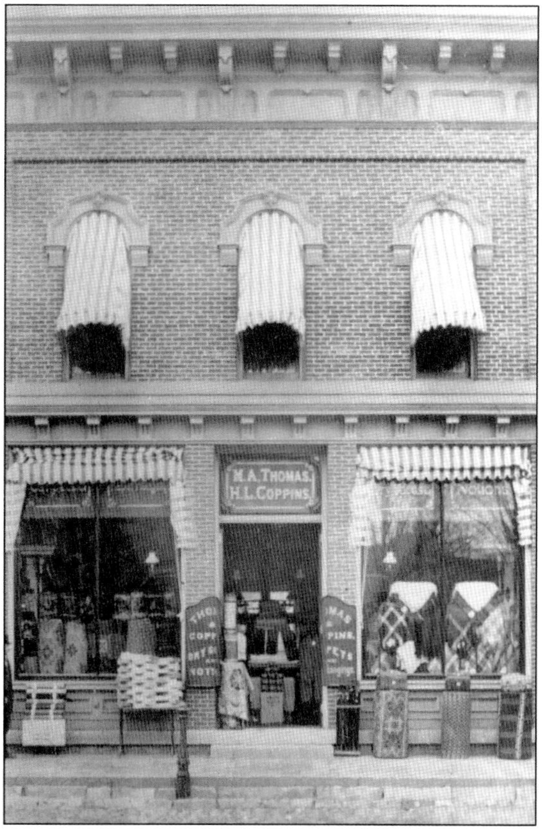

Hopkins Drug Store, as seen in this photograph dated around 1880, sold a wide range of goods to the people of the community. While the building is still standing, it now houses an art gallery and children's educational resource. The empty lot to the right of the building is now the Keeseville Free Library, which blocks the view of the Prescott Factory in the background of this photograph.

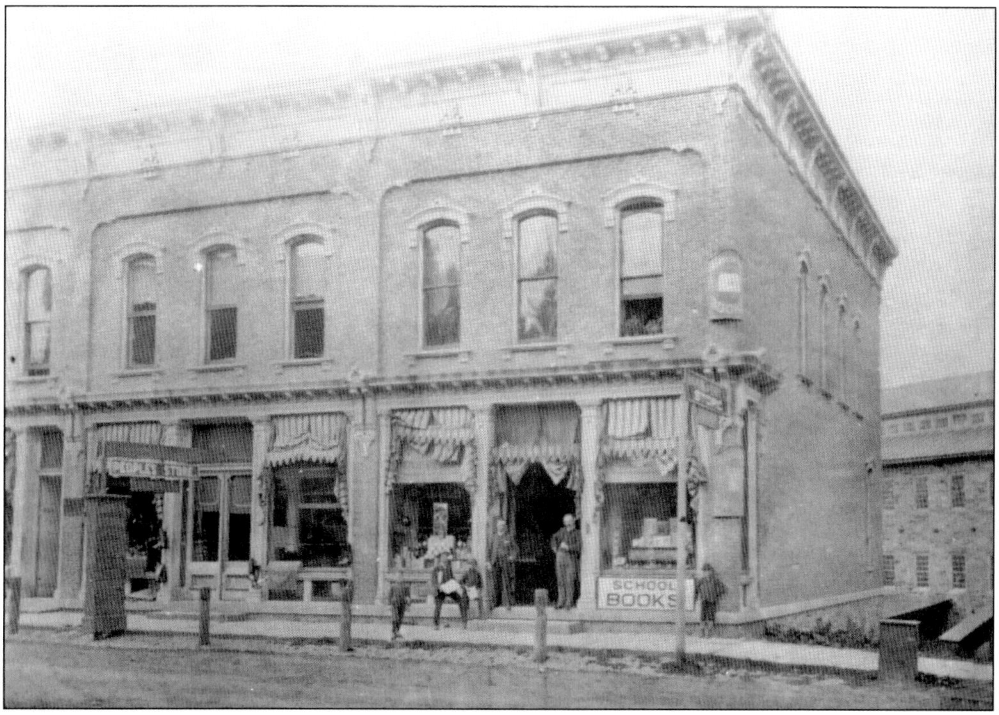

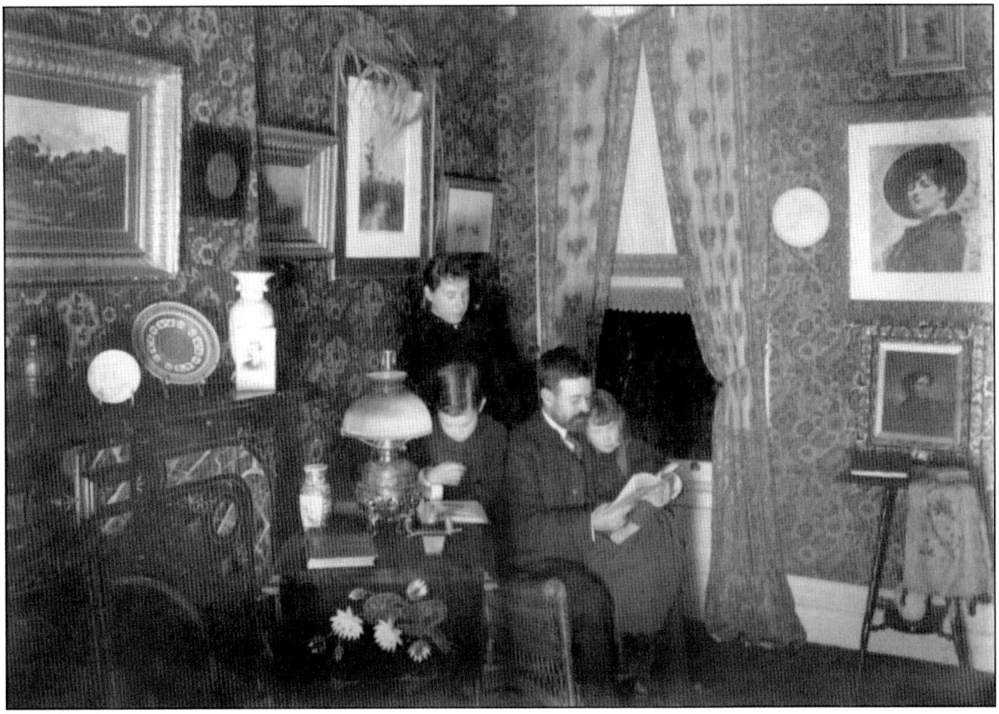

The Shields family poses in the parlor in this undated photograph. Nearly all of the predominant houses of Keeseville were built by master builder Senecal Perry or his son Isaac.

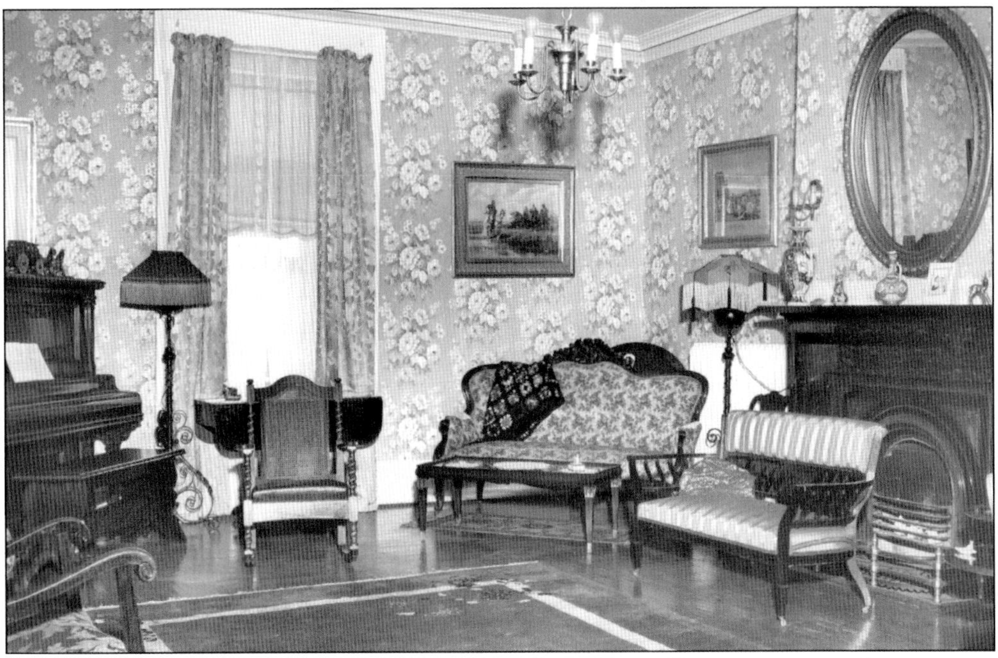

This is the parlor of Martin Rennell's Keeseville residence. Rennell was a prominent businessman in the hotel industry and owned several in the Port Kent area as well as the general store near the boat dock. Rennell was also instrumental in bringing tourists to the area through his position as secretary of the Adirondack Resort Association.

This undated photograph highlights the spiral staircase in the Rennell home. A popular feature, many homes in the community contain these freestanding spiral staircases. The Anderson Falls Heritage Society is in the process of documenting them all as to location and architecture.

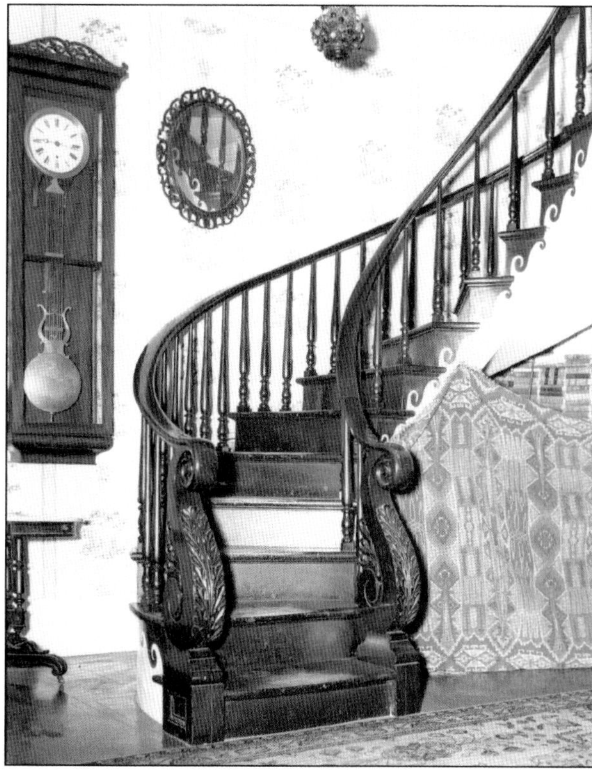

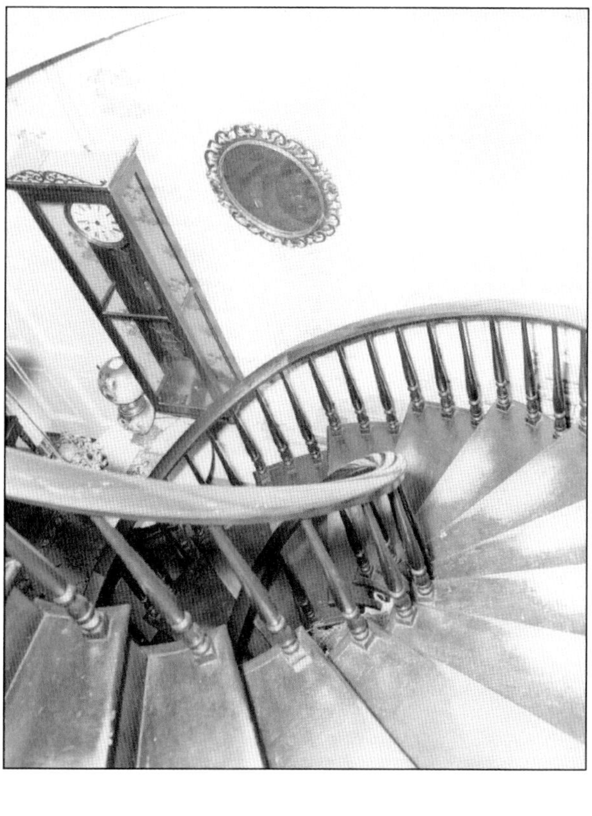

This view from the second floor of the Rennell home emphasizes the curve to the spiral staircase and provides a unique view of the clock and mirror. Some of the spiral staircases in the community carry on to a third floor.

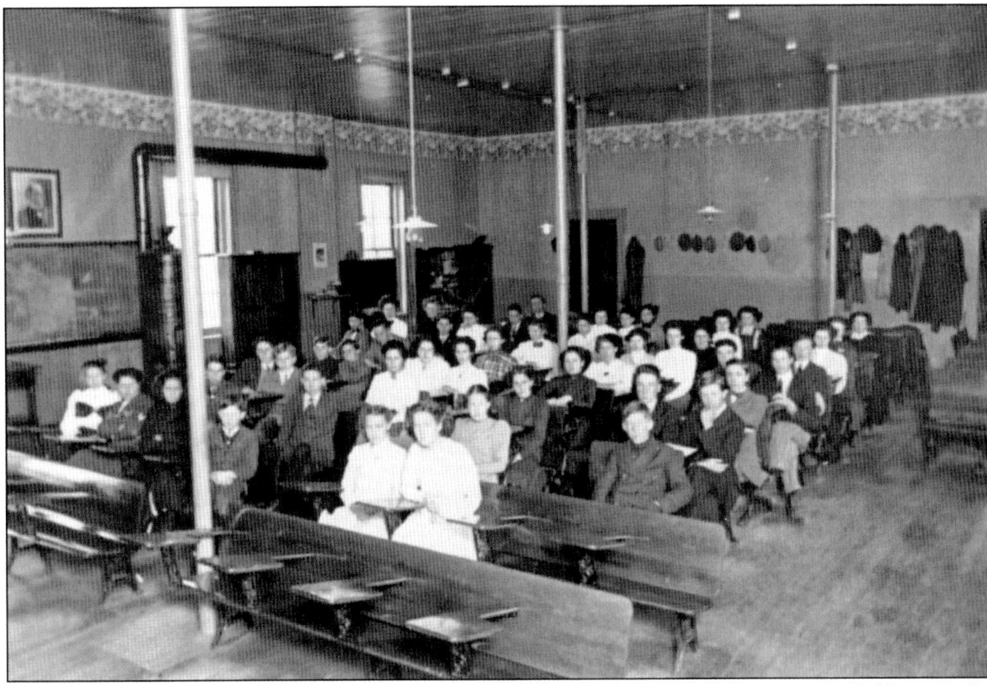

Pictured here in 1910 is the Keeseville High School. In 1870, there were over 800 children in the community, and only 200 of them attended school. In 1936, the old building was demolished, and a new one was erected as a central school in 1939.

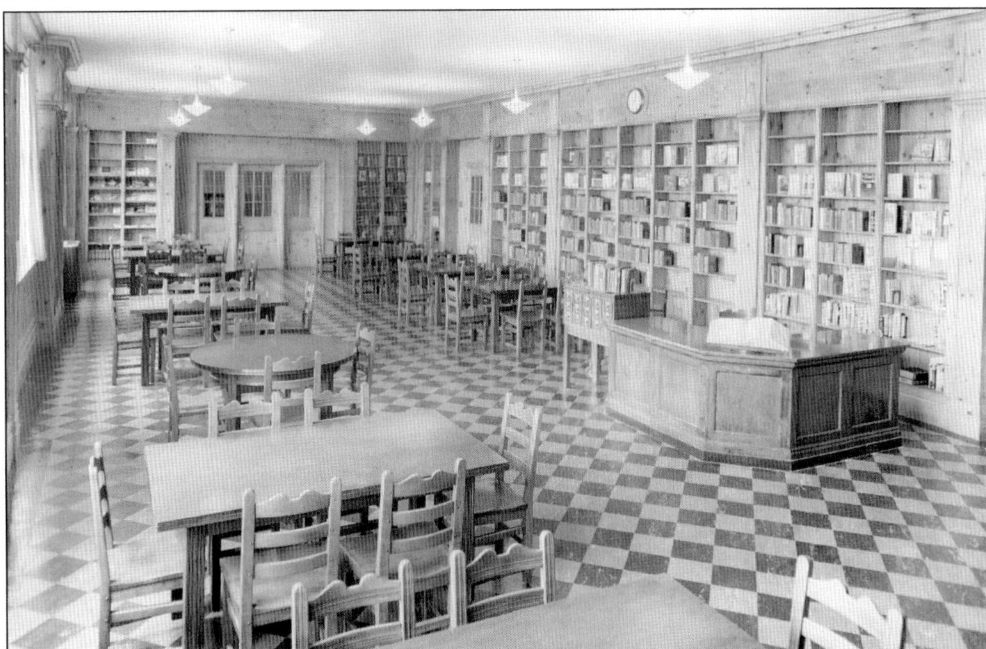

This was the Keeseville Central School Library as it appeared between the 1950s and 1960s, featuring built-in wooden bookcases on the walls around the entire library and a tile floor. Near the librarian's desk is a small card catalog file cabinet for keeping track of all the books.

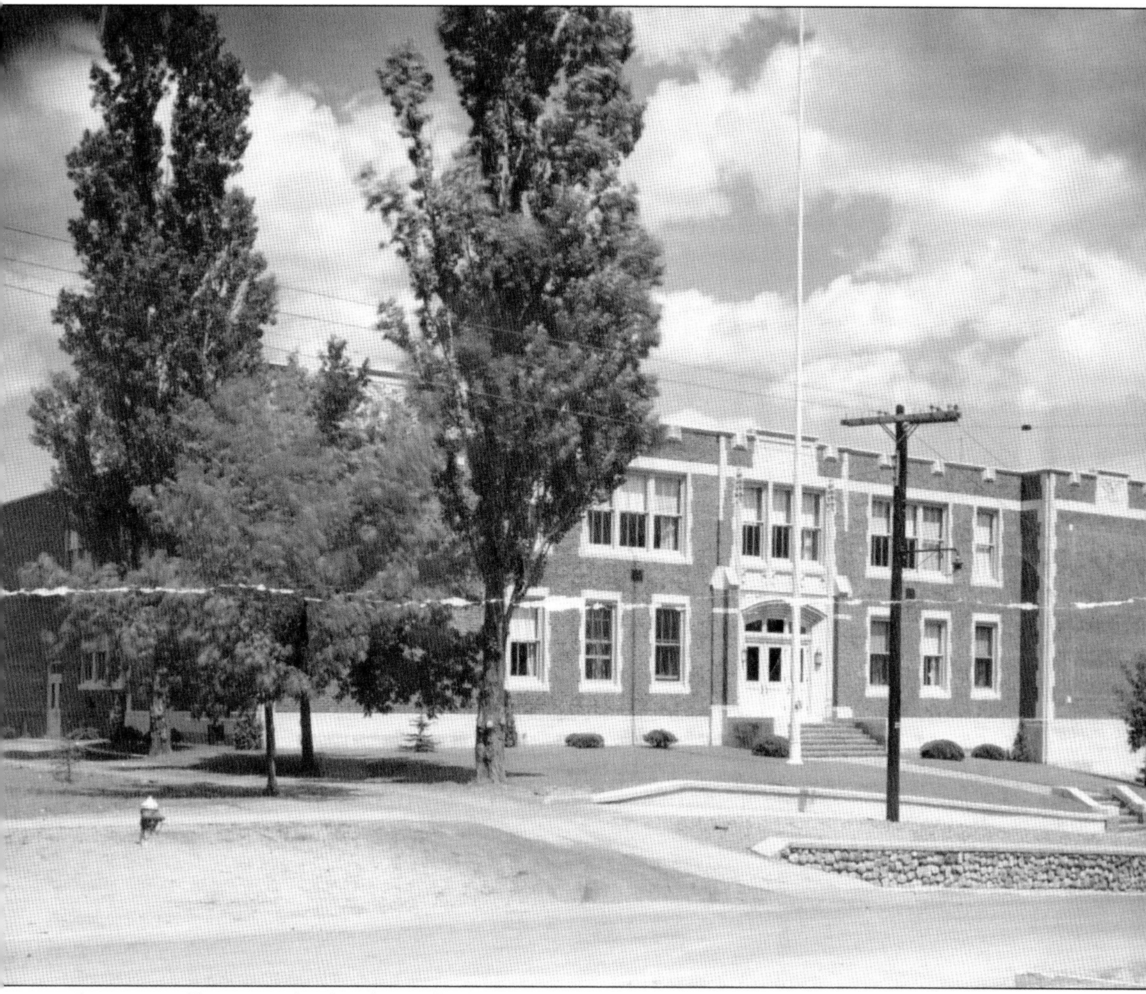

The Keeseville Central School was the home for area students from 1939 until 1972. As the local population dwindled, elementary schools in Keeseville and nearby Ausable Forks were established, and a combined middle and high school was built between the two communities. After closing as a school, the building became home to the Keeseville village offices as well as the first home for the Anderson Falls Heritage Society. A building across the street was renovated for the offices, and the society moved into a house at 96 Clinton Street, leaving the school building empty.

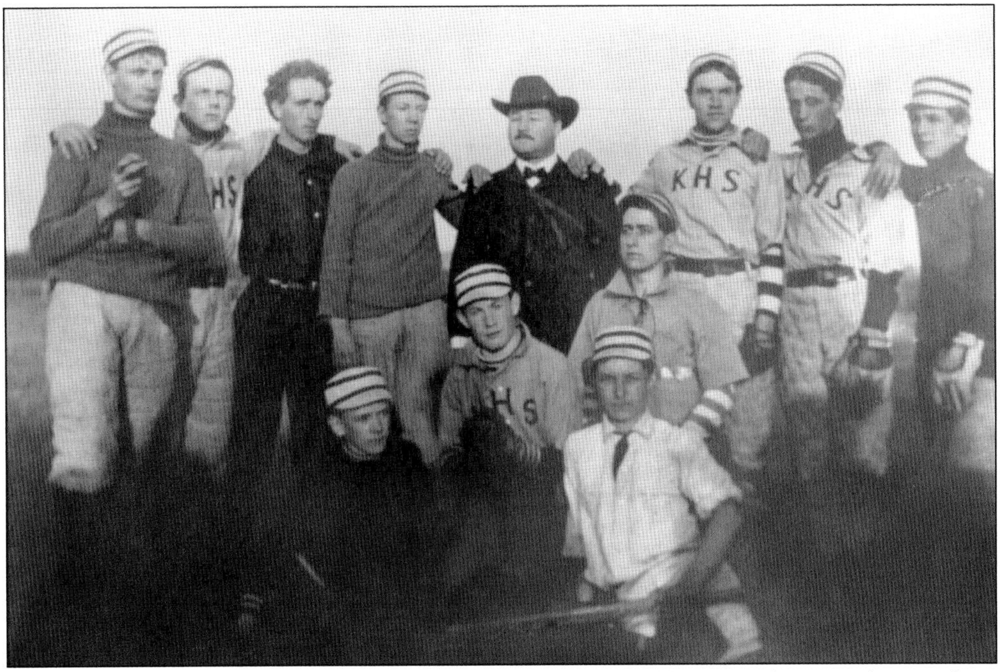

This undated photograph shows the Keeseville High School baseball team. In the 1930s, homemaking was taught to girls, and using tools, woodworking, and metalworking was taught to boys so they could find employment right out of school.

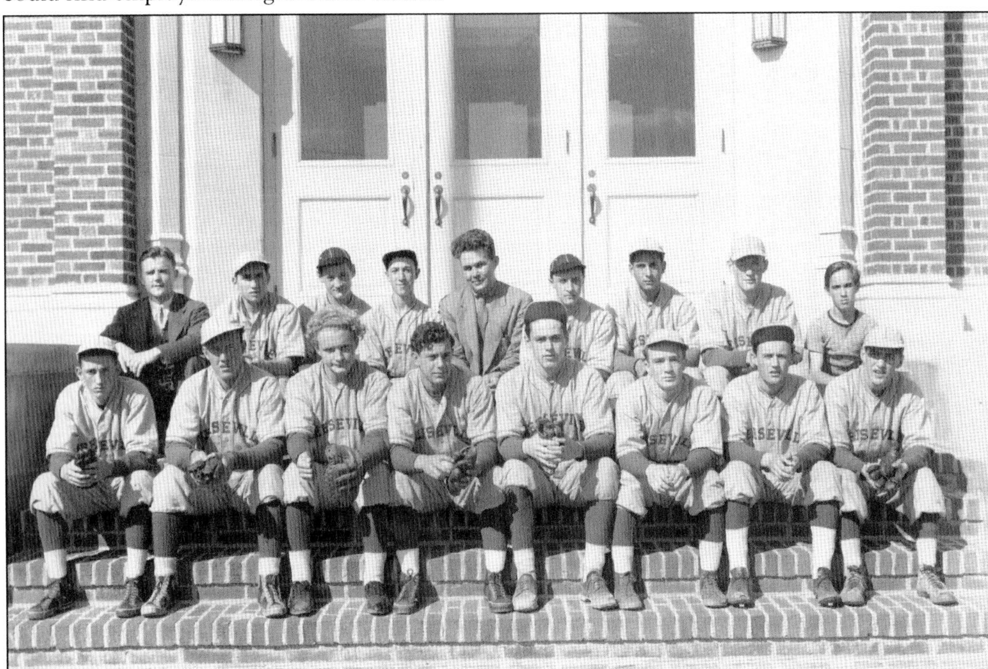

Sitting on the steps of the school building is the Keeseville High School baseball team of 1938 and 1939. In addition to formal instruction, the school offered students courses in physical education as well as band, clubs, and access to a library.

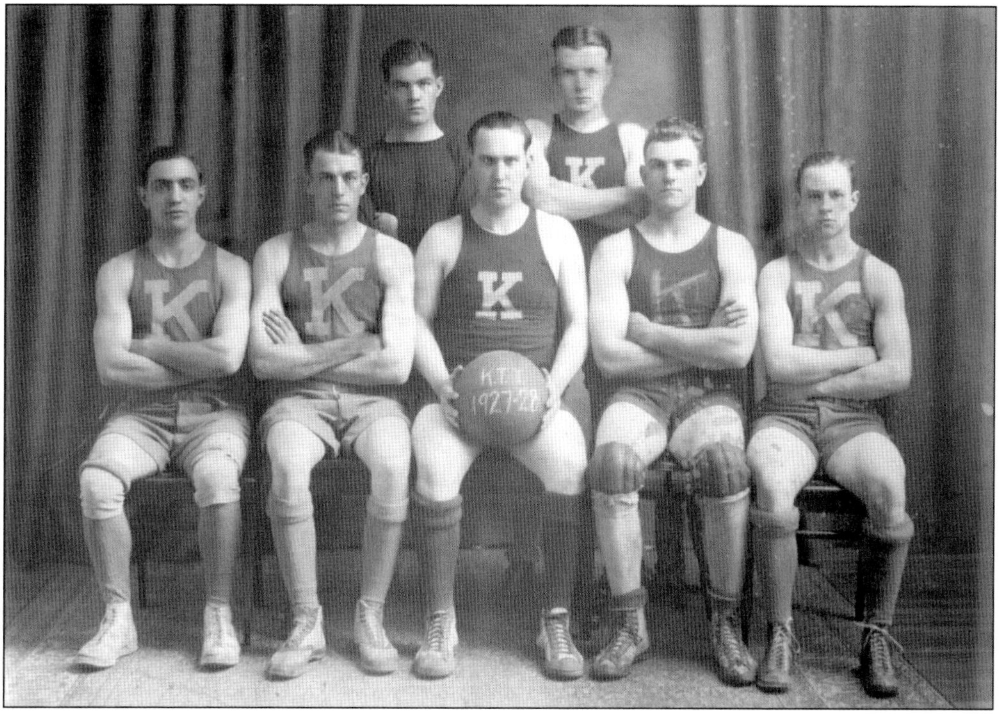

Members of the Keeseville basketball team pose in 1927. Note the Ks on the athletes' jerseys are all different; at this time, uniforms were often handmade by the proud parents of the players.

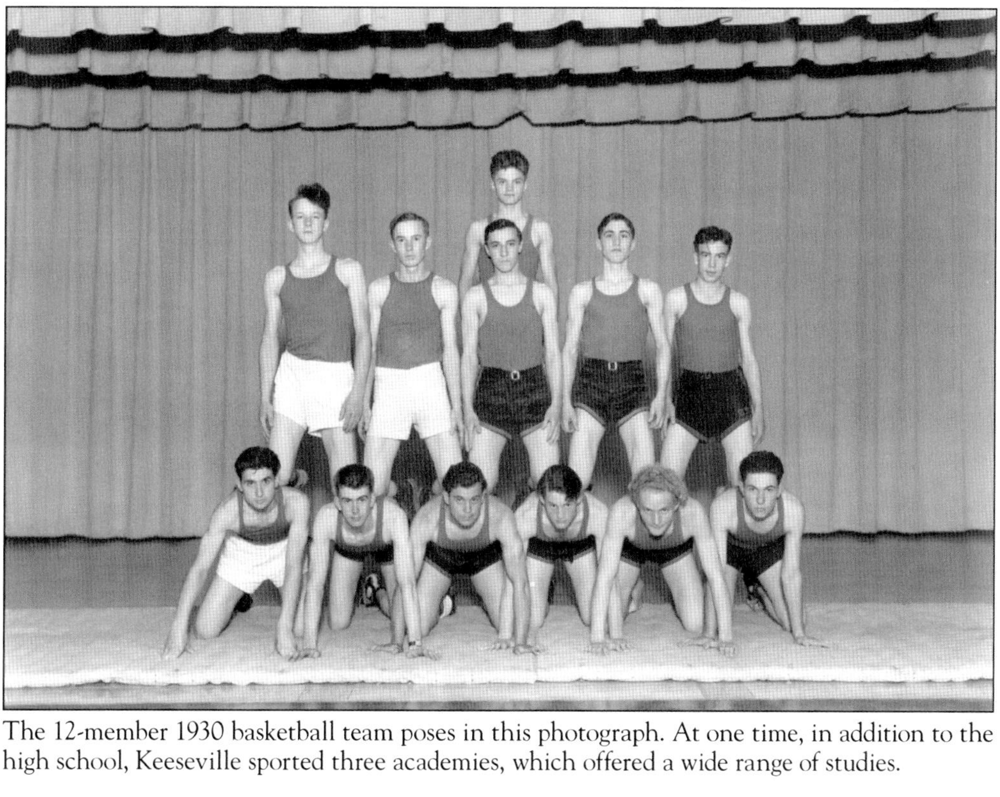

The 12-member 1930 basketball team poses in this photograph. At one time, in addition to the high school, Keeseville sported three academies, which offered a wide range of studies.

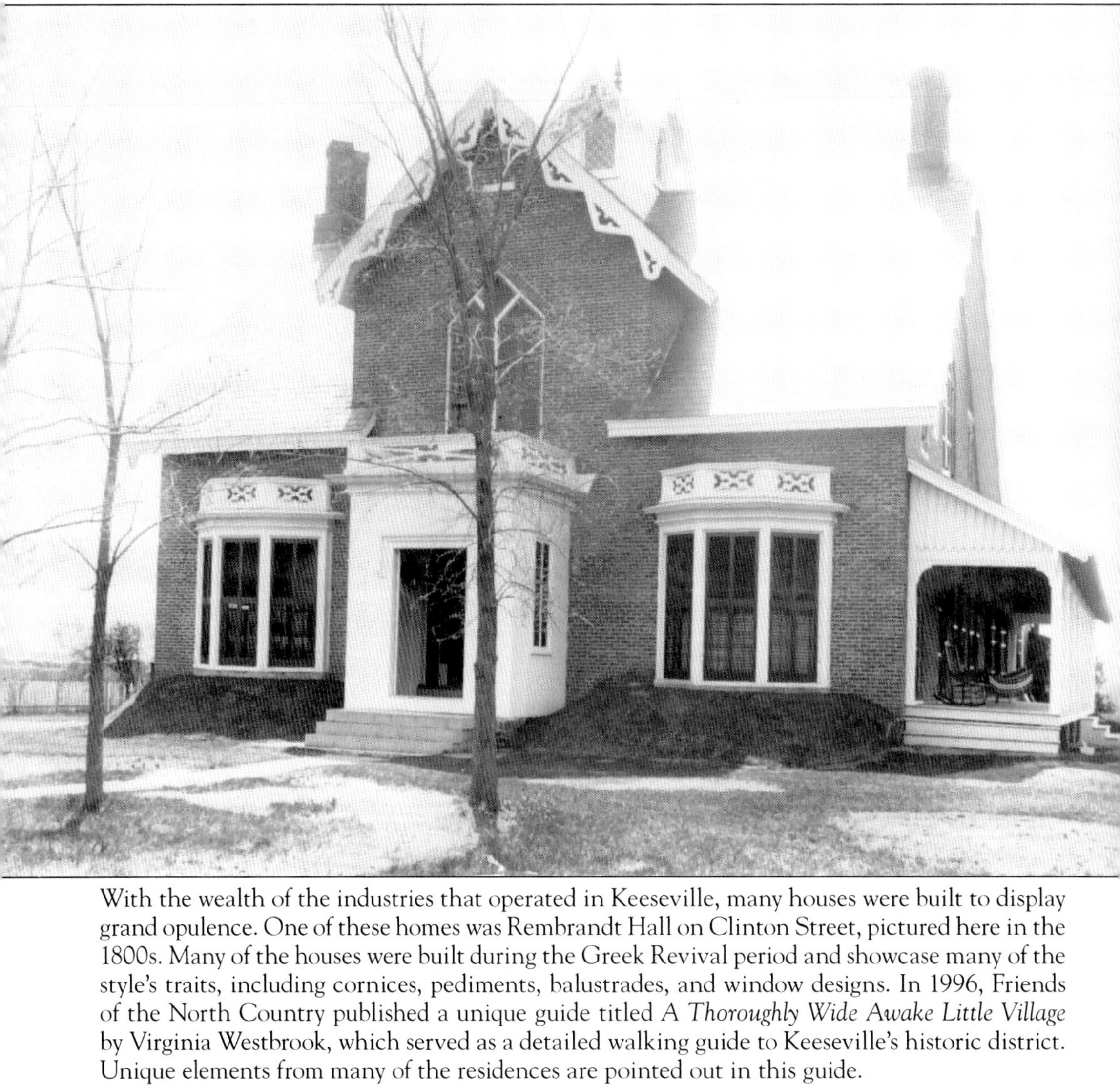

With the wealth of the industries that operated in Keeseville, many houses were built to display grand opulence. One of these homes was Rembrandt Hall on Clinton Street, pictured here in the 1800s. Many of the houses were built during the Greek Revival period and showcase many of the style's traits, including cornices, pediments, balustrades, and window designs. In 1996, Friends of the North Country published a unique guide titled *A Thoroughly Wide Awake Little Village* by Virginia Westbrook, which served as a detailed walking guide to Keeseville's historic district. Unique elements from many of the residences are pointed out in this guide.

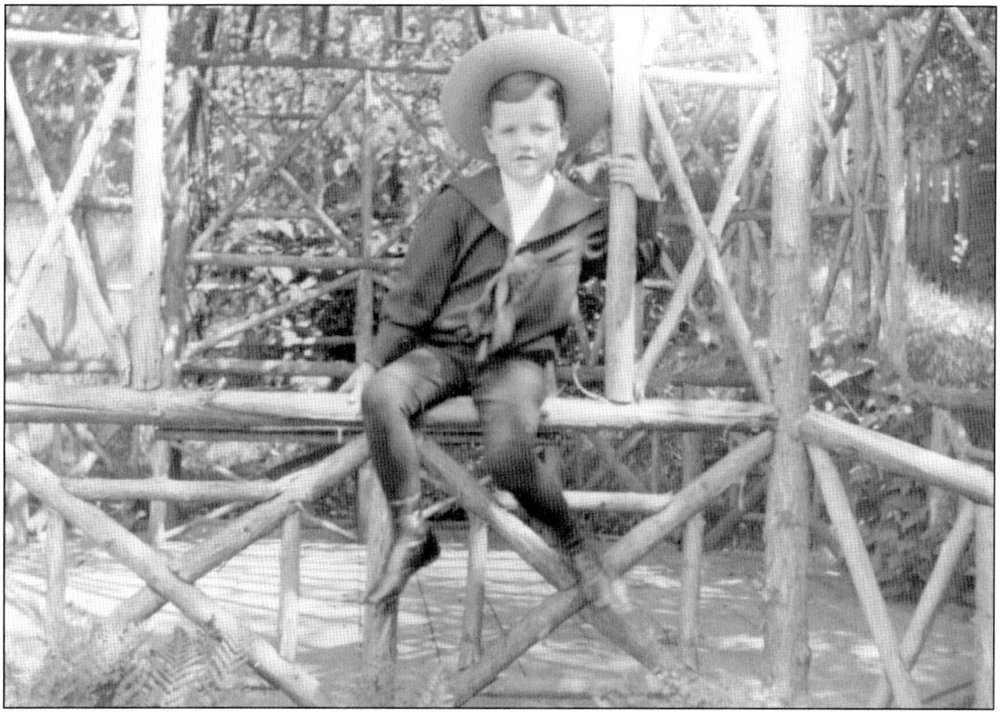

Not only were the houses grand in style, but their yards were also over the top. Gorgeous gardens were cultivated, and tours would develop towards the end of the season to show off the impressive yard work. Children's play areas also were given a grand treatment, as seen in this undated photograph of a young boy playing on a homemade jungle gym at the Fletcher House on Beach Street.

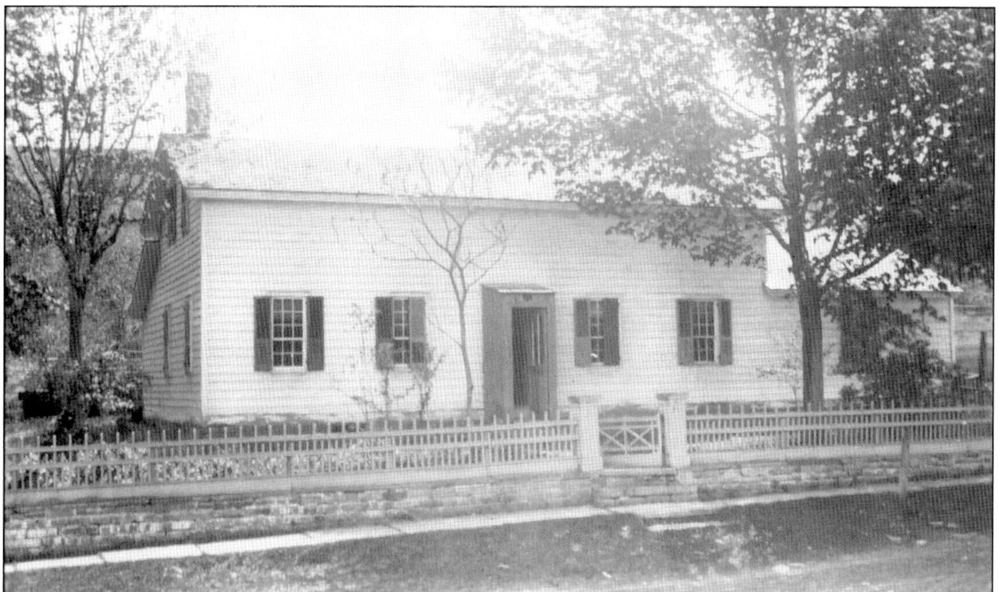

Samuel Keeler had a modest one-story house on River Street near the Upper Bridge. Generally, domiciles in Keeseville took on one of two looks, either the traditional, smooth-line box houses or the ostentatious grand mansions patterned after the Greek Revival look.

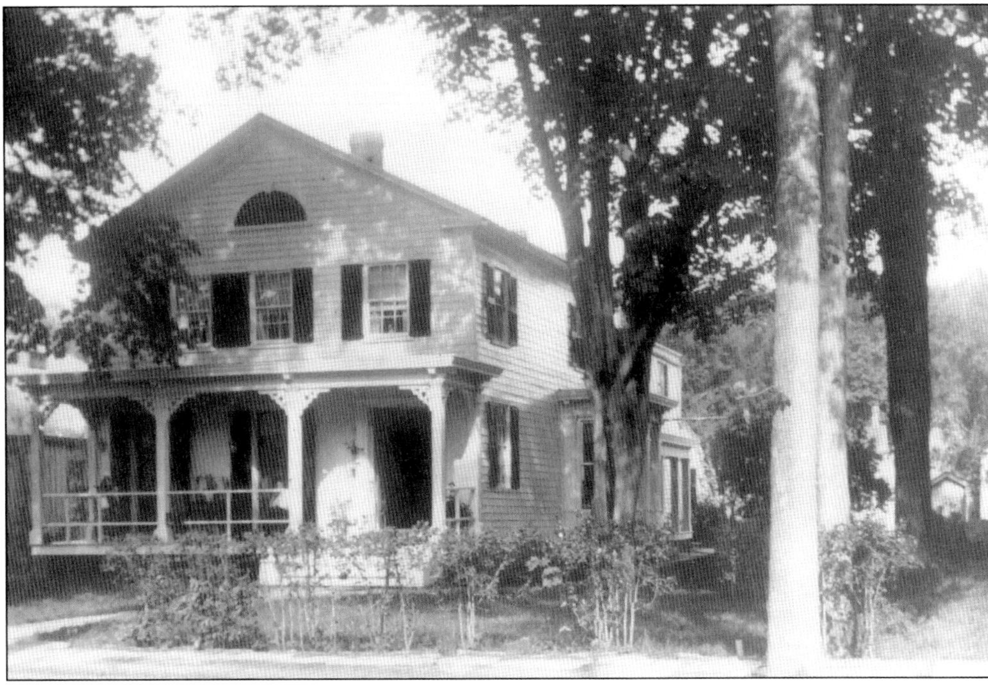

This undated photograph shows the Luther Whitney House on Front Street. Whitney operated the harness business by the First Bank of Essex County. This house is no longer standing, as the portion of Front Street on which it stood became a parking lot in the mid-1900s.

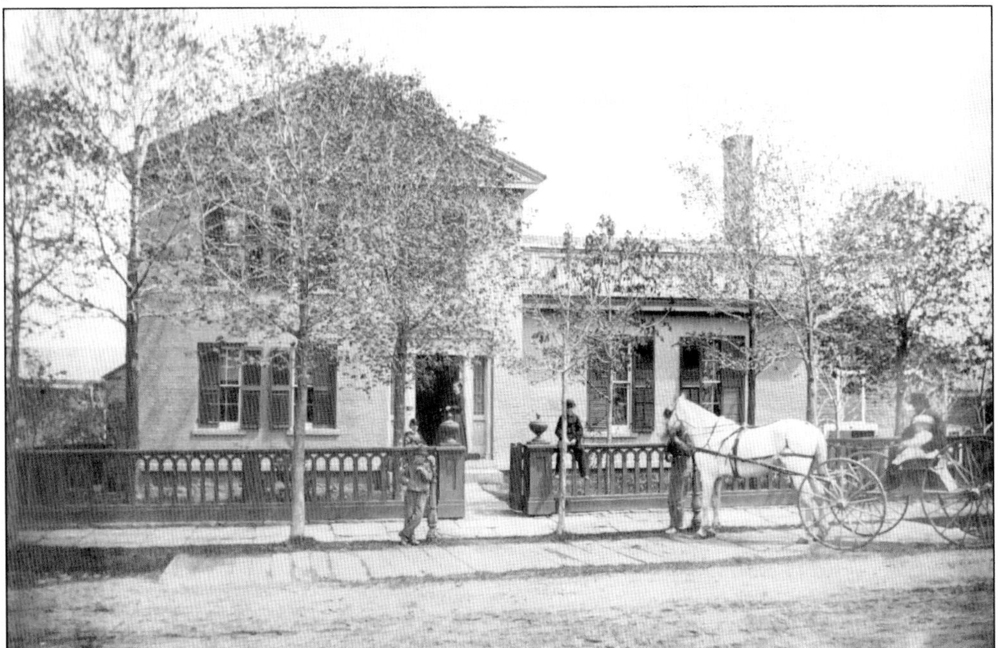

Pictured here in the mid-1800s is the Walter Greene House on Pleasant Street. Pleasant Street was the home of Keeseville dignitaries such as Edmund Kingsland Baber, Daniel Dodge, and artist Emmitt Pine.

This is the home of N. Kingsland and family. In the 1880s, Kingsland was the most prominent name in Keeseville business with the Kingsland Opera House and the Kingsland's Block of businesses. Popular legend has it that E.W. Kingsland and W. Mould had a footrace that began on the Arch Bridge with the two running in opposite directions and meeting once in the middle near Ausable Chasm before meeting again back on the Arch Bridge. Mould was the winner of the race.

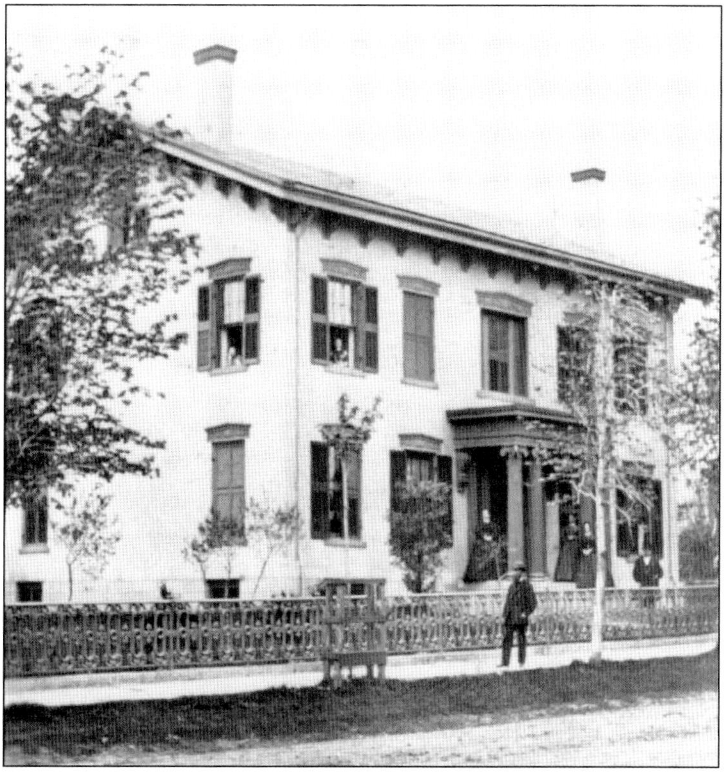

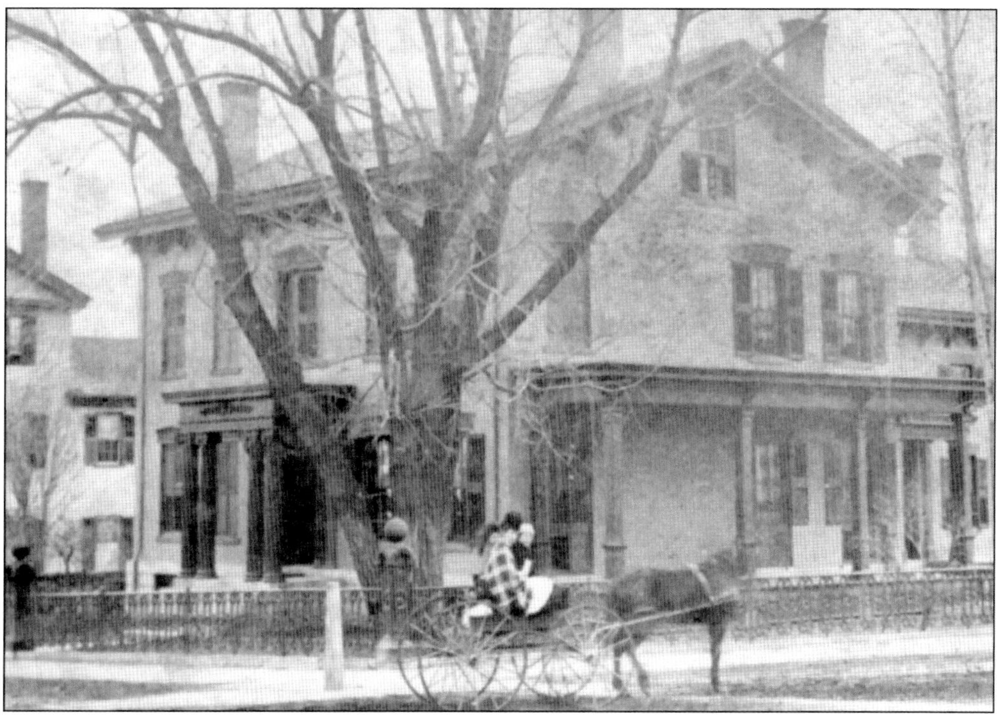

Pictured here is another view of the N. Kingsland House on a snowy Keeseville winter day. Today, Pleasant Street is part of Route 9N, which runs north and south through New York.

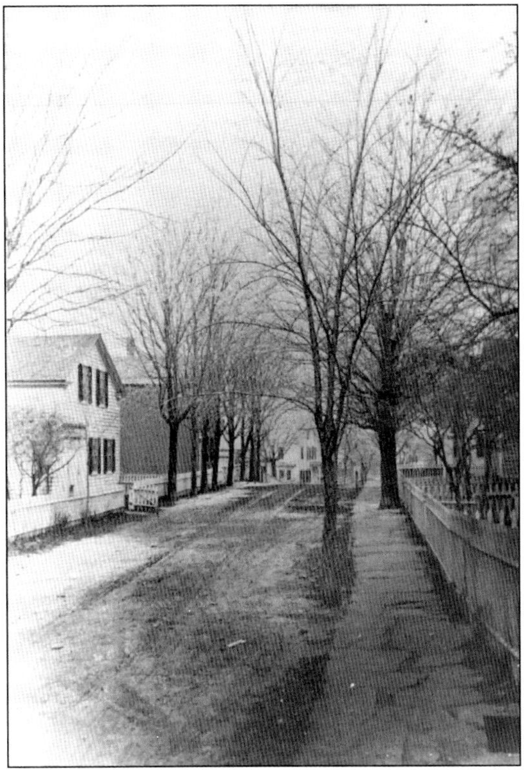

This 1880 photograph shows the Mills House on Beach Street. Beach Street, just off Main Street, was a popular home for well-to-do factory workers and shop owners due to its proximity to downtown and the factories on the other side of the river.

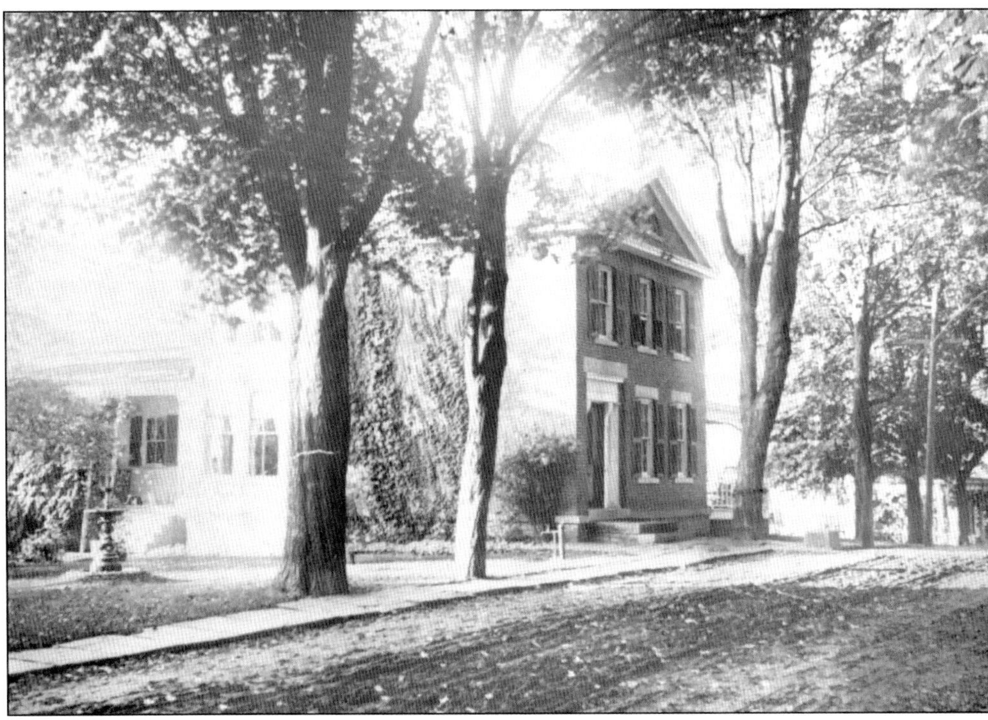

This photograph, taken prior to the 1900s, shows a stately house on Beach Street. The house features the clean architectural lines common in many of the homes built early in Keeseville.

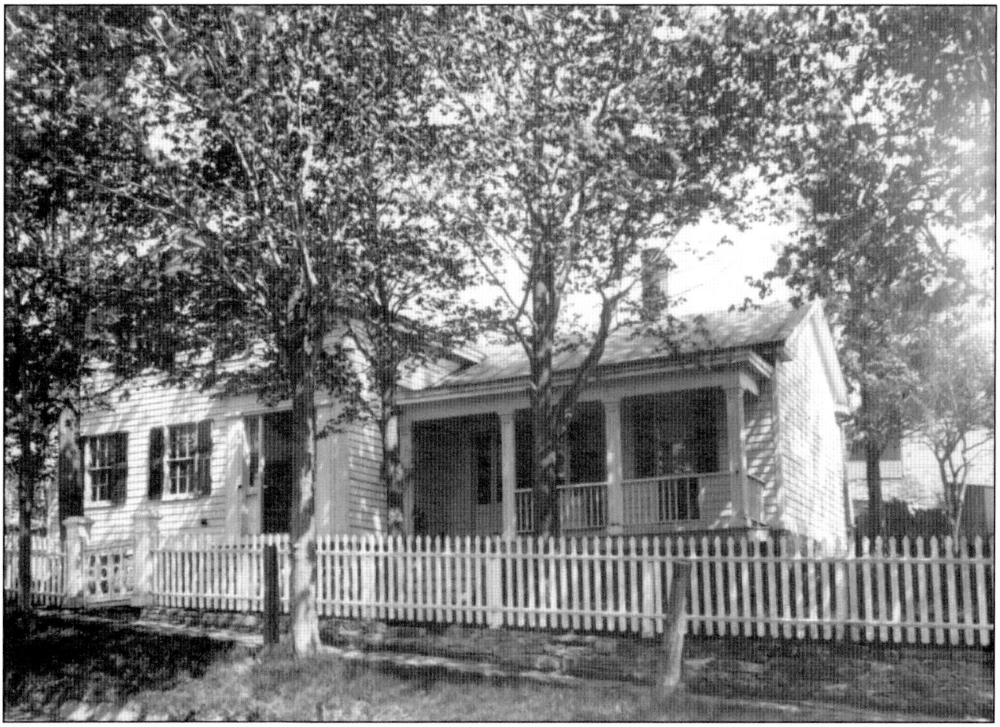

The residence of Viola Durham, located on Kent Street, is the subject of this undated photograph. A common feature to many of the residences outside of the main streets of Front and Main was the picket fence seen here.

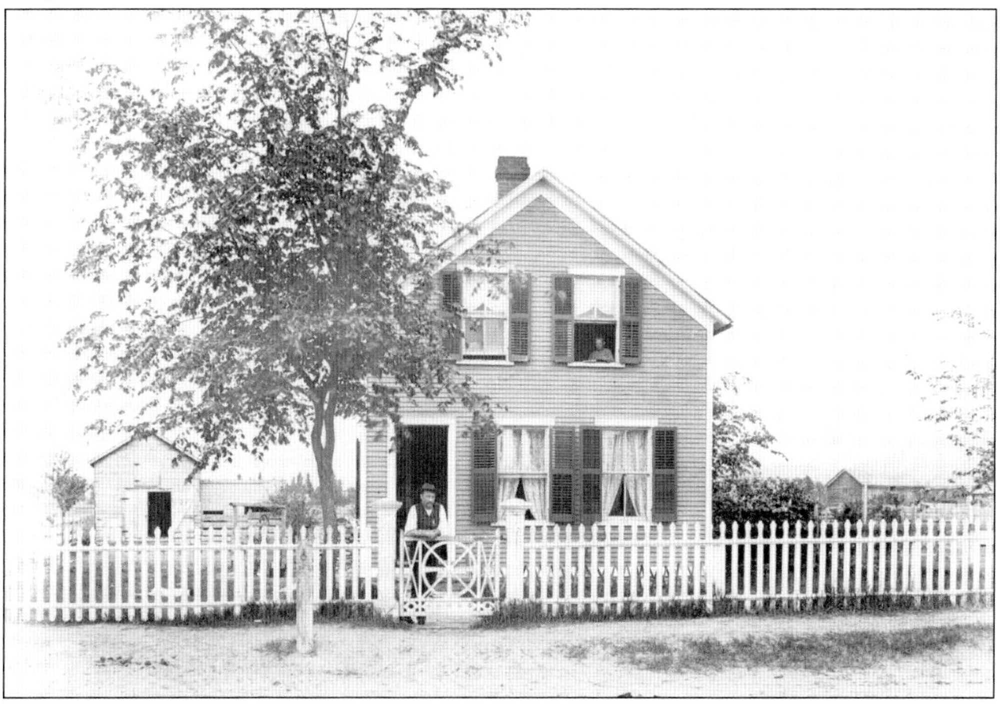

In this undated photograph, H. Savage leans against the front gate of his house.

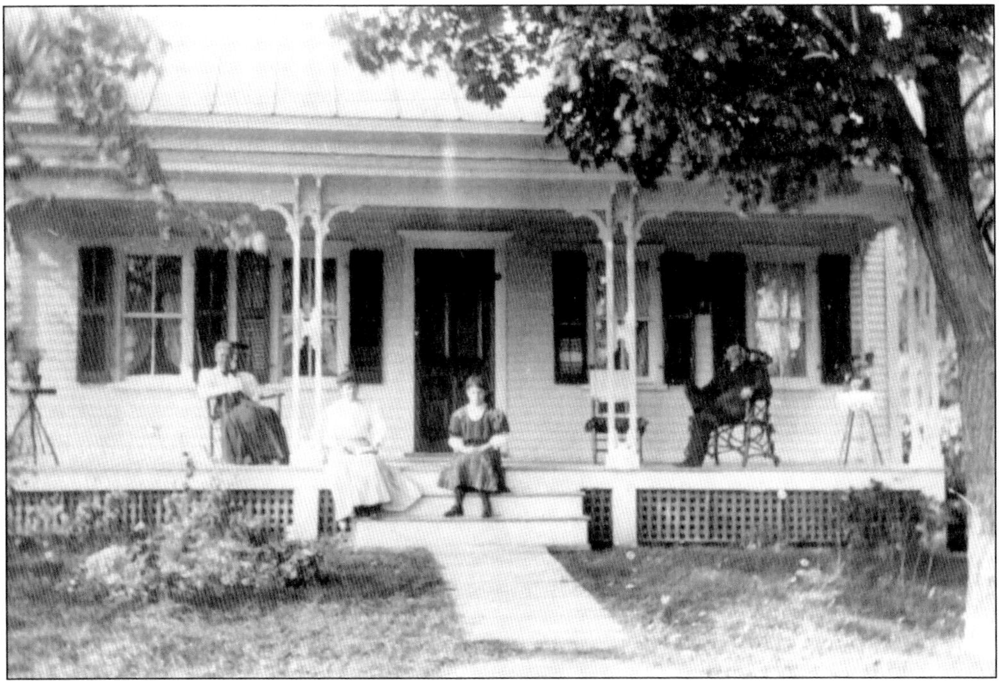

Edward Dumollin's family poses on the front porch of their home, which was later sold and became known as the Hubert Toomey House. The four front posts highlight the cornice architecture popular in Keeseville buildings.

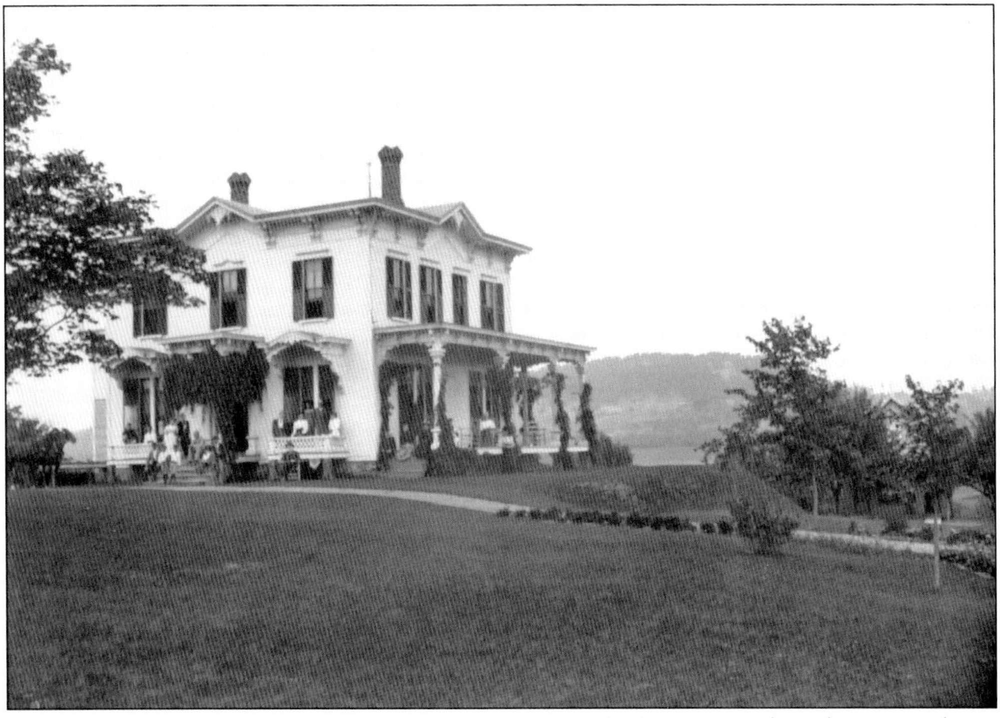

This undated photograph shows the Clawbonny Hotel, which once stood on the Mace Chasm Road. It was destroyed by fire in 1911. This is now known as the Beckwith Farm.

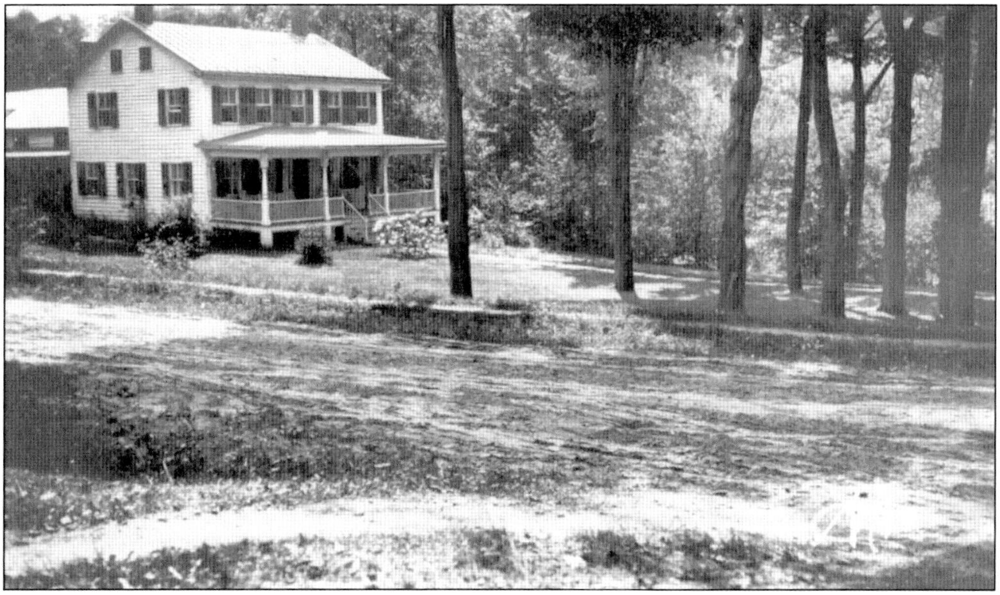

This 1830 photograph shows one of the earlier houses built in the Keeseville area prior to the popular Greek Revival style that sprang up several years later. This house features the clean-cut lines and square shapes common in early residences.

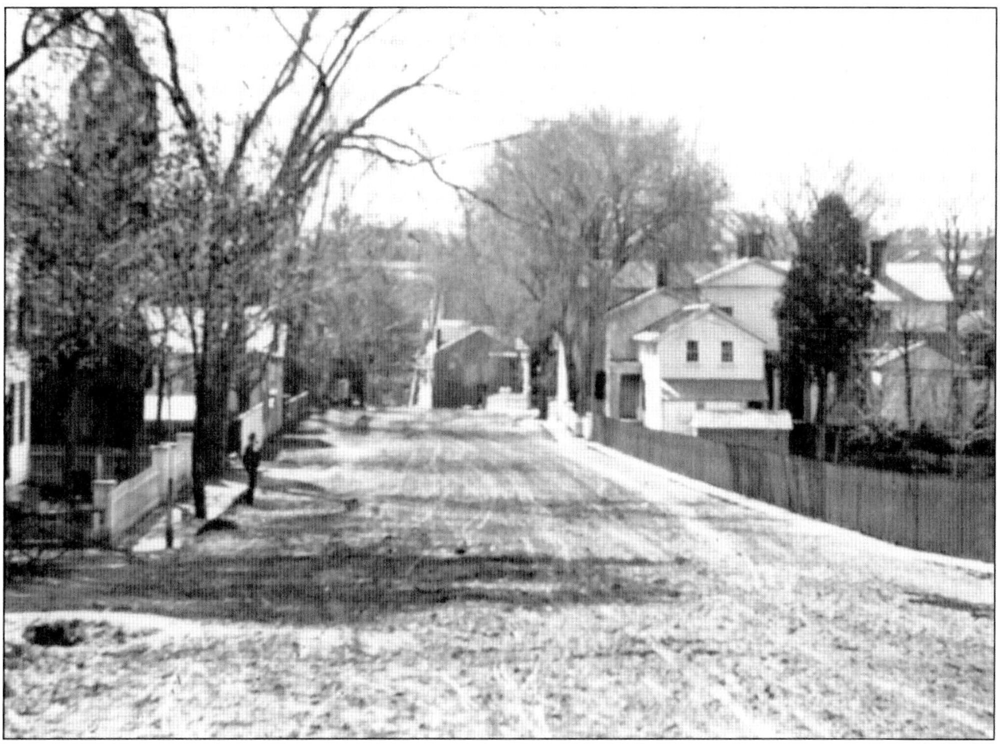

One of the main roads off Front Street was Clinton Street, pictured here in the 1870s. This photograph was taken partway up Clinton Street, with Front Street crossing at the center. Today, the Chesterfield town offices are located on the first corner of Clinton Street. Clinton Street is the home of St. Paul's Episcopal Church, built in 1853.

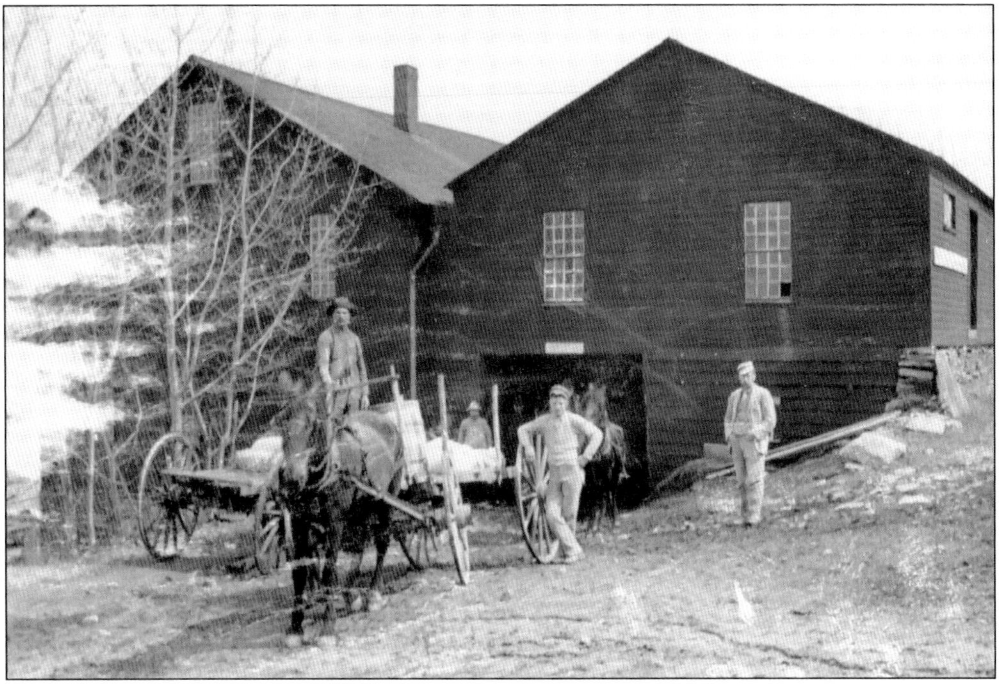

The gristmill utilized the powerful water of the Ausable River at the upper dam location. The gristmill was built in 1815, one of the first operations in the Keeseville area, and it continued to operate well until the end of the 1800s.

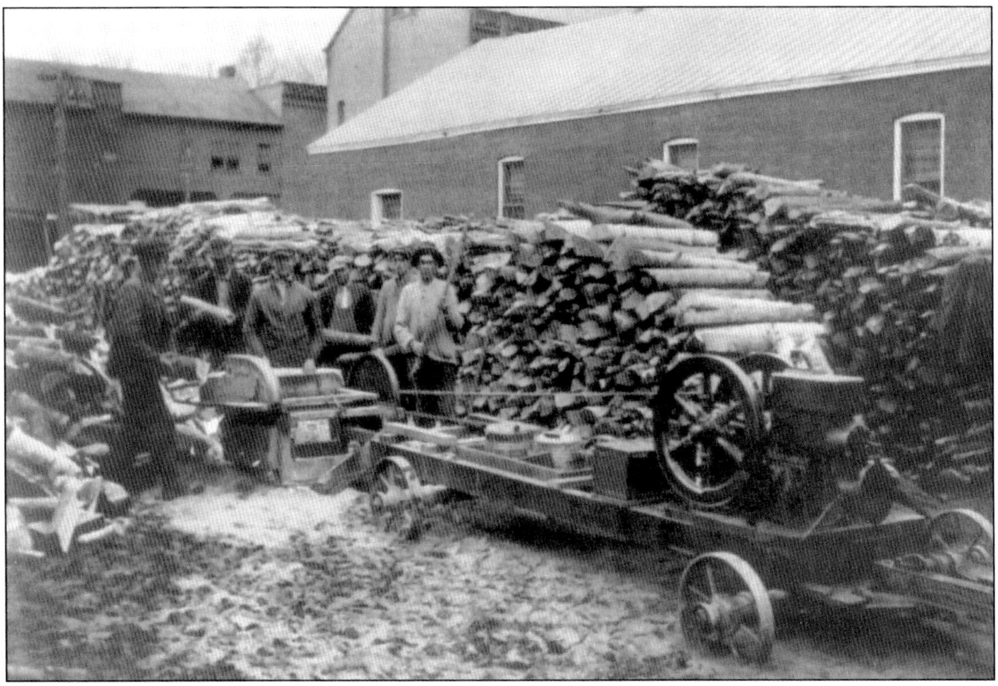

This undated photograph shows workers shaping the lumber that would be used in the many factories along the Ausable River, from pulp mills to furniture stores. Adirondack timber and iron ore were important natural resources for the local businesses.

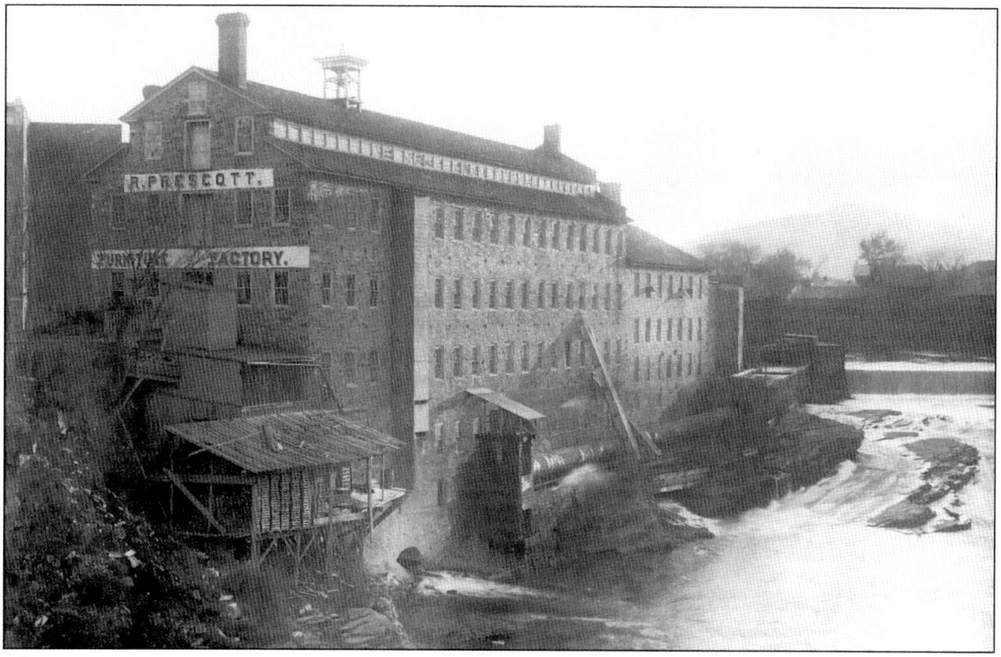

This 1880s photograph shows the R. Prescott Furniture Factory, which ran along the edge of the Ausable River in downtown Keeseville. Just visible running alongside the factory is the large pipe that water rushed through to generate power for the factory as well as the exhaust venting that allowed water to run back into the river.

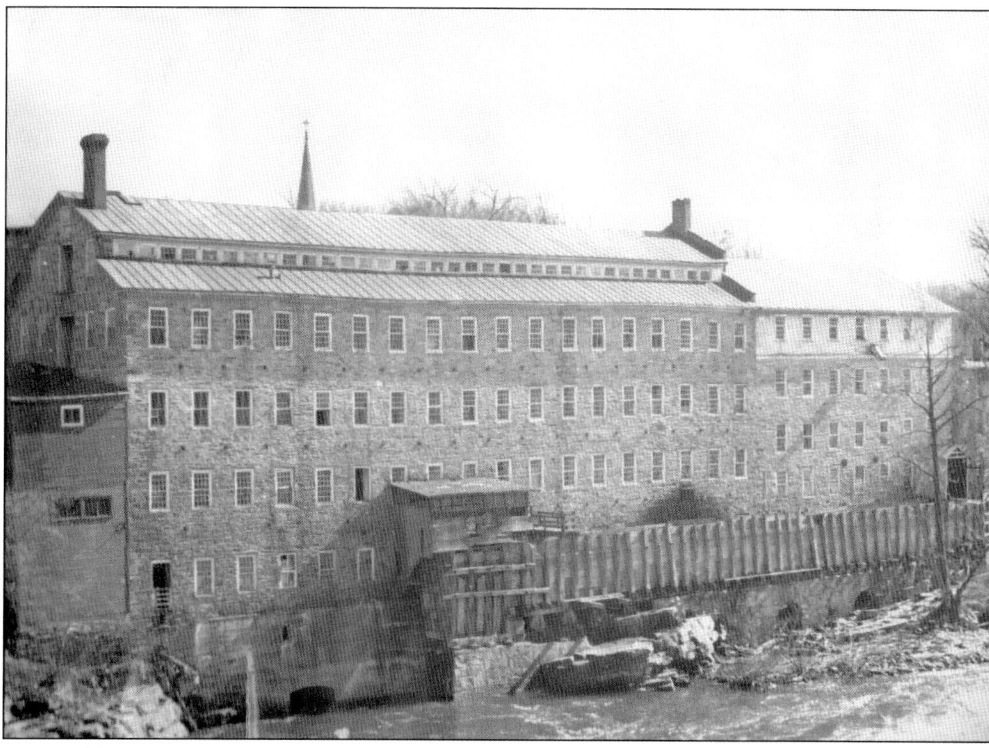

Pictured here is another view of the R. Prescott manufacturing plant.

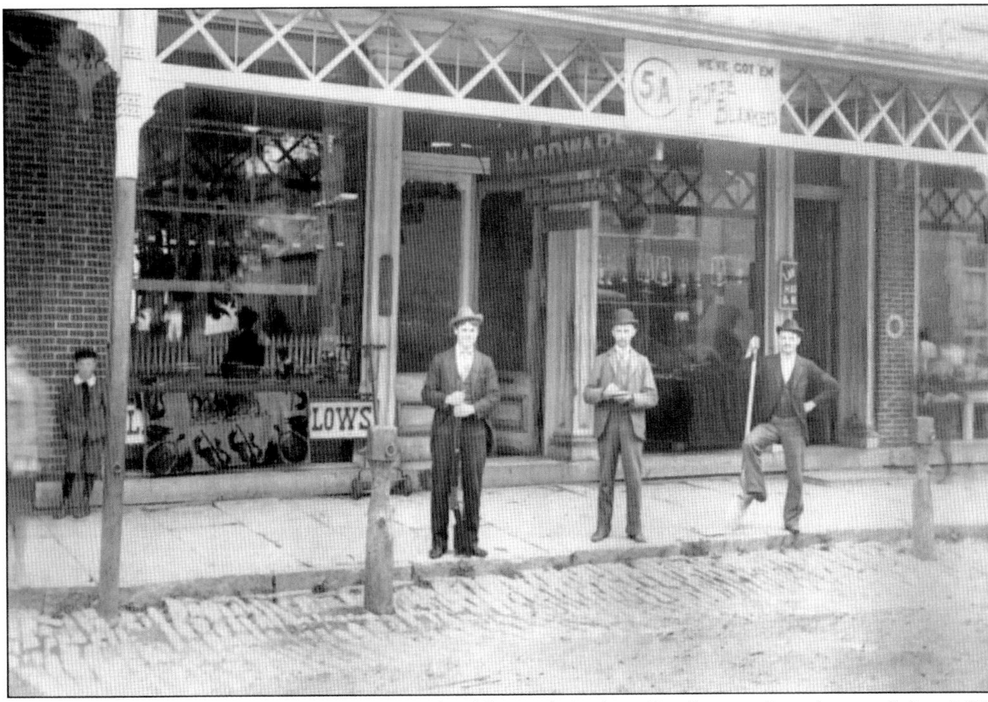

From left to right, Robert Hayes, A.W. Shields, and Arthur Boule stand in front of the A.W. Shields and Company Hardware Store on Front Street in this undated photograph.

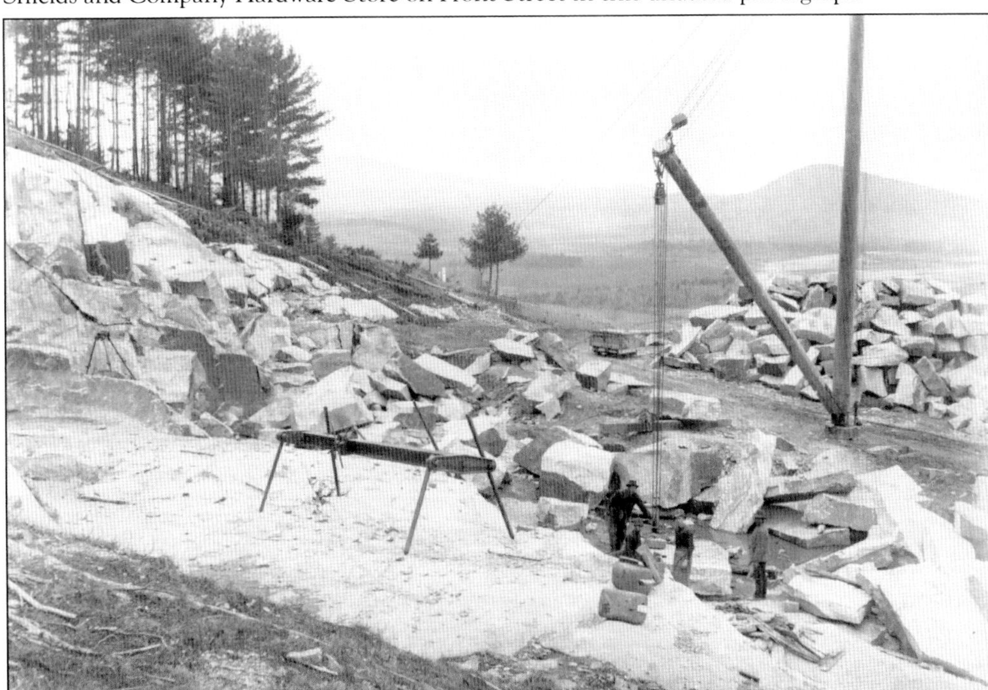

The Ausable Granite Quarry provided the stone that went into the building of many of the factories and homes in the area, as well as the material used for the sidewalks in the 1880s. It also provided the material for the Arch Bridge.

This 1890 insurance map shows the interior of the huge Ausable Nail Factory, which ran alongside the Ausable River in downtown Keeseville. With the many forges, fires were a constant risk, creating a need for itemized schematics of the operation, from the location to means of securing the facility.

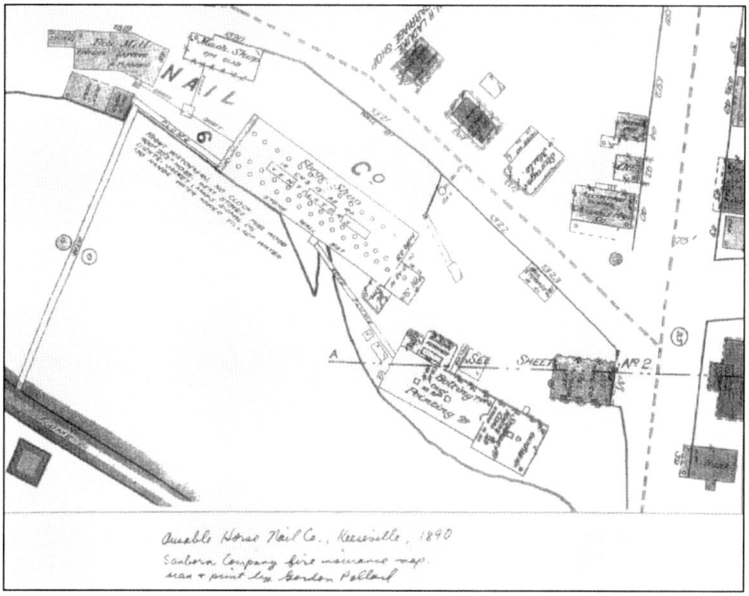

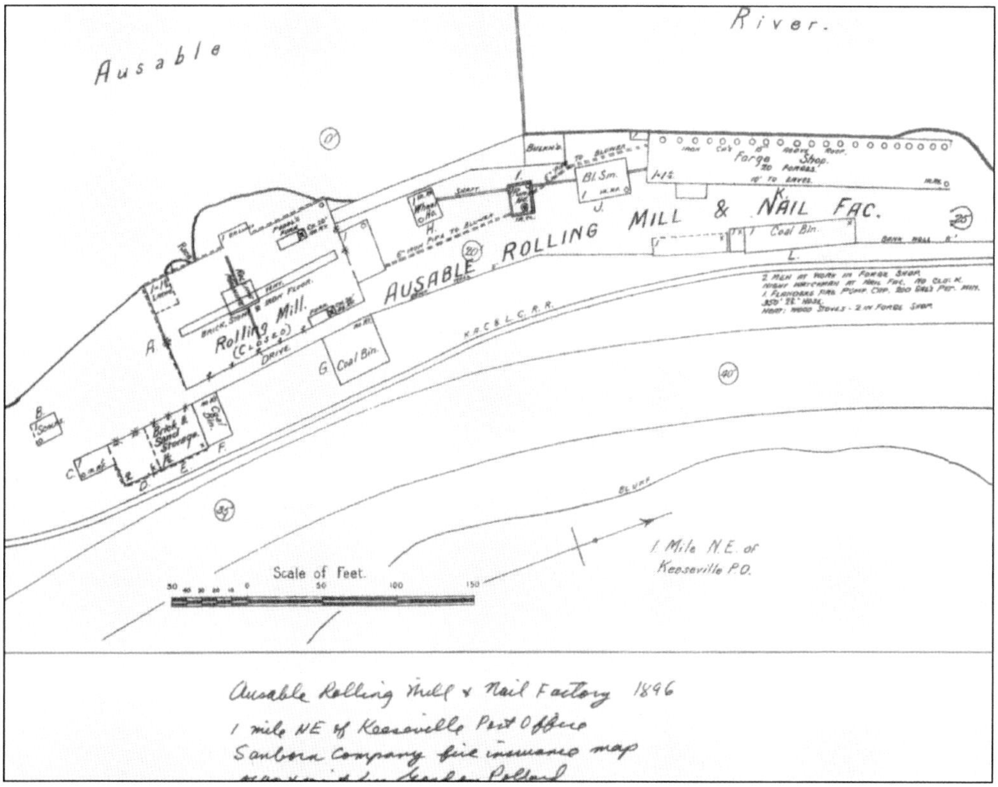

Drawn six years later, another insurance map sketches the Ausable Rolling Mill and Nail Factory. At this point, the factory was using 20 forges for its production.

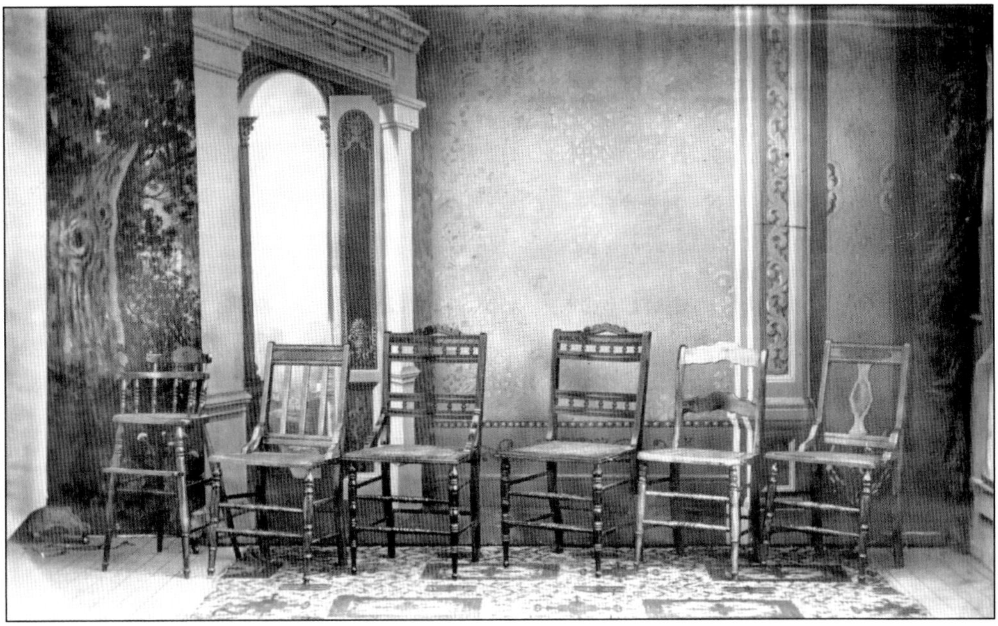

In its highly stylized showroom, six examples of chairs available are presented that were manufactured in the R. Prescott Furniture Factory and Store. Rufus Prescott purchased the location, known as the Yellow Shop, and manufactured his furniture starting around 1856.

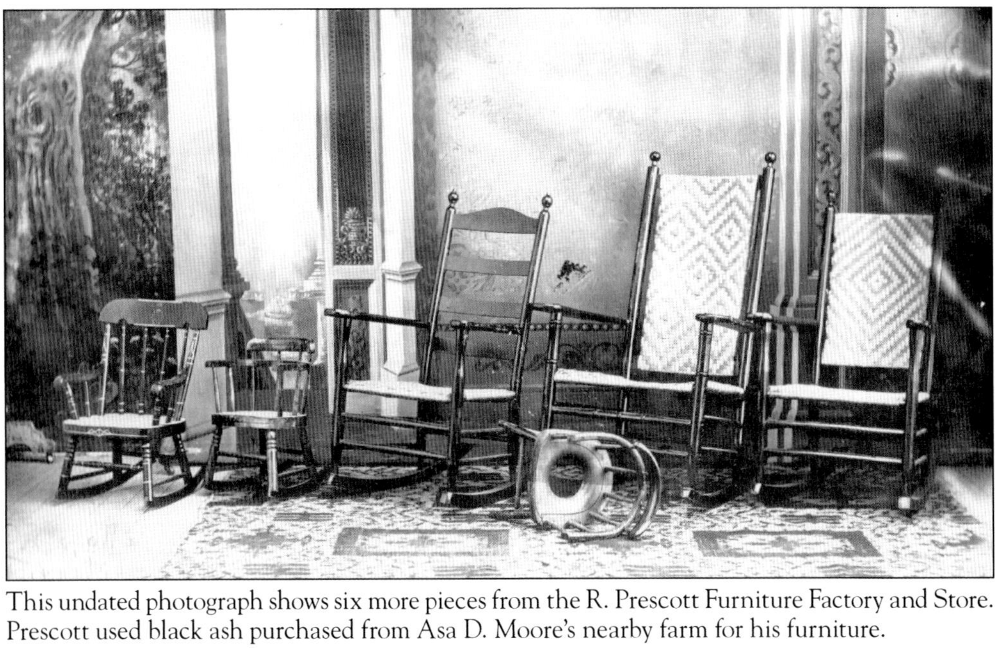

This undated photograph shows six more pieces from the R. Prescott Furniture Factory and Store. Prescott used black ash purchased from Asa D. Moore's nearby farm for his furniture.

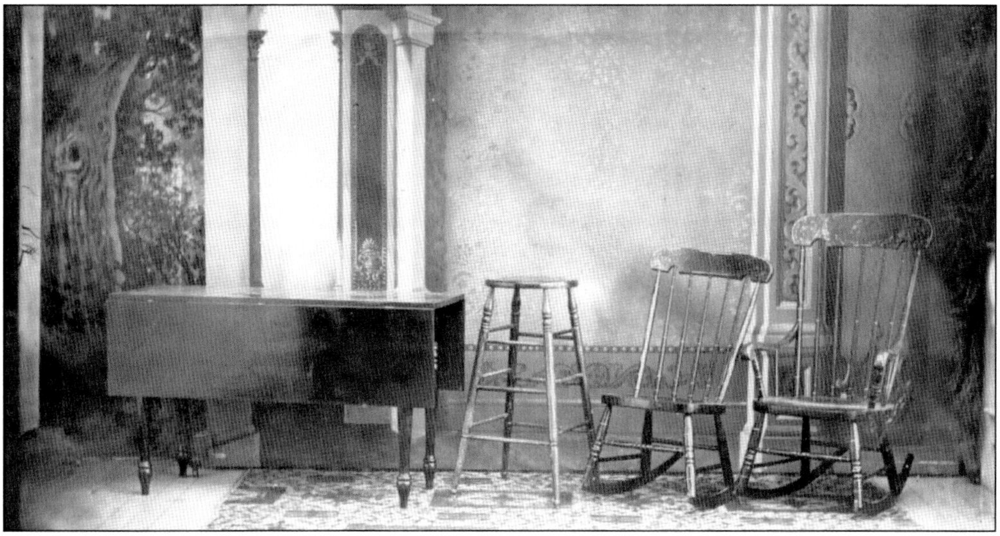

Rufus Prescott and his son were craftsmen who could generate high-quality furniture in their factory. In 1878, the factory employed 60 workers. The company formally incorporated in 1888 in a new location after a fire destroyed the entire business, forcing it to relocate.

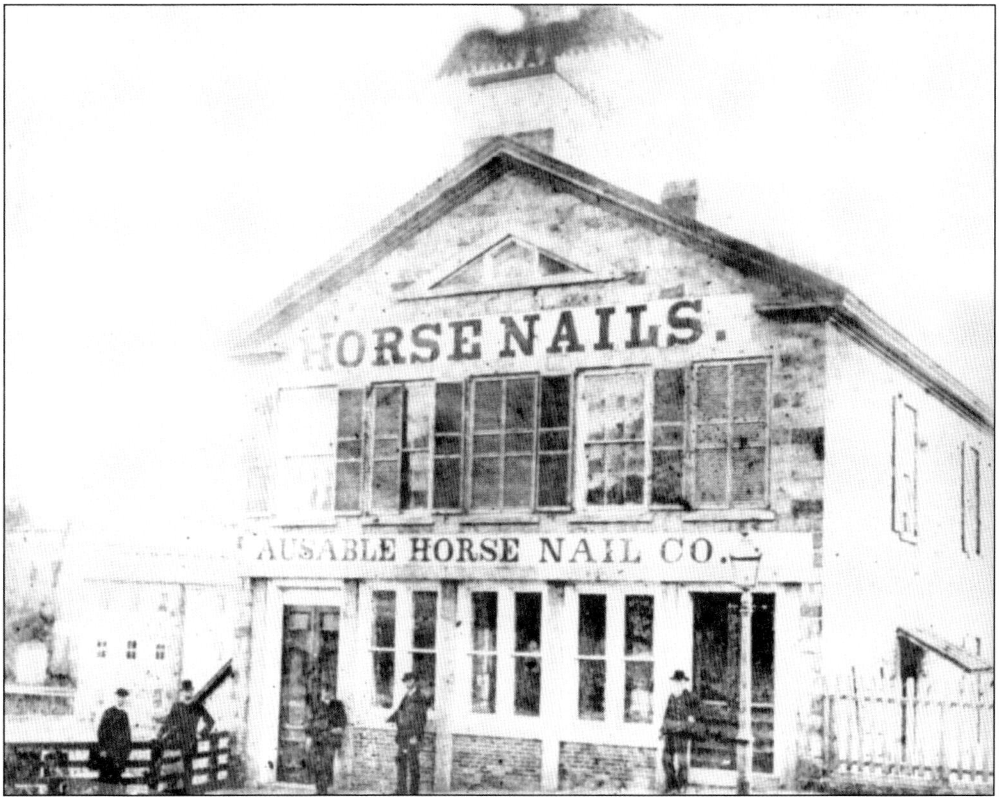

The storefront of the Ausable Horse Nail Company on Main Street in Keeseville appears in all its glory in this undated photograph. The gilded wooden eagle spreads its wings on the rooftop. Today, the building (without the eagle) is the home of the Adirondack Architectural Heritage, an organization dedicated to preserving local history, directed by local historian Steven Engelhart.

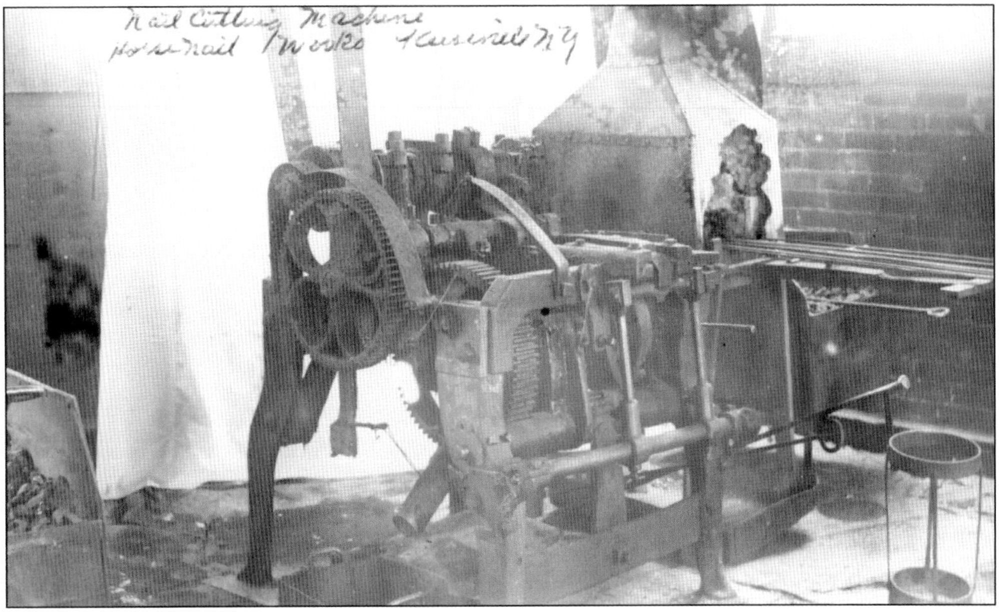

In an upstairs workshop in the horse nail factory headquarters on Main Street, Daniel Dodge spent a period from 1848 to 1862 designing and perfecting machines that could produce horse nails from iron ore at high speeds.

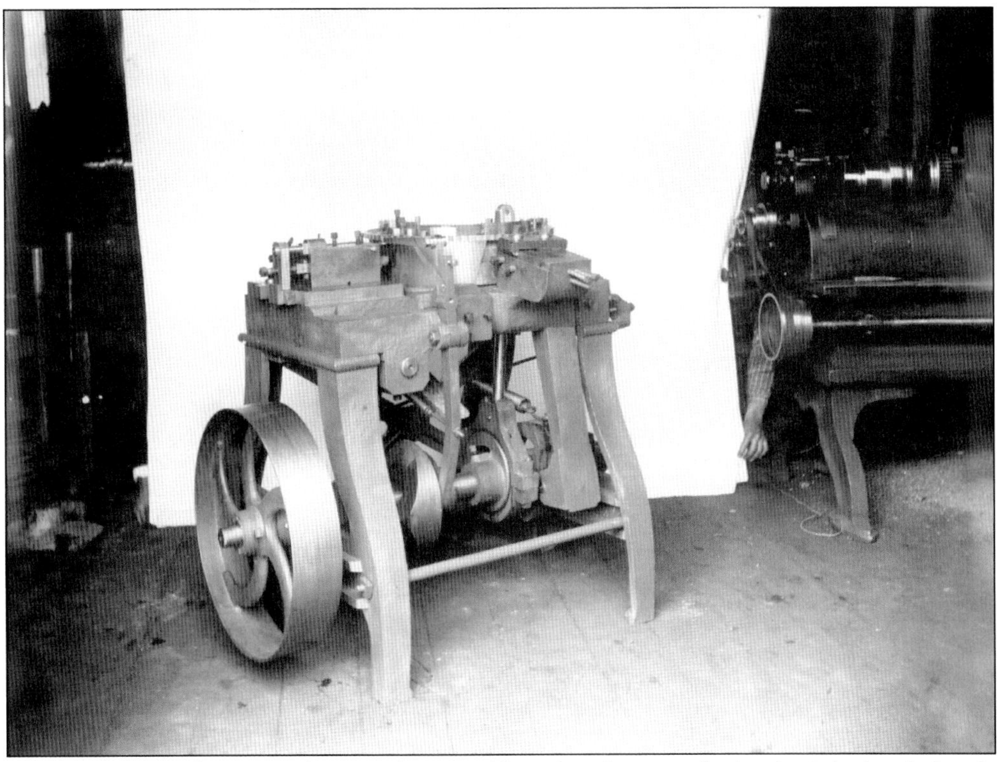

Revolutionary in design, Dodge's machine could produce horse nails that had the head already attached. Previously this was a lengthy three-step process from shaping to affixing the head to the point. Boys operating 50 machines could each produce 40 nails per minute.

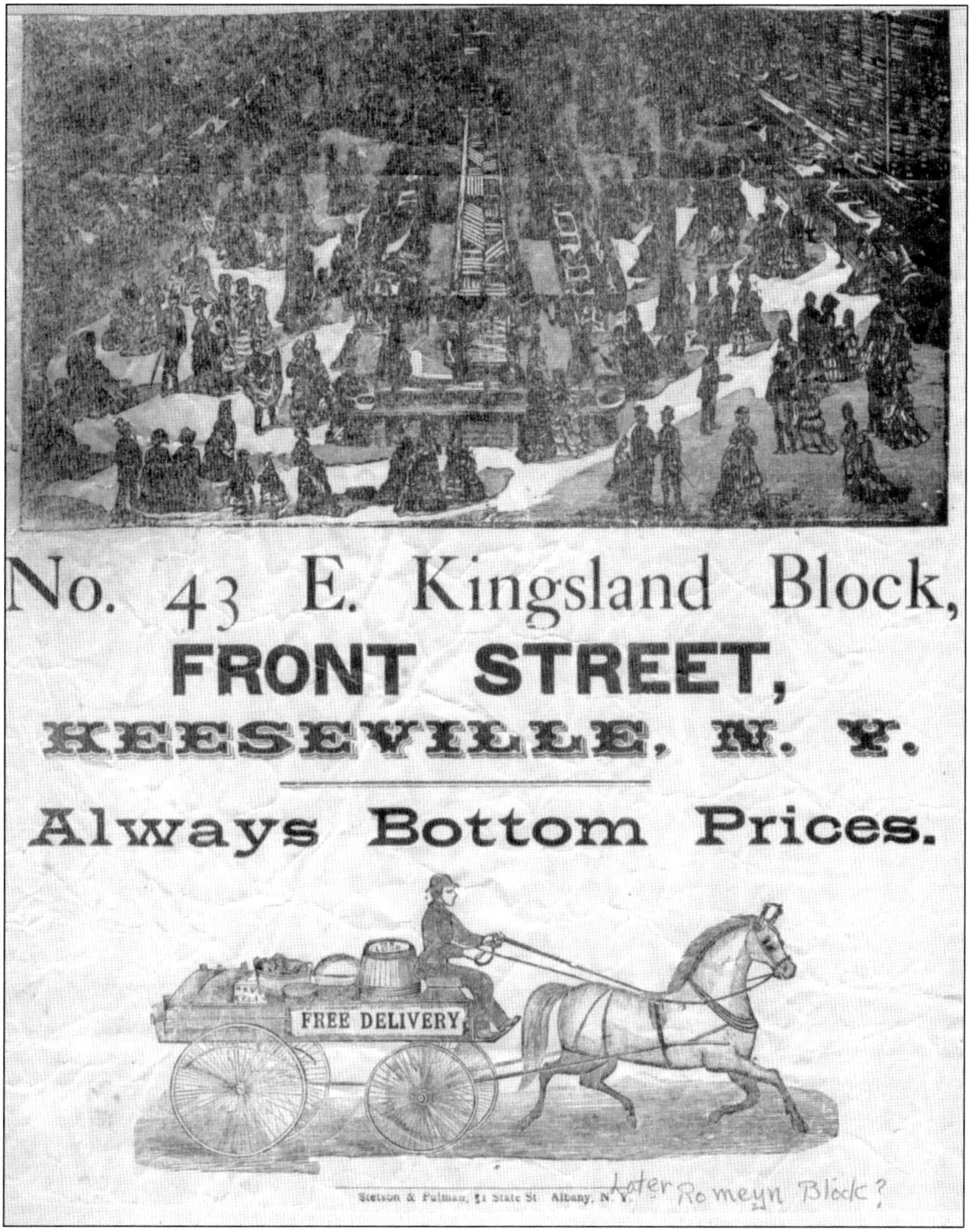

This full-page advertisement shows the mid-1800s business block known as Kingsland's Block. By 1847, Keeseville had a population of 2,700 and sported a rolling mill, two grist and flour mills, a wagon shop, a cabinet store, three sawmills, a foundry, a bank, an academy, eight dry goods and general stores, 12 grocery stores, two drugstores, a bookstore, two clothing stores, three other stores, two printing plants, two saddle and harness shops, four tailor shops, three wheelwright shops, and 12 blacksmith shops. At this time, E.W. Kingsland and his son were fully involved in the business and politics of the village of Keeseville, owning several key buildings and businesses, running the opera house, and holding office as well as positions on numerous committees. Business was indeed booming along the Front Street area.

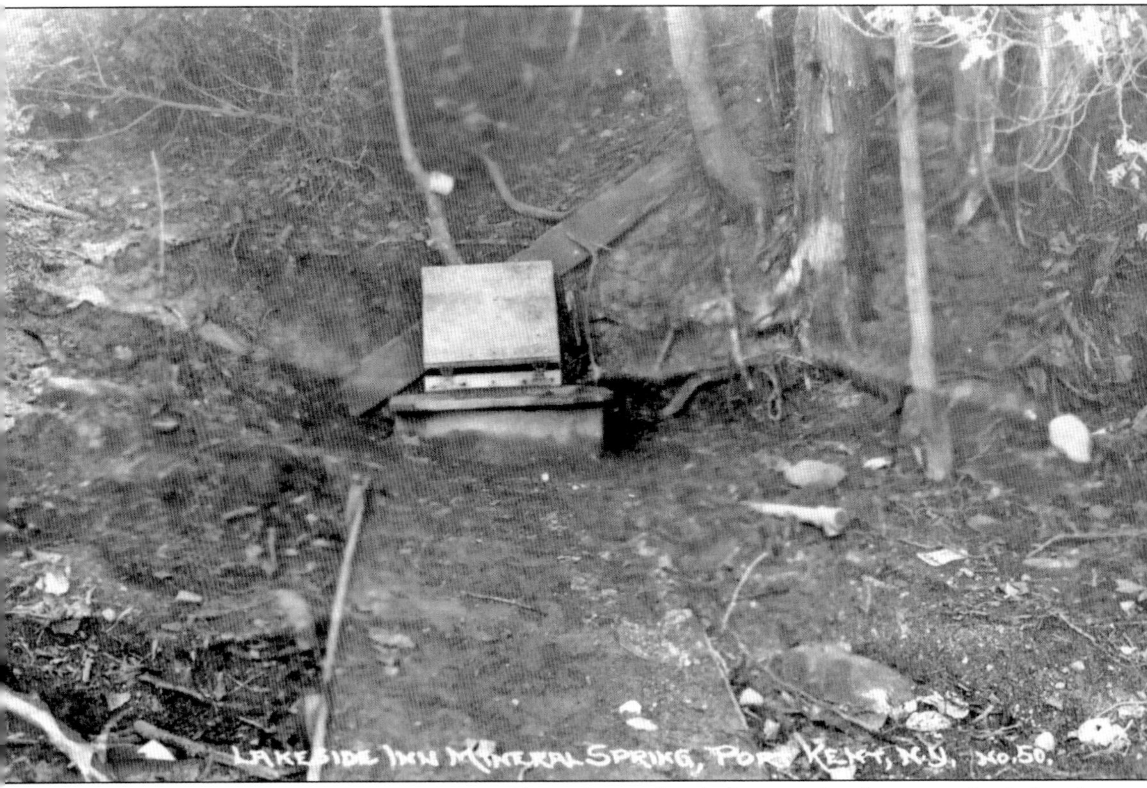

The fountain of a mineral spring is visible in this undated photograph taken near the Lakeside Inn in Port Kent. It was actually in Keeseville that mineral springs would turn into a lucrative business with Dietade Mineral Springs.

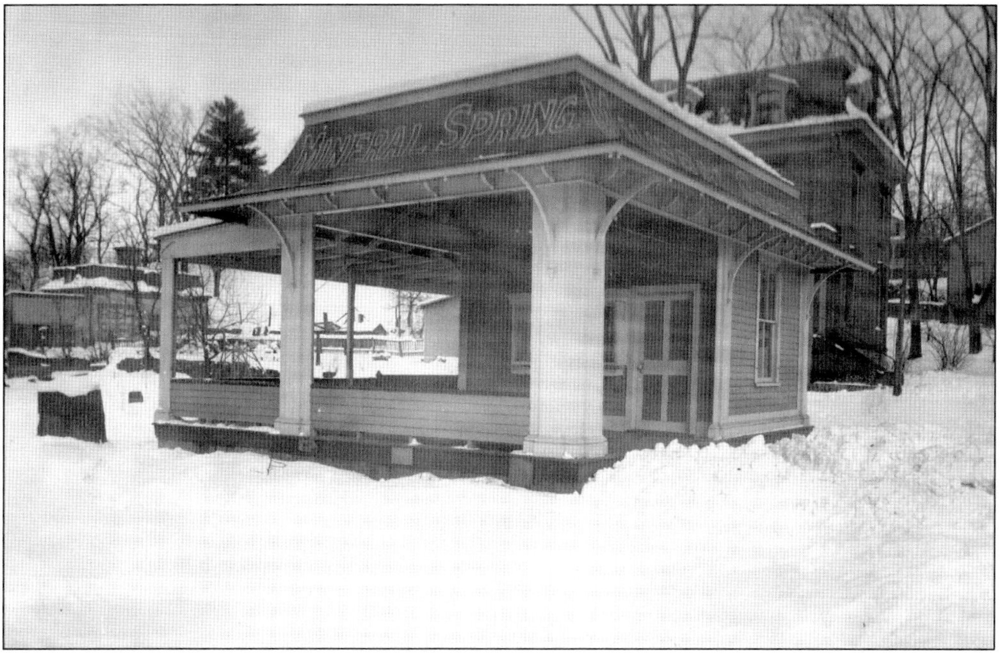

The Mineral Springs Store in the 1900s is shown here. In March 1915, a chemical analysis of the spring water was made, revealing the great amount of mineral matter that was in the solution.

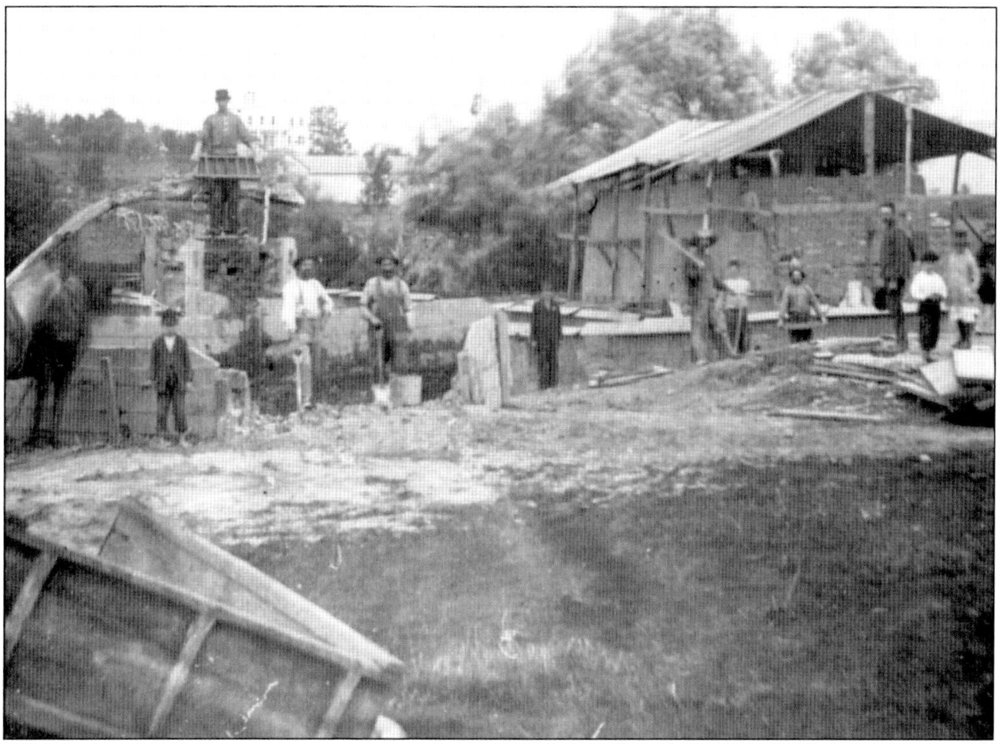
Mace Chasm Road, running between Keeseville and Ausable Chasm, was home to many farms and stone businesses, including the Mussen Brickyard, seen in this 1870 photograph. On the hill in the background is the Clarence Daughty House.

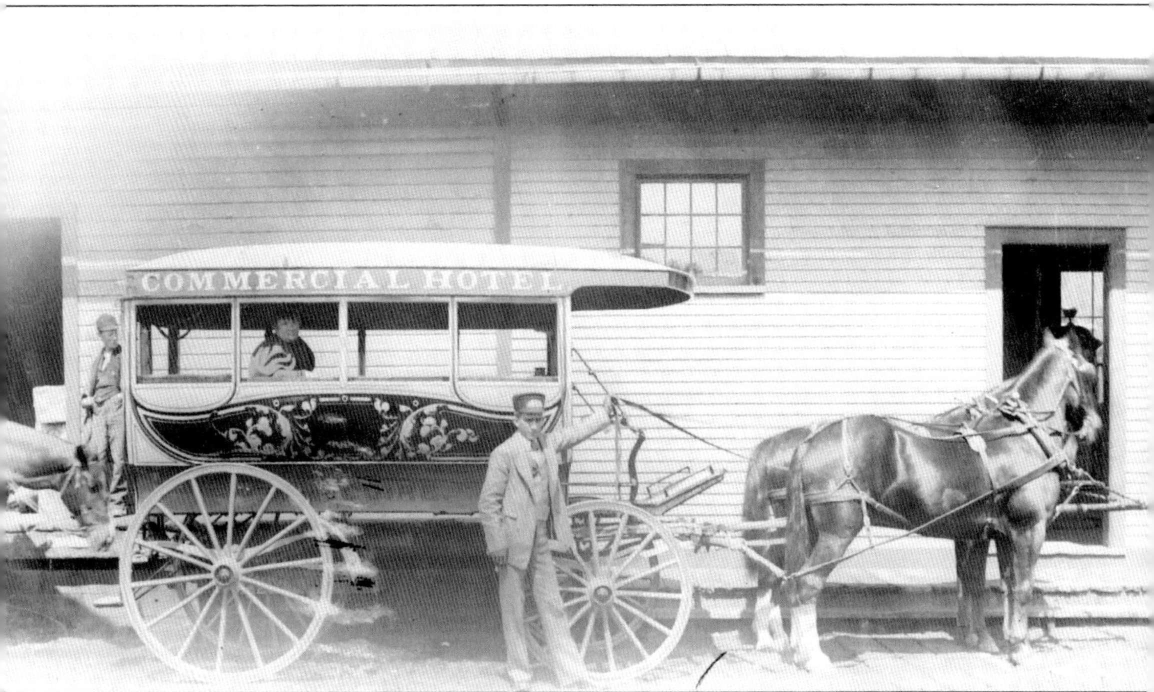

The commercial bus that transported passengers from the Keeseville station of the peanut railroad to the depot in Port Kent is pictured here between 1890 and 1900. Once there, passengers could travel by rail north to Plattsburgh and Montreal or south to Albany and New York City or by ferry across to Vermont. The railroad operated from 1890 until 1920, traveling a five-mile stretch. The railroad was set up one way, meaning the train traveled backwards on the ride back to Keeseville. To get over the deep gorge at Ausable Chasm, a cantilever bridge was designed and built. According to Poor's Railroad Manual of 1890, the line averaged 4.55¢ per mile for passengers. The railroad was established by businessmen of Keeseville to transport the heavy iron and wood-manufactured goods to the train station and ferry quicker than horses could carry the heavy loads.

With large quantities of wood always present and the hot fires of many forges, wildfires were a harsh reality for Keeseville. In 1876, many residents of Keeseville are seen standing around the rubble of Front Street after a particularly devastating fire destroyed most of the buildings.

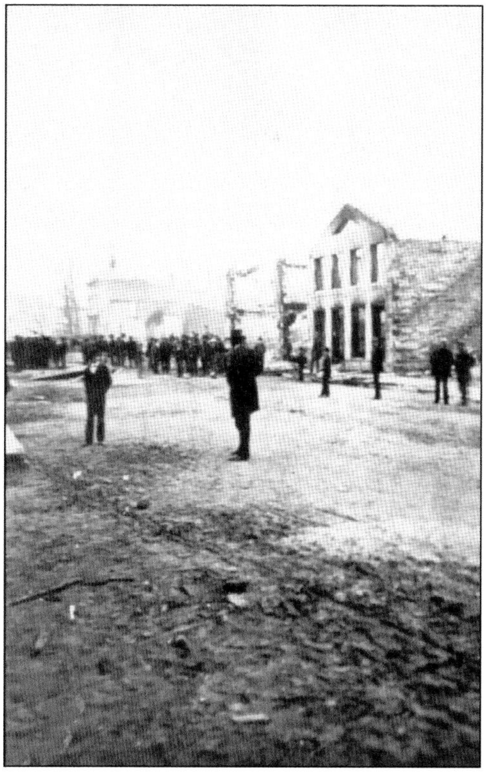

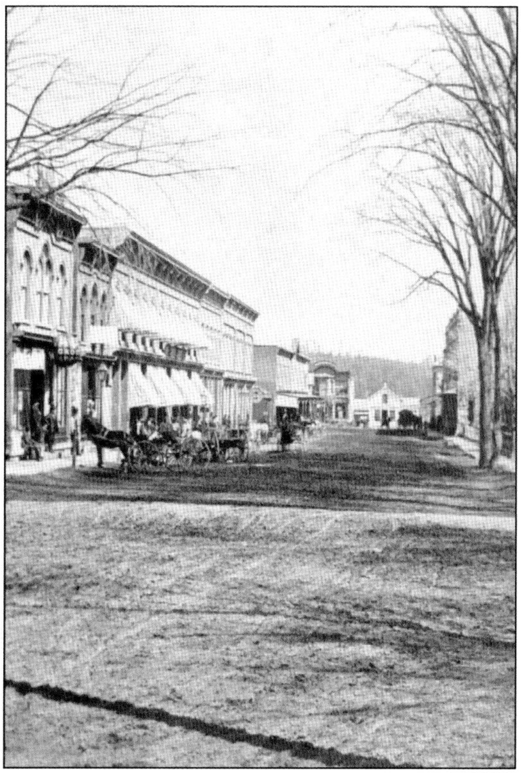

After the fire of 1875, Front Street was rebuilt and appears much the same today. In 1878, the Keeseville Fire Department was formed, with Henry M. Mould as chief engineer. Hose and hook and ladder companies were formed at this same time. The fire department was one of the earliest volunteer fire departments in the country.

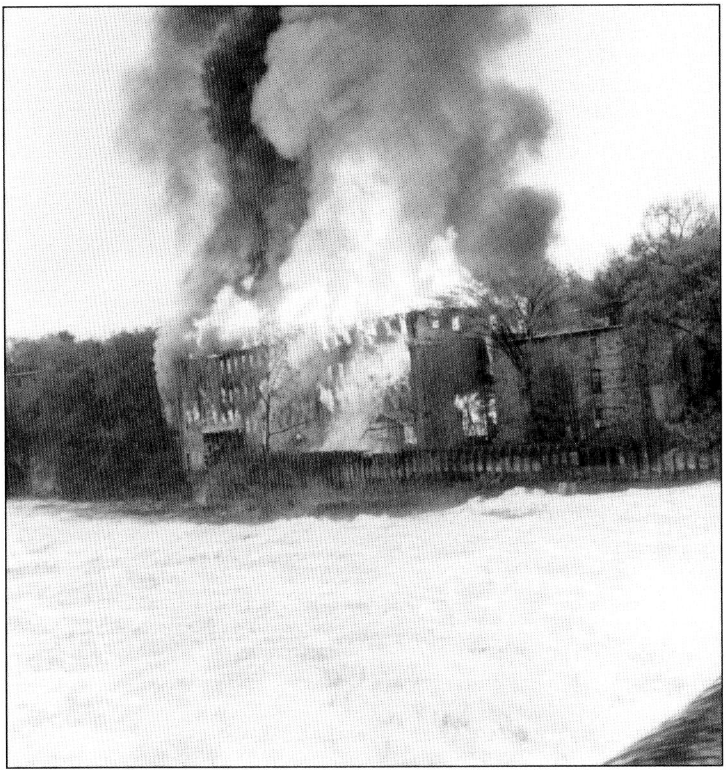

May 29, 1969, was the date of the last enormous fire in the Prescott Mill. With so many pulp and wood products, fires in the factory would get out of control quickly. The Ausable River creates a natural barrier for the downtown Keeseville area.

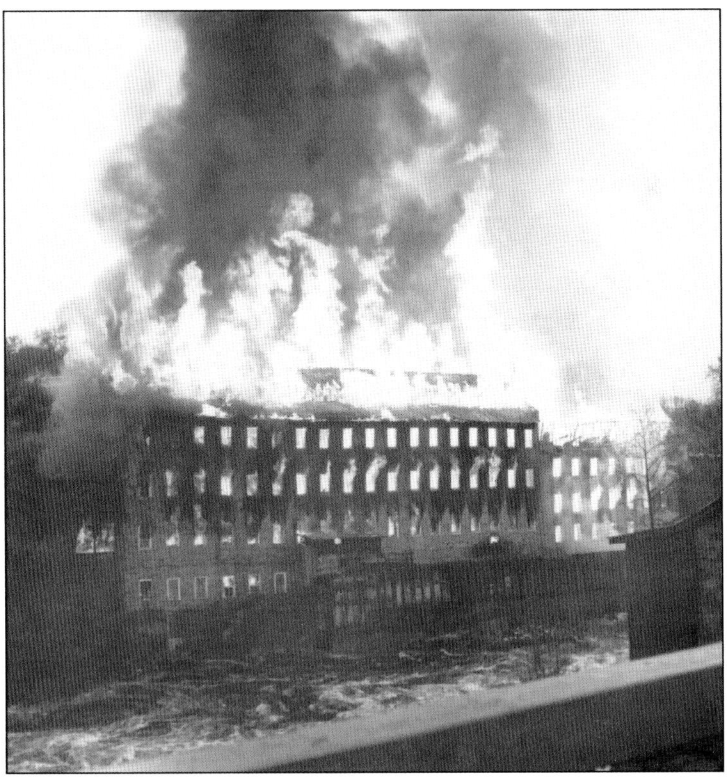

Another photograph shows the 1969 Prescott Mill fire. A fire in the early 1800s in the factory ignited the wooden support posts of the nearby bridge, causing it to collapse. The next design of the bridge was all in metal to prevent this from happening again.

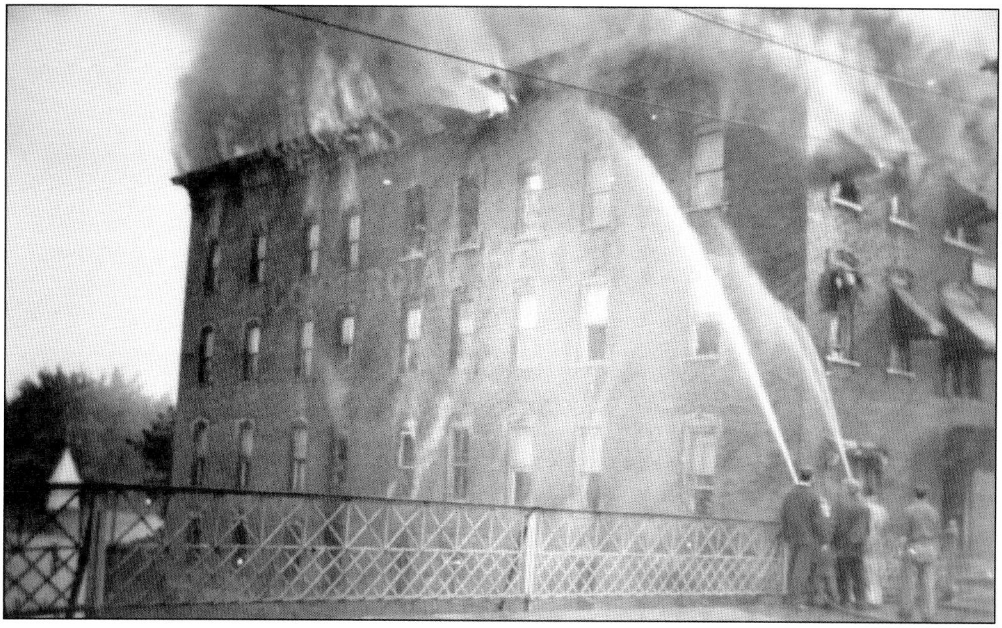

In 1940, a fire destroyed the Commercial Hotel, owned and operated by Adolphus Brelia and Anthony Santor. The hotel stood next to the Arch Bridge, on which firefighters are standing while they attempt to tame the conflagration.

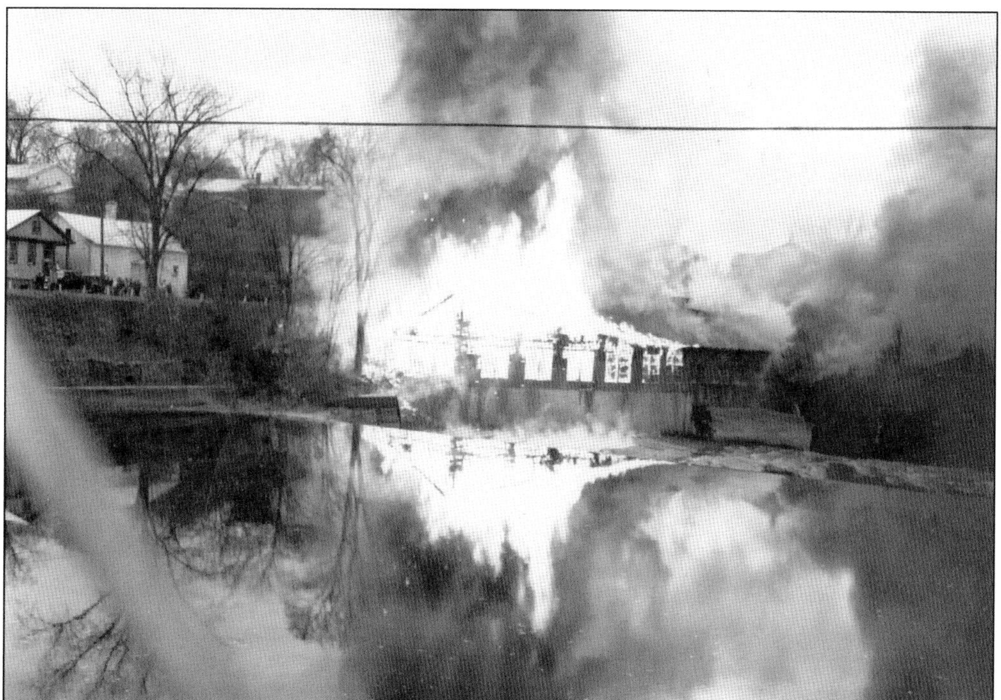

Flames are seen reflected in the still water of the Ausable River as Prescott Plant No. 2 goes up in flames on October 28, 1952.

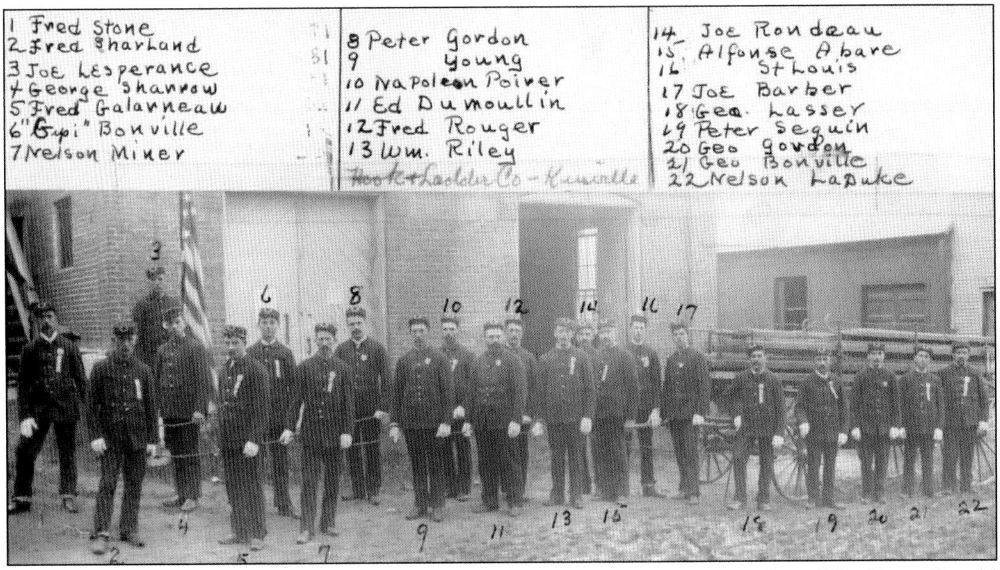

Pictured here is the hook and ladder team of Keeseville prior to 1900. In the 1970s, Pres. Gerald Ford paid a visit to the nearby Plattsburgh Air Force Base. During presidential visits, medical and fire teams were to be on standby at the location to react quickly to any situations that may arise. For his visit to the area, President Ford requested the presence of the Keeseville Fire Department Ambulance in acknowledgement of its distinction of being one of the first American all-volunteer fire departments.

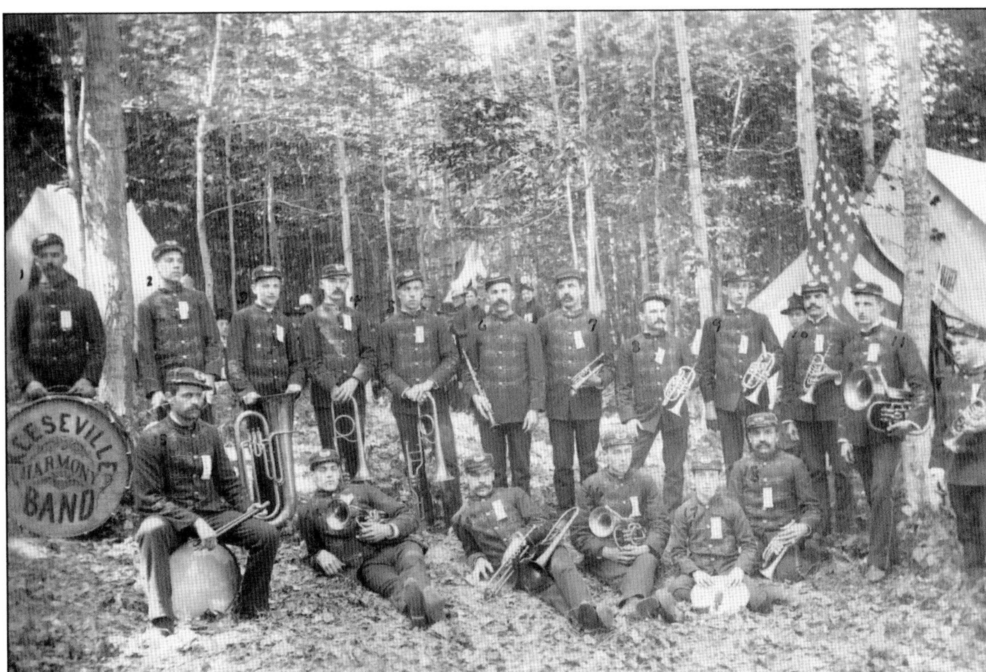

Keeseville was home to a professional uniformed marching band, the Keeseville Harmony Band. Here the members pose in a field in June 1890.

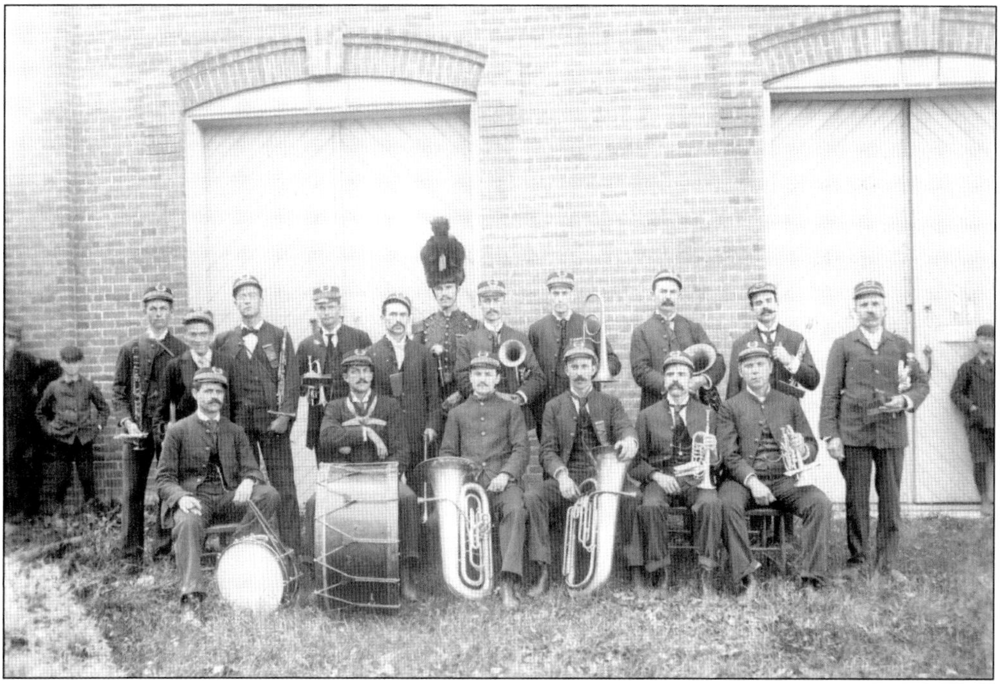

The Keeseville Harmony Band lasted from 1890 until its last performance in 1920. The group was made up entirely of dedicated volunteers from the Keeseville area. They performed for special occasions as well as at local fairs and events. This photograph shows the band in 1898.

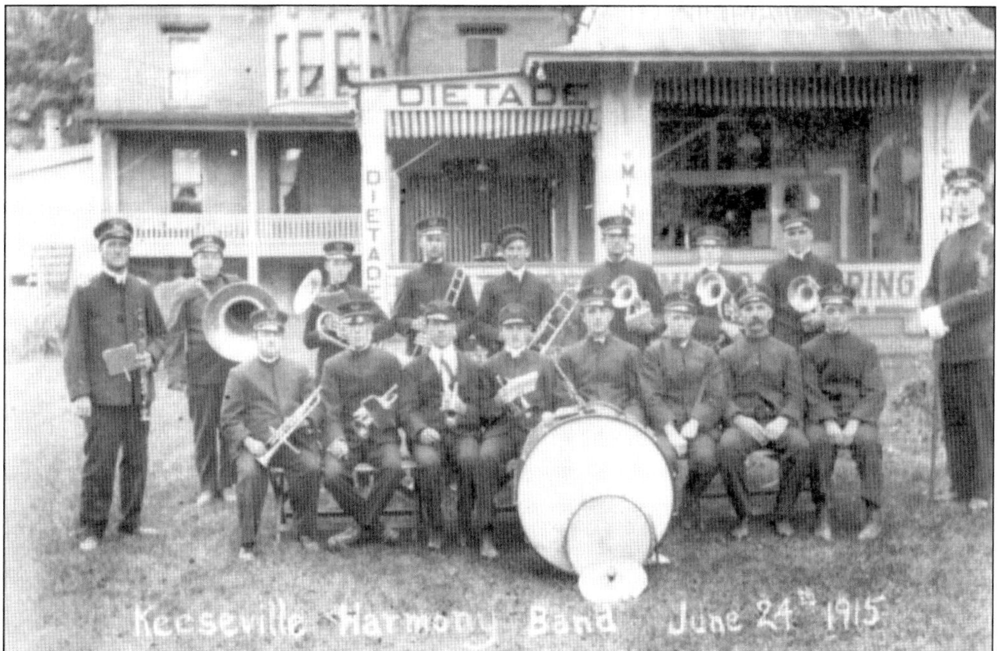

The Keeseville Harmony Band poses in front of the Dietade Mineral Springs Store on June 24, 1915. As members grew older, young Keeseville men were quick to replace them, keeping a steady membership for the active marching band.

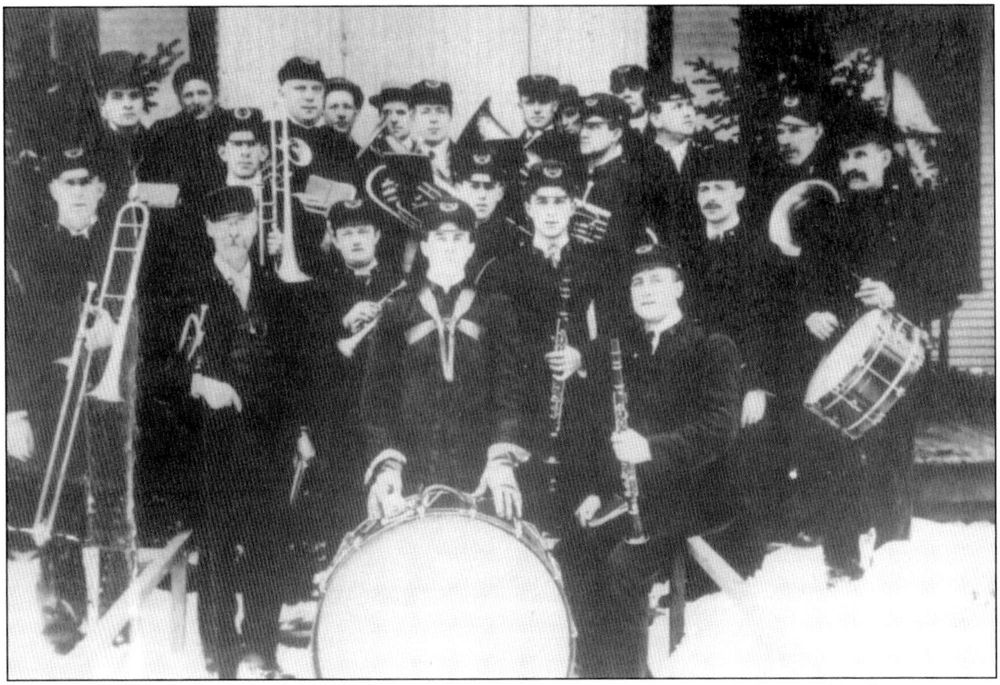

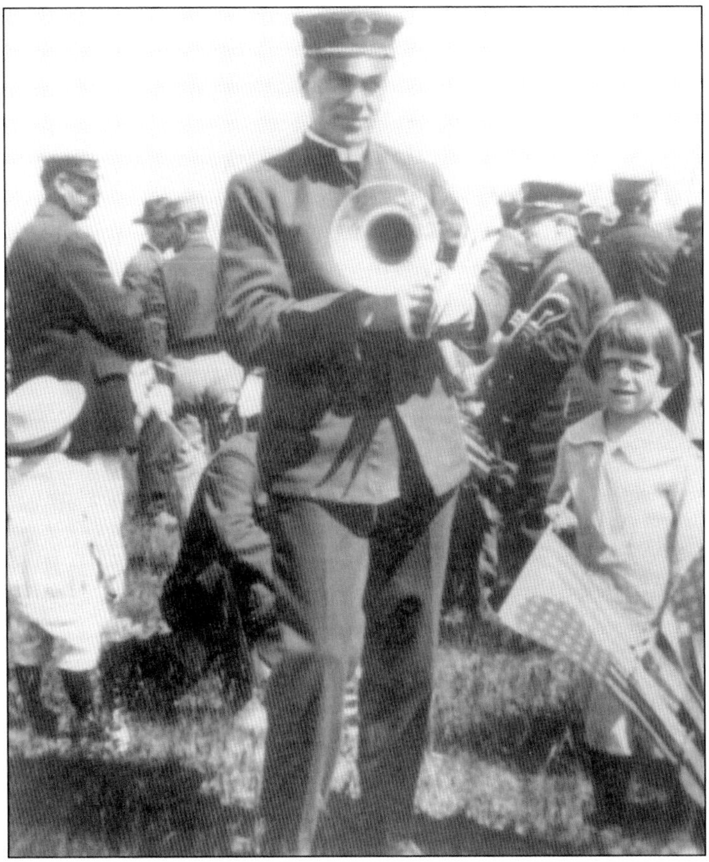

This undated photograph shows the members in a slightly different uniform at the time. The Keeseville Harmony Band operated totally on its own finances, purchasing all its own equipment. Mothers and wives of the members often made their uniforms by hand.

This undated photograph shows George Bradley of the Keeseville Harmony Band posing amongst the crowd at one of its performances. Some of the members played with the group its entire 30-year run.

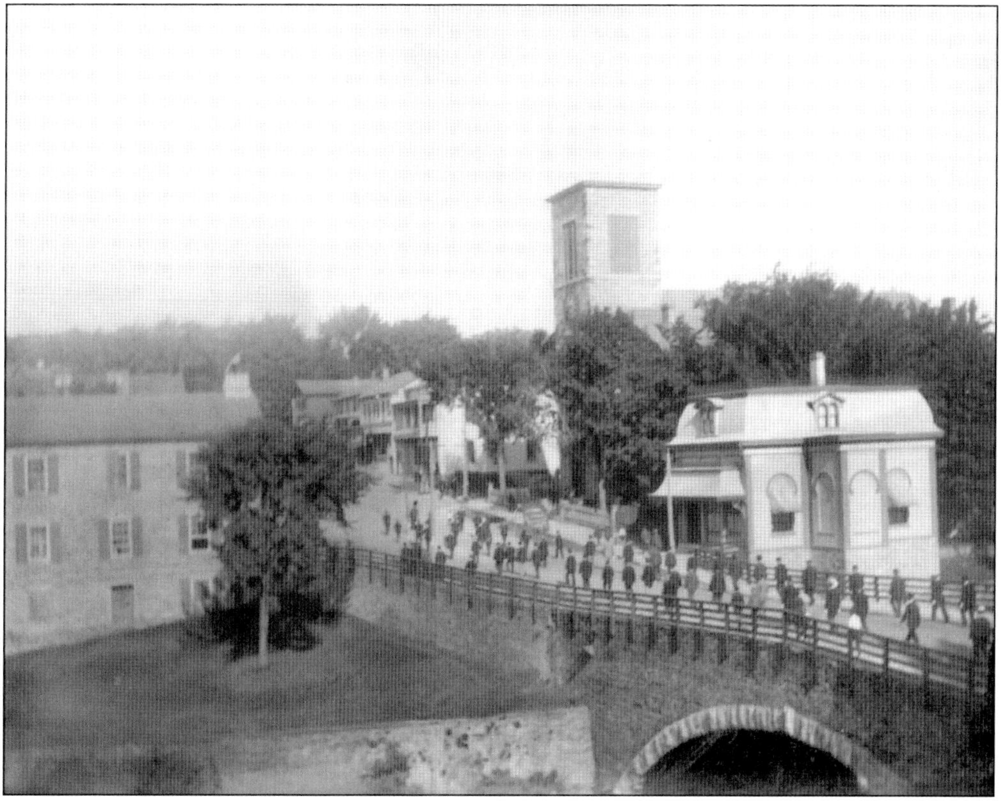

A parade is seen crossing the Arch Bridge in 1900. The event was the St John the Baptist Society annual parade. In one year from this parade, St. John's Church would be built up the hill in the direction the marchers are marching.

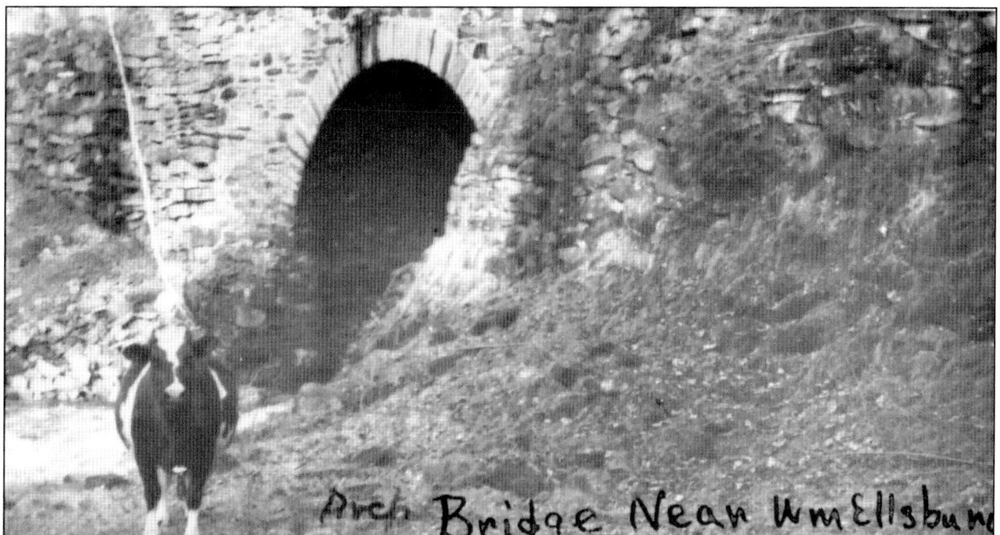

This pre-1950 photograph shows a lonely cow standing next to a small arch bridge near William Ellsbury's residence. The bridge would collapse into the water in 1950. Cows and sheep were bred on the outskirts of the Keeseville area.

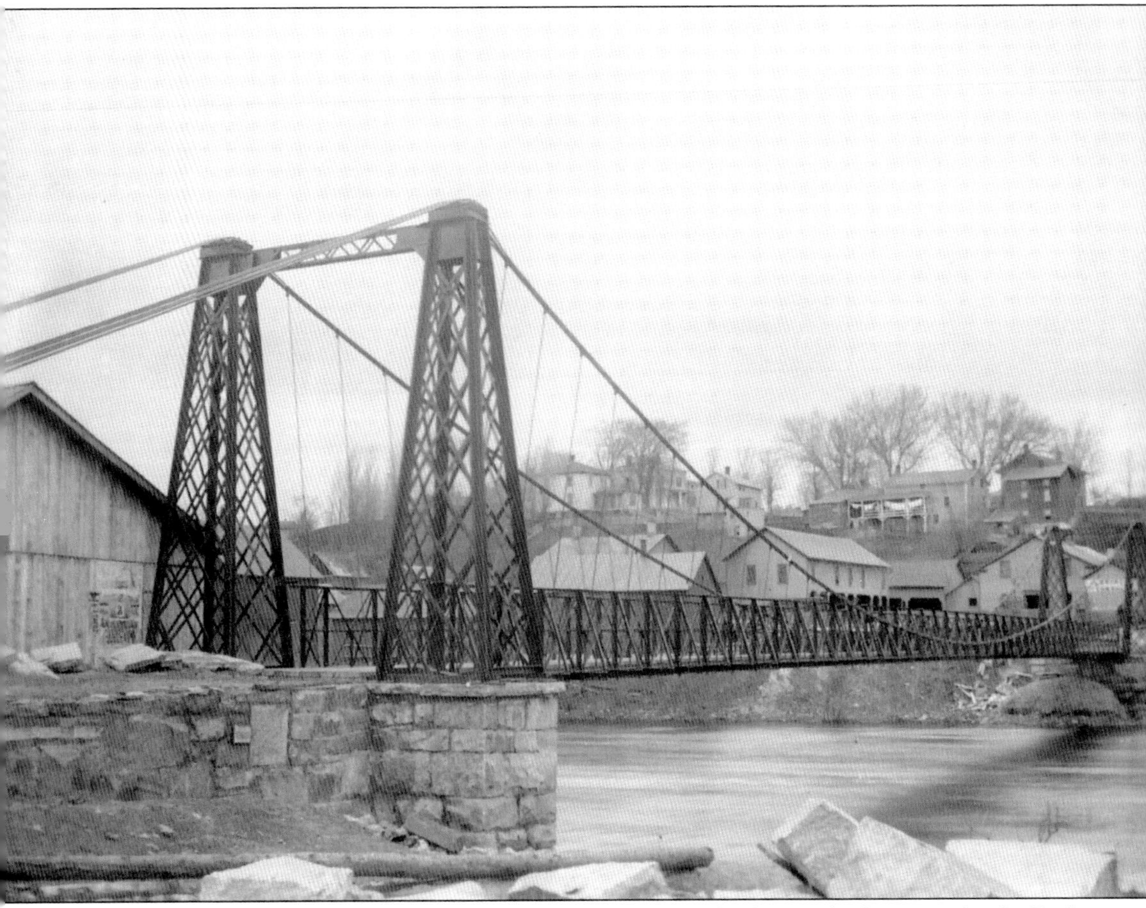

One of the three main bridges in Keeseville, the suspension bridge was built in 1888 by the Berlin Iron Bridge Company of East Berlin, Connecticut. The bridge spans an impressive 240 feet across the river. It was named a National Historic Engineering Landmark along with the iron truss bridge and Keystone Arch Bridge in 1987. In 1840, an earlier suspension bridge spanned the river in the same spot. Sadly, a marching band in 1842 proved too much stress for the bridge, and a link snapped, dropping the bridge and about 40 marchers into the river. There were 13 casualties. The suspension bridge, constructed and pictured here in 1888, is still in use today.

The iron truss bridge, photographed by Arthur Cumber almost 100 years after its construction, is the third of the National Historic Landmark bridges. The bridge is currently in need of repairs and closed to public use. No plan is yet in place to repair the bridge; it requires the efforts of two counties, as the bridge connects Essex and Clinton Counties in New York.

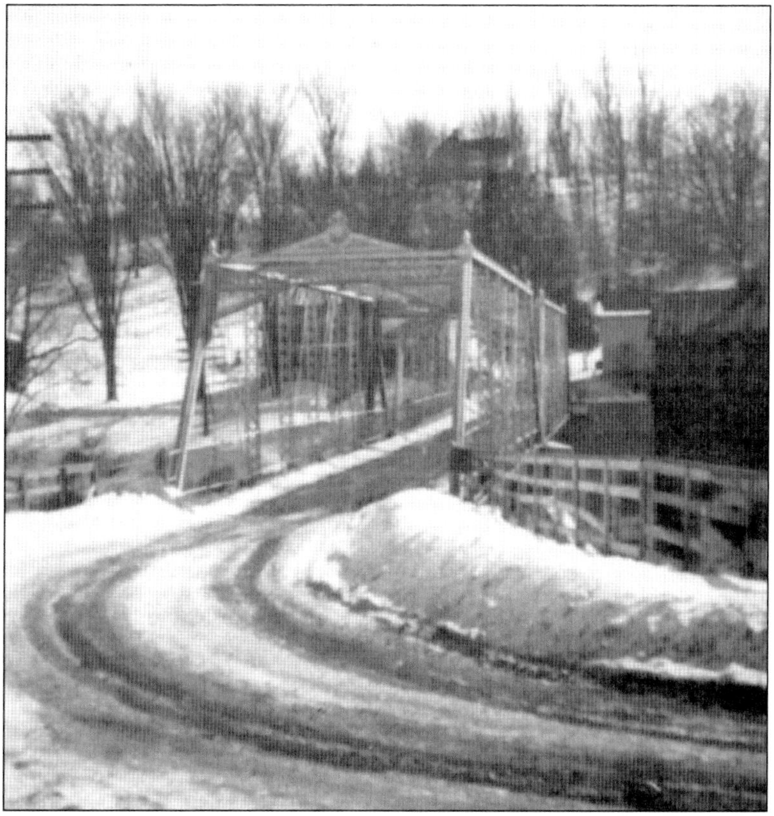

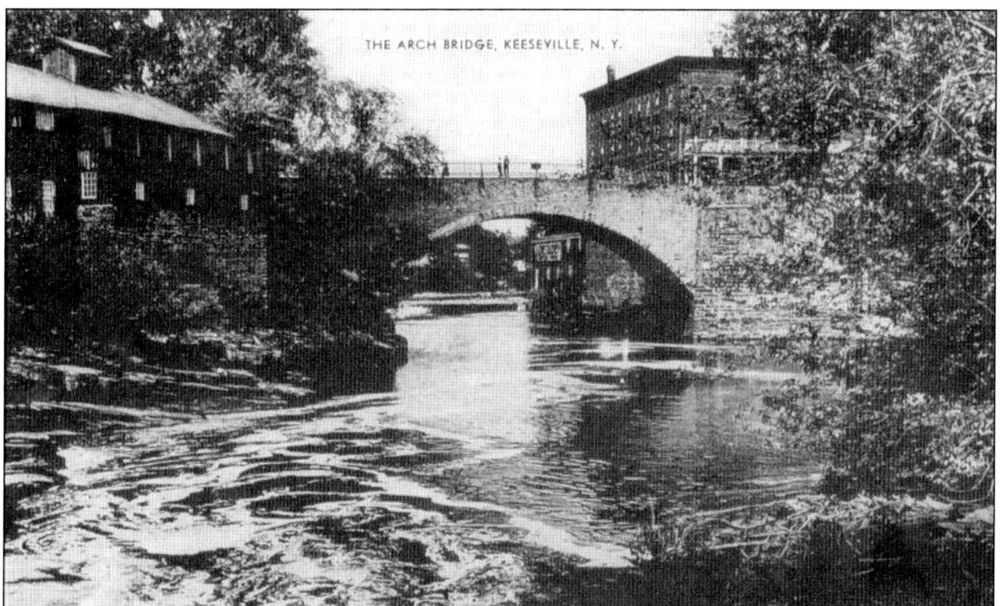

The most recognizable of the three historical bridges is the Arch Bridge, pictured here sometime in the late 1800s. The bridge, designed by Solomon Townsend, is a keystone design in which the keystones put pressure on each other to stabilize the entire arch.

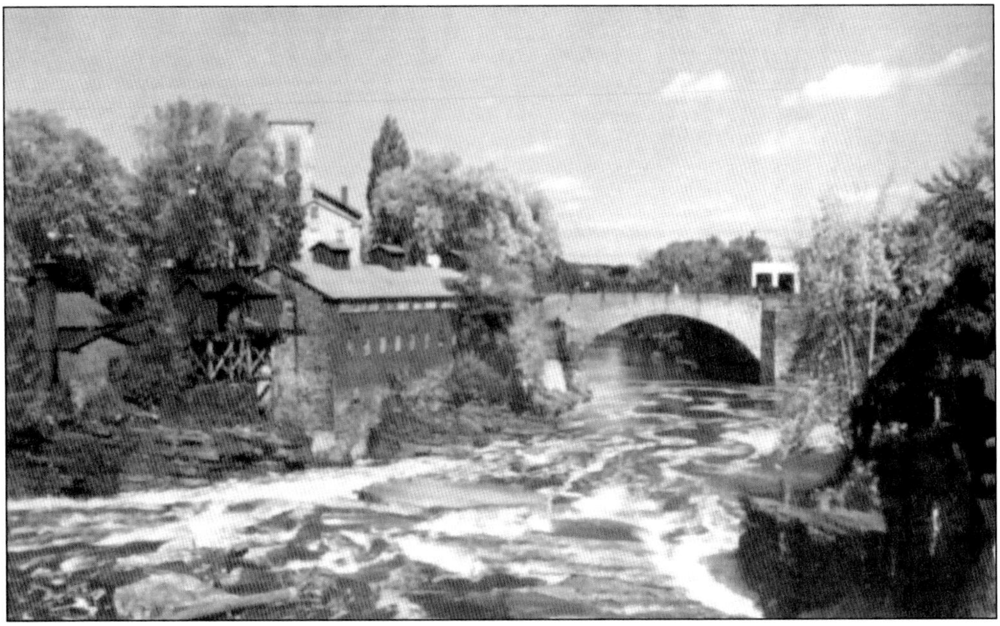

This undated photograph of the Arch Bridge highlights the waters in the foreground continuing to the falls at Ausable Chasm. With the lodge hall towering on the left, the Prescott plant in the foreground, and the stone Arch Bridge spanning the river, this iconic image is popular for postcards and street flags.

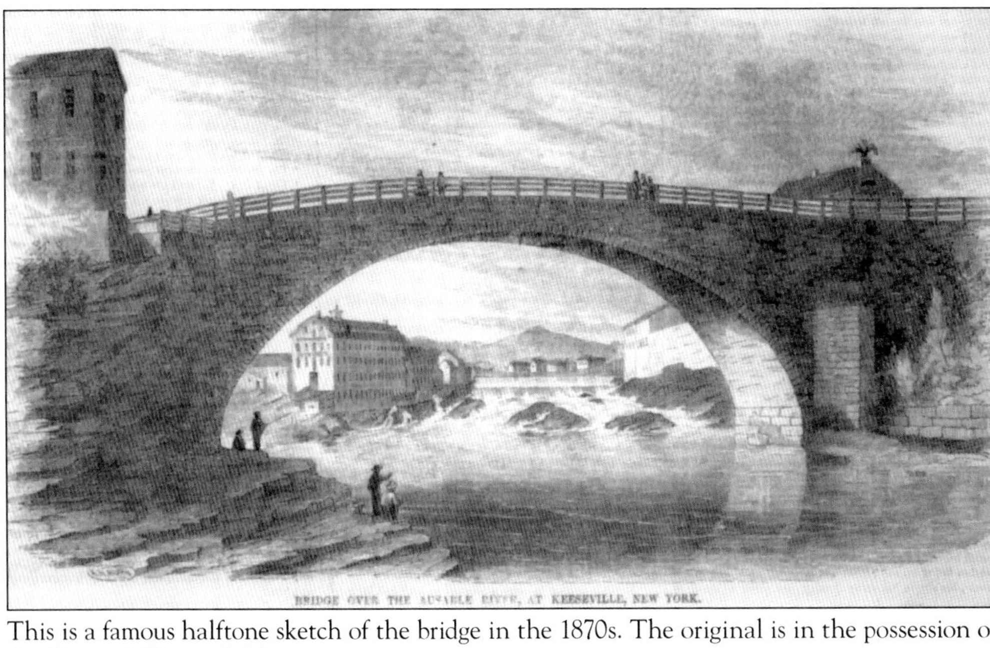

This is a famous halftone sketch of the bridge in the 1870s. The original is in the possession of the Town of Chesterfield.

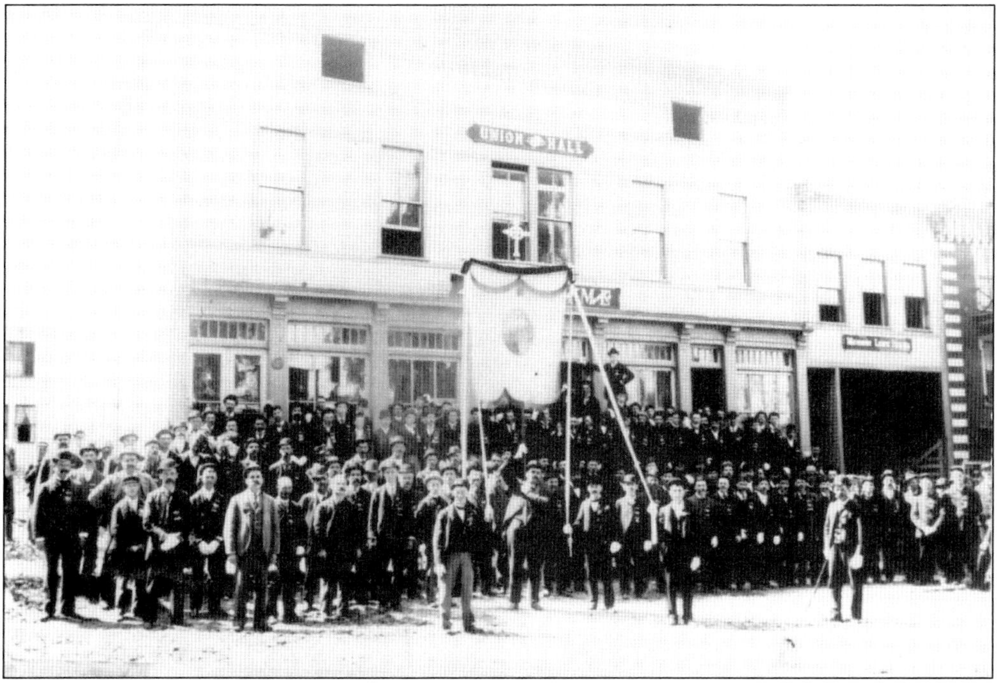

The St. John the Baptist Society stands in front of the Union Hall sometime between 1880 and 1890. The Congregational Society was organized in 1806, with the Baptist Society incorporating in 1826. The numerous denominations held their services in the yellow schoolhouse building until the construction of the churches throughout Keeseville.

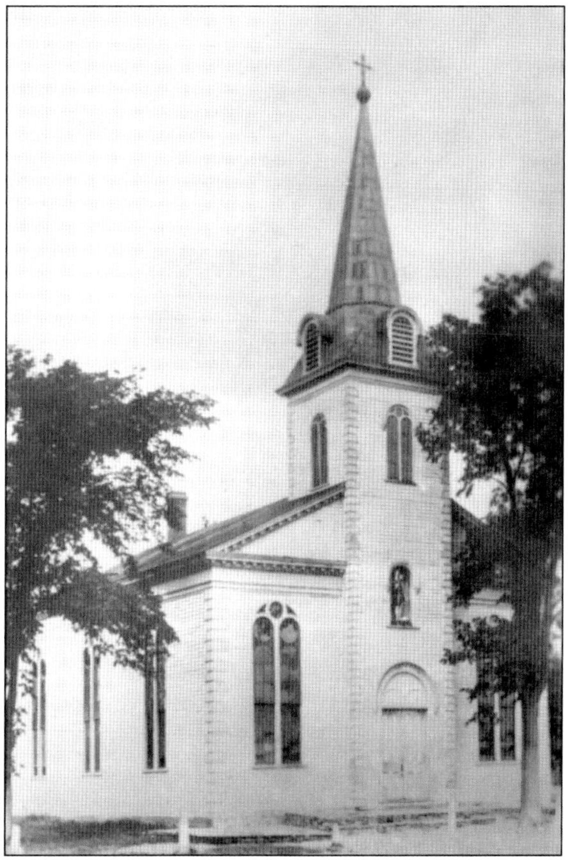

This undated photograph shows the original St John's Church. As with many communities in the area, early settlers came either from the north or south, creating two very distinctly different Catholic groups. Differences between French settlers and Irish often led to two churches. The area Baptists first organized as a society in a log cabin in 1791. The Baptist church was built in 1853 on Front Street in Keesville.

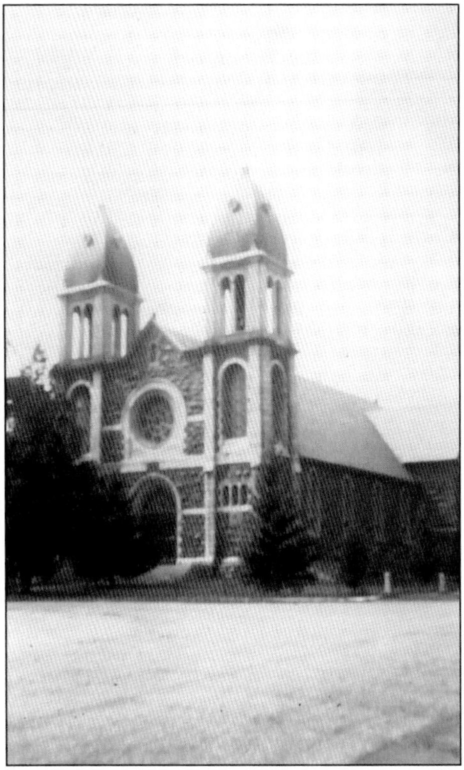

St. John the Baptist Church was first built in 1901, but it had to be rebuilt after a fire in 1926. This building is still in use today for the Catholic population of Keeseville.

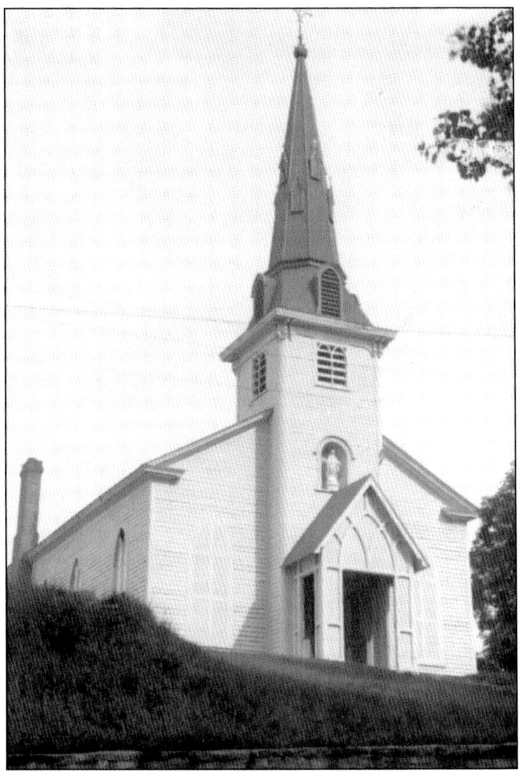

The Little White Church on the Hill is a popular local name for the Church of the Immaculate Conception, which was first built in 1835. The church still celebrates masses for the Catholics of Keeseville.

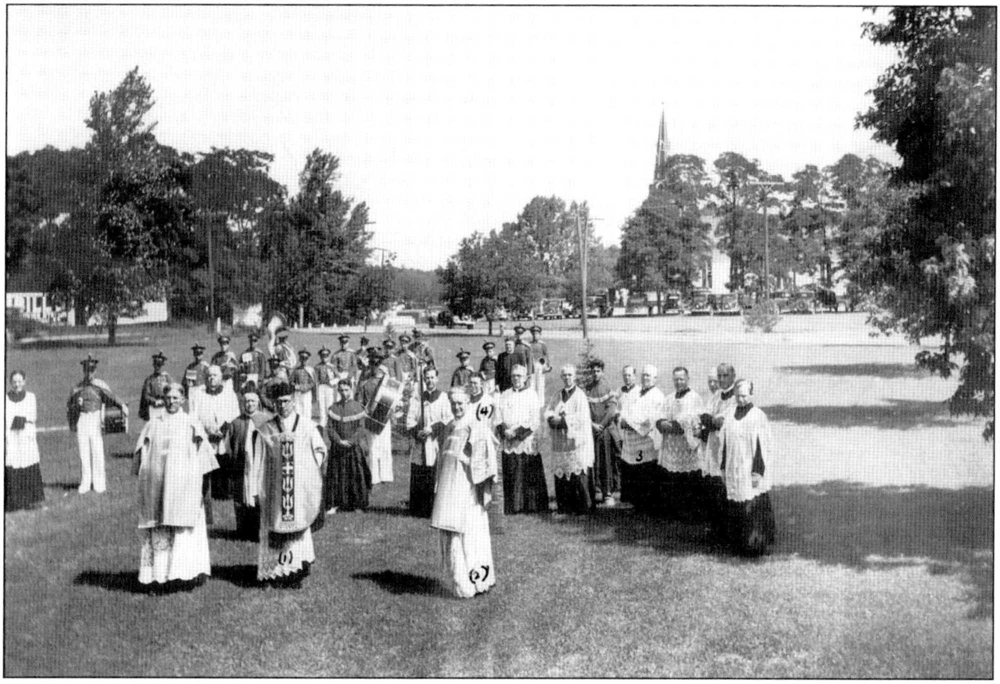

In the summer of 1935, the Church of the Immaculate Conception celebrated its 100th anniversary with all due pomp and ceremony, including bishops and other dignitaries from around the state in attendance.

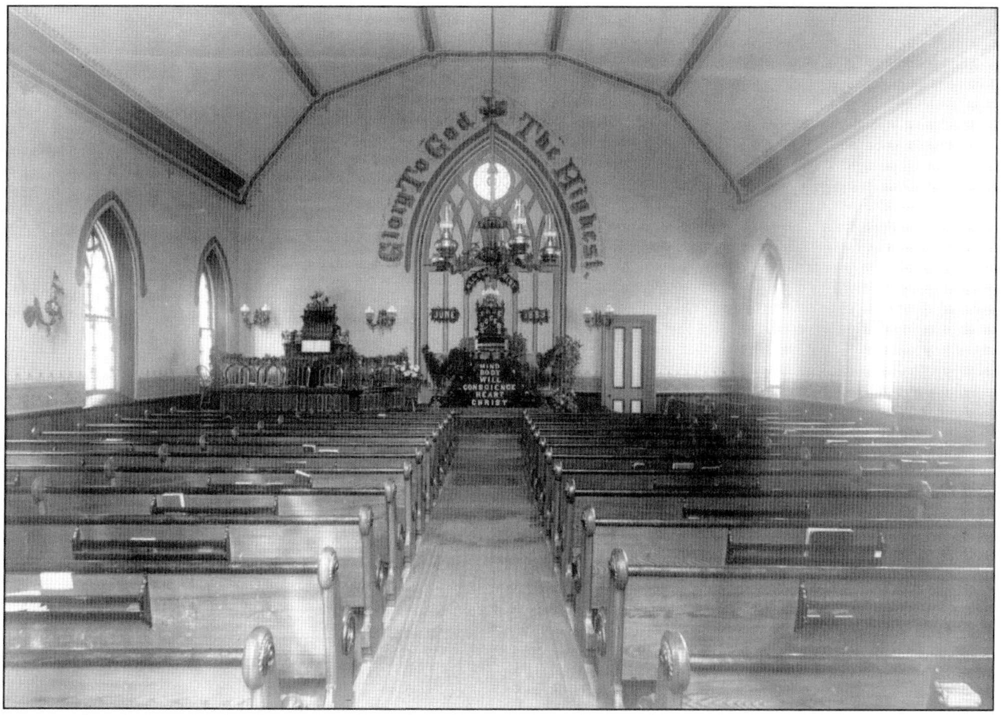

Pictured is the interior of the Methodist church in Keeseville, New York, in June 1889. It burned in 1878 and was rebuilt as it is today.

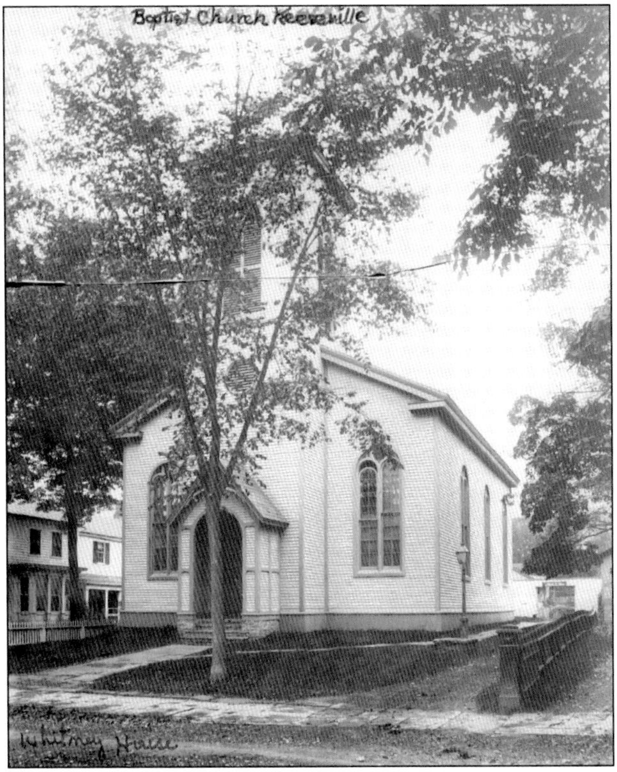

The Baptist church on Front Street is shown next to the Whitney House in this undated photograph. The church was demolished in 1970.

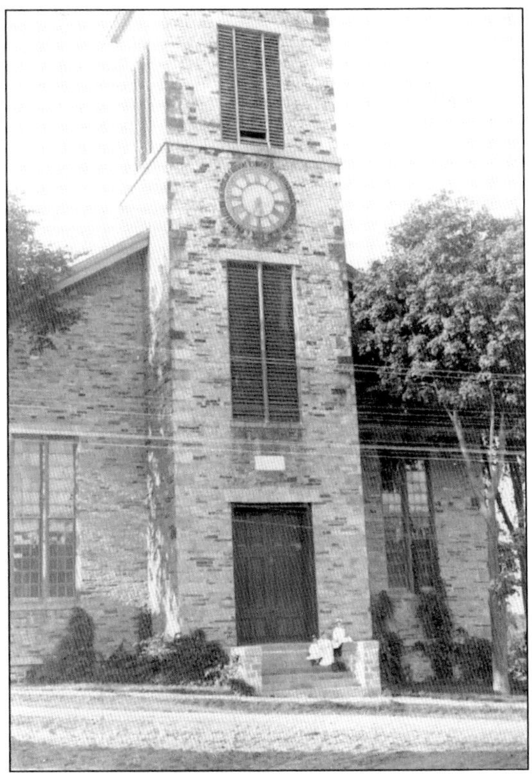

Children are sitting on the front steps leading into the Congregational Presbyterian Church of Keeseville in 1910. The church was built using local sandstone in 1852. Later it would be used as a Masonic lodge. The clock still keeps proper time and is regularly serviced.

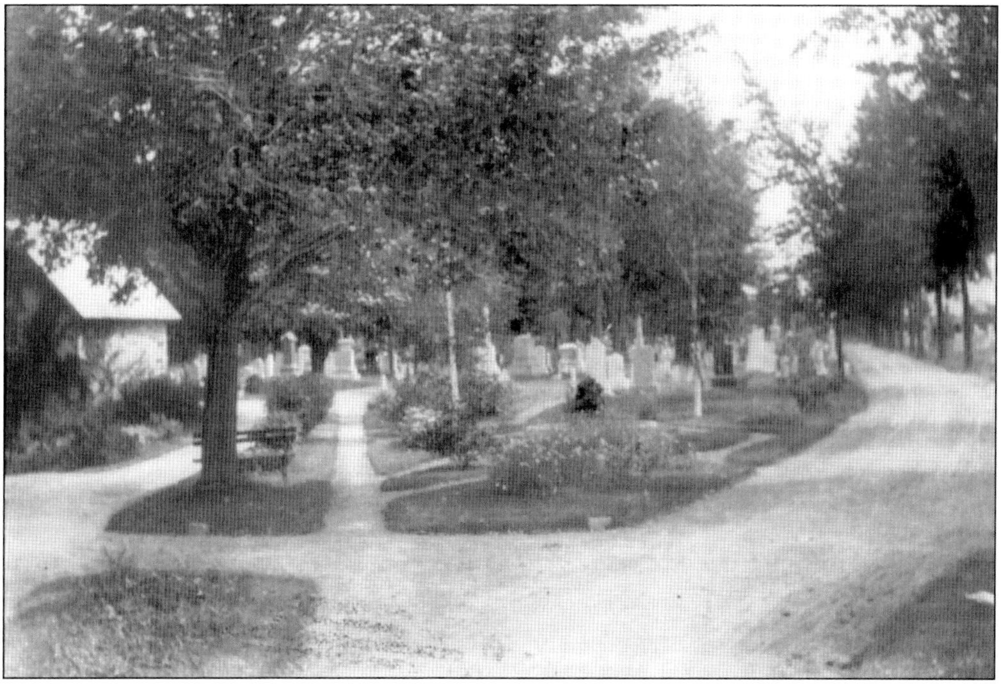

The Evergreen Cemetery is the oldest of the cemeteries located in the village of Keeseville and the townships of Ausable and Chesterfield. Numerous graves of veterans are here as well as many of the prominent residents of early Keeseville.

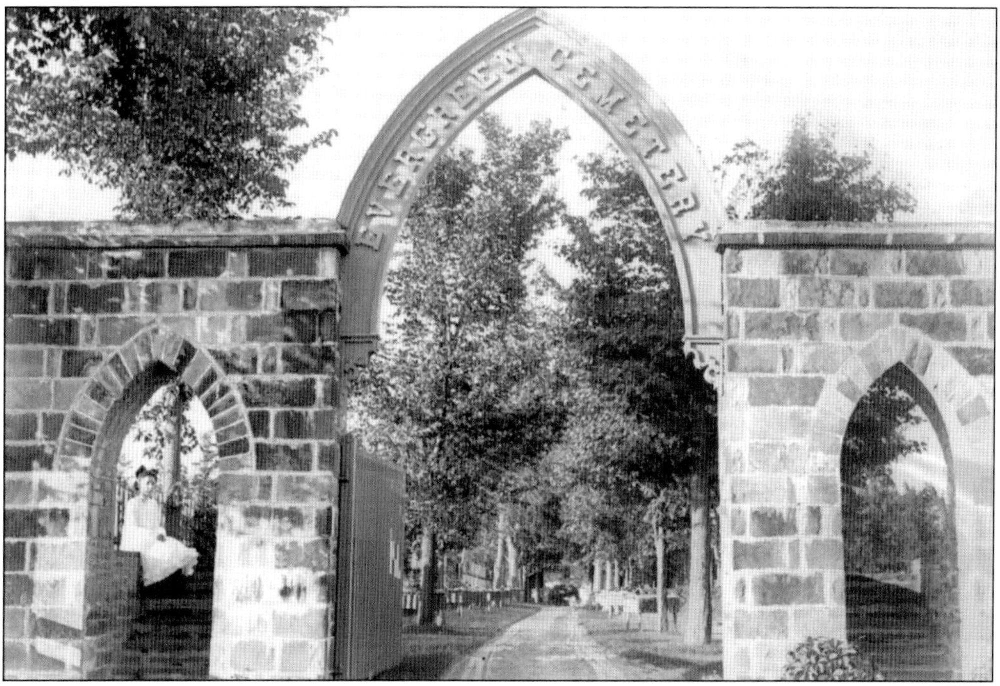

The original stone gate for the entrance of the Evergreen Cemetery is shown in this undated photograph. Included among the more than 2,000 interments are three US Congressmen, a member of the New York State Legislature, and a Civil War Union army officer.

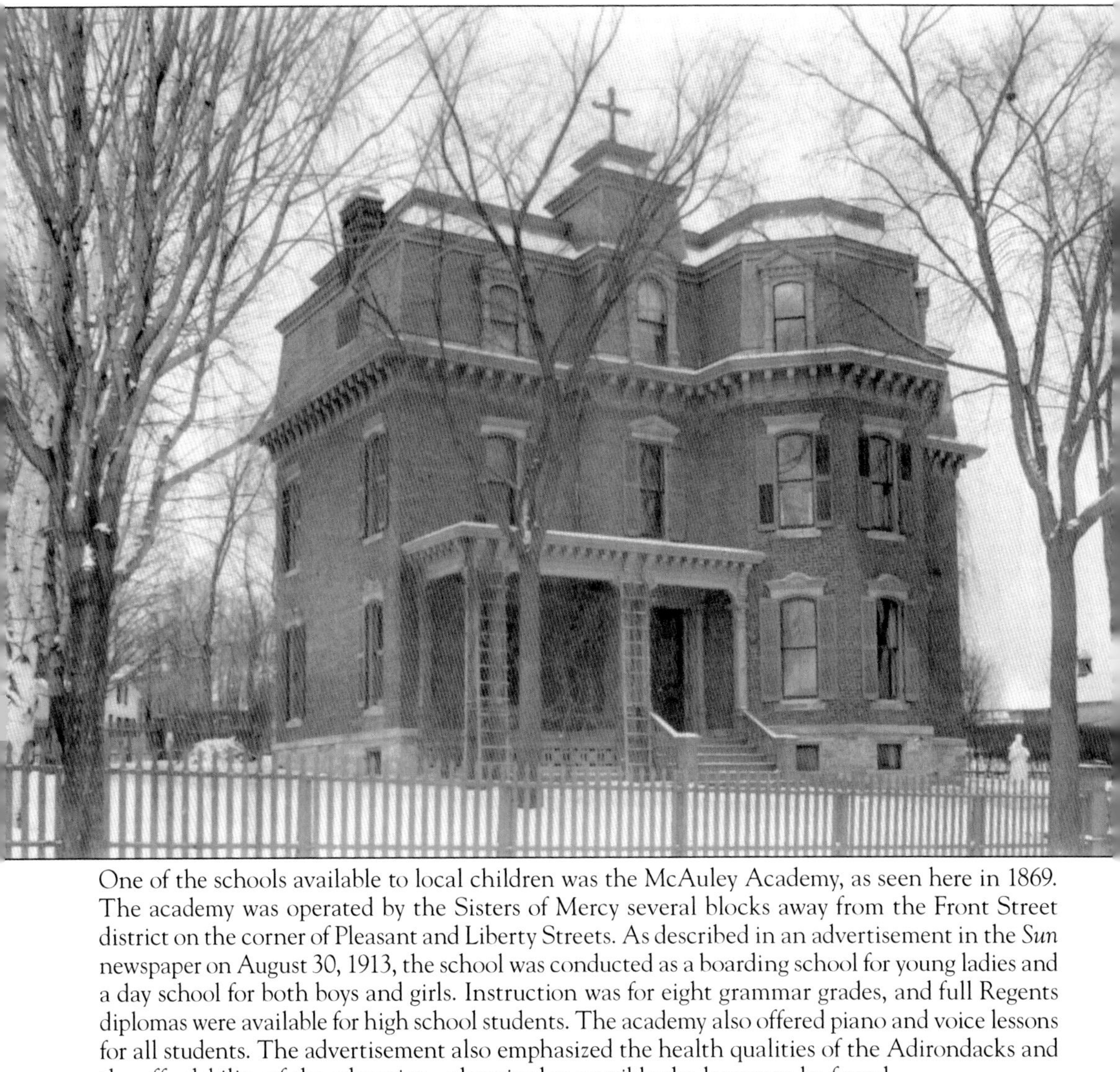

One of the schools available to local children was the McAuley Academy, as seen here in 1869. The academy was operated by the Sisters of Mercy several blocks away from the Front Street district on the corner of Pleasant and Liberty Streets. As described in an advertisement in the *Sun* newspaper on August 30, 1913, the school was conducted as a boarding school for young ladies and a day school for both boys and girls. Instruction was for eight grammar grades, and full Regents diplomas were available for high school students. The academy also offered piano and voice lessons for all students. The advertisement also emphasized the health qualities of the Adirondacks and the affordability of the education, advertised as possibly the lowest to be found.

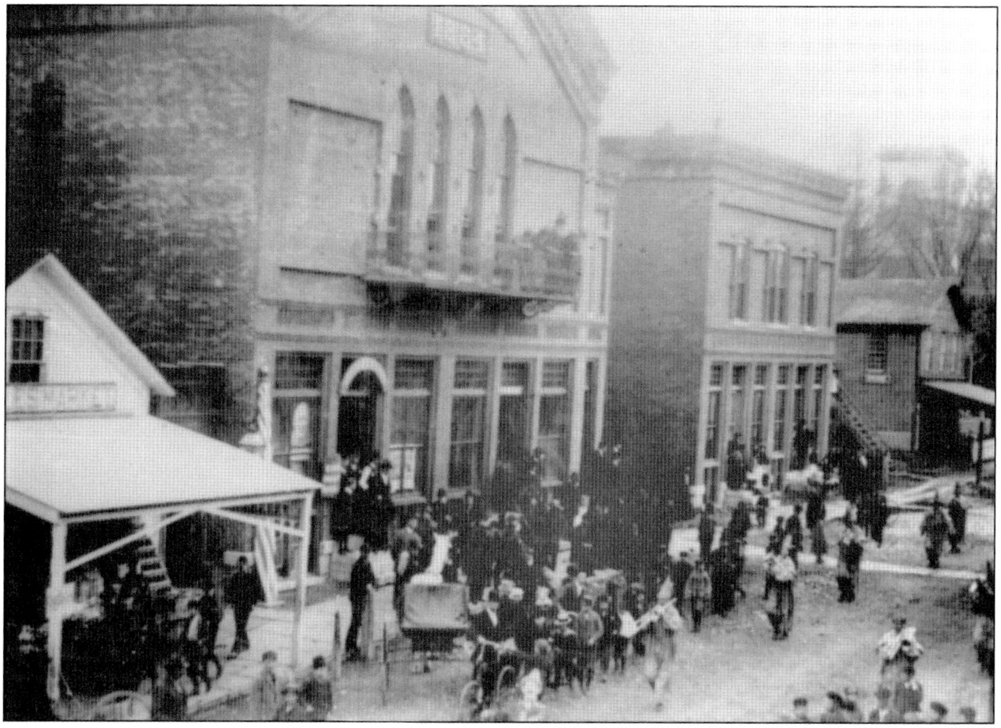

This 1880s photograph shows a parade going past the Kingsland Opera House on Front Street. From the 1880s until well into the 1900s, the Kingsland Opera House was the main source for entertainment, with plays, operas, vaudeville performances, and smaller presentations.

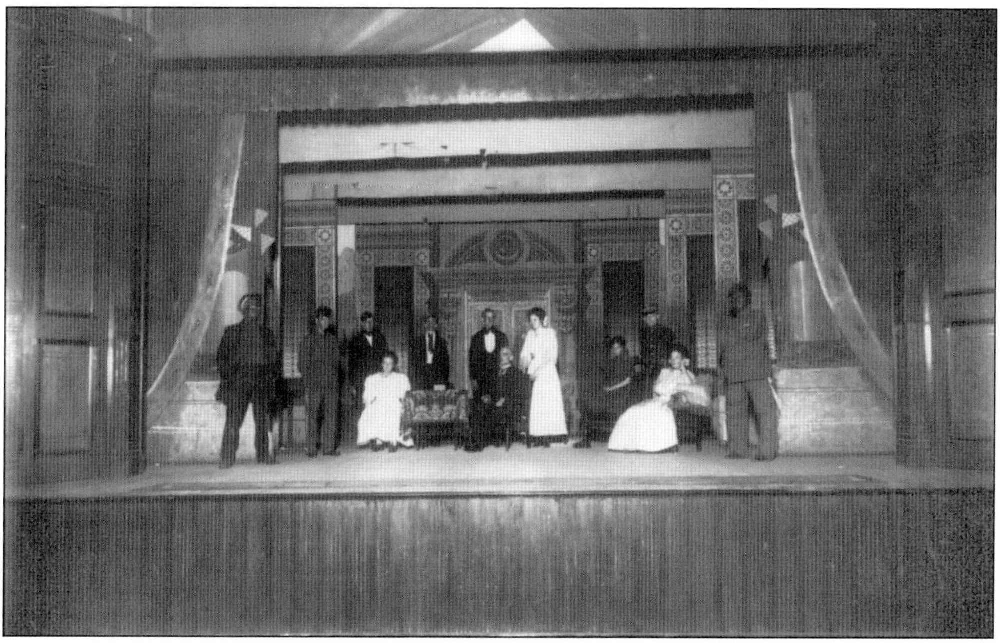

This undated photograph presents the main stage as set up for the production of a play, with the cast posing for the photograph. The opera house was operated by the Kingsland family, who were by this time the predominant businessmen of the community.

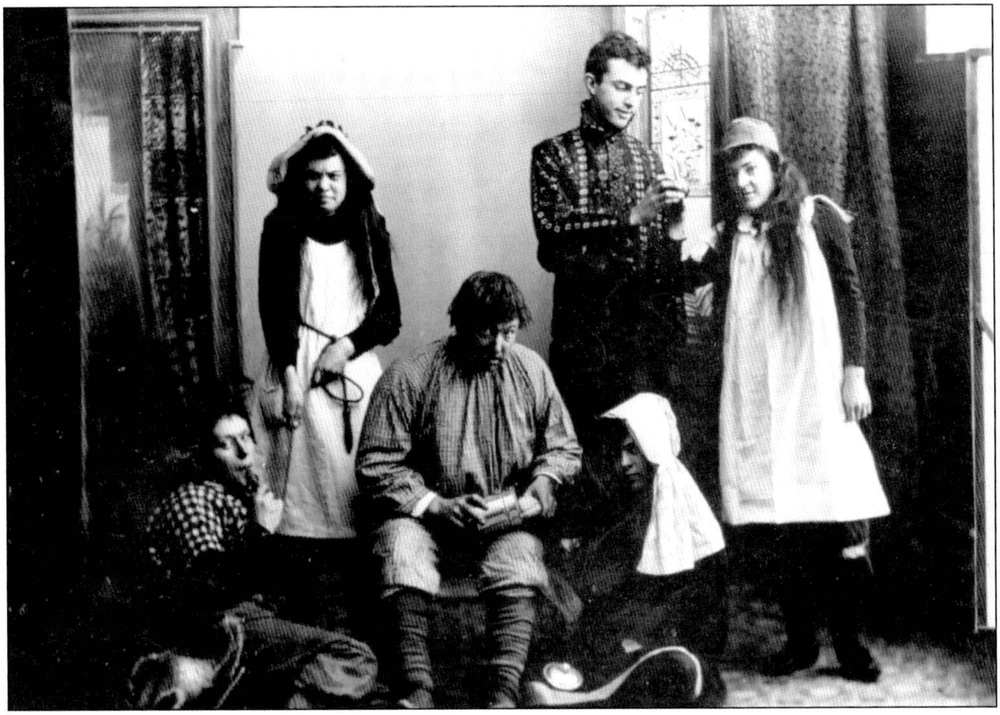

The cast for a small play production poses in 1890. Most of the performers were local residents, but others did come from away to participate in the myriad of productions that were constantly running in the opera house.

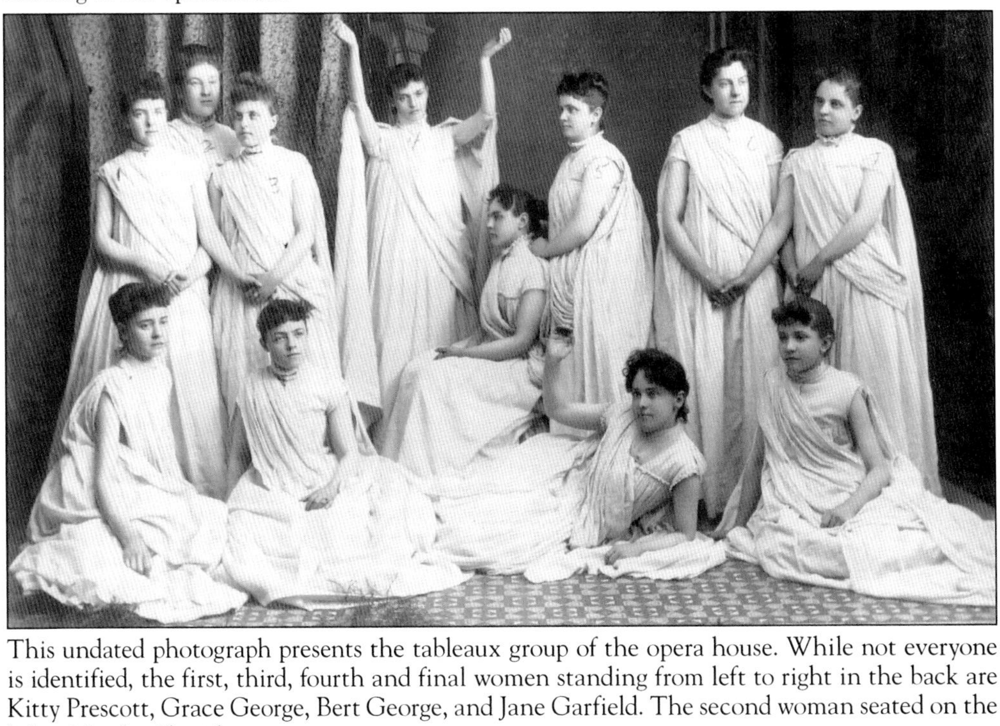

This undated photograph presents the tableaux group of the opera house. While not everyone is identified, the first, third, fourth and final women standing from left to right in the back are Kitty Prescott, Grace George, Bert George, and Jane Garfield. The second woman seated on the left is Martha Sheridan.

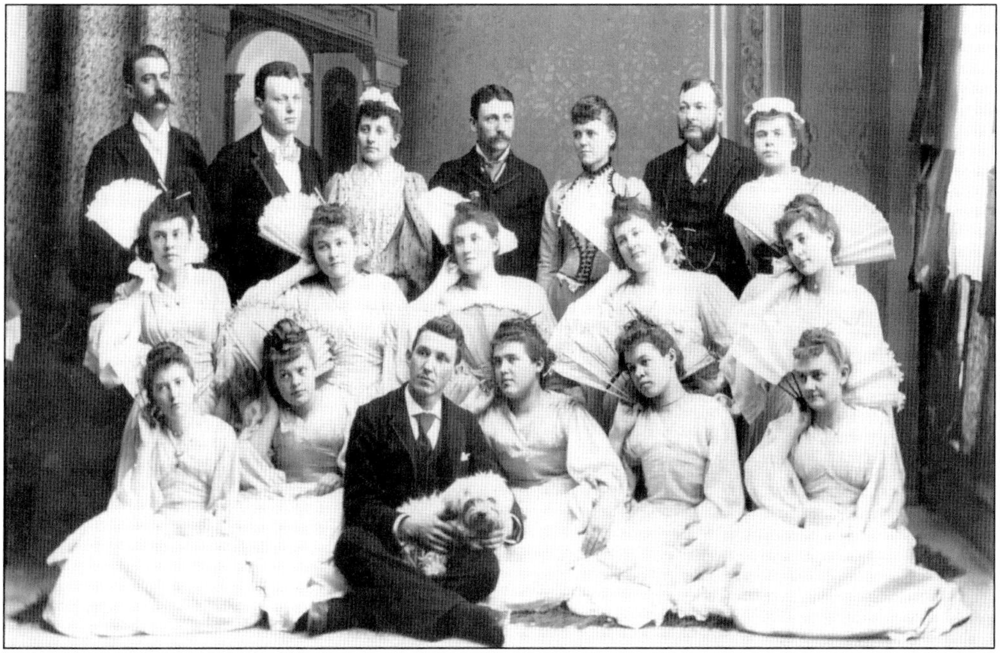

The Frederick Standish performers pose with the Fan Drill Girls before a performance at the opera house. Many productions were performed by local residents, but outside groups passing through the area would often perform onstage as well.

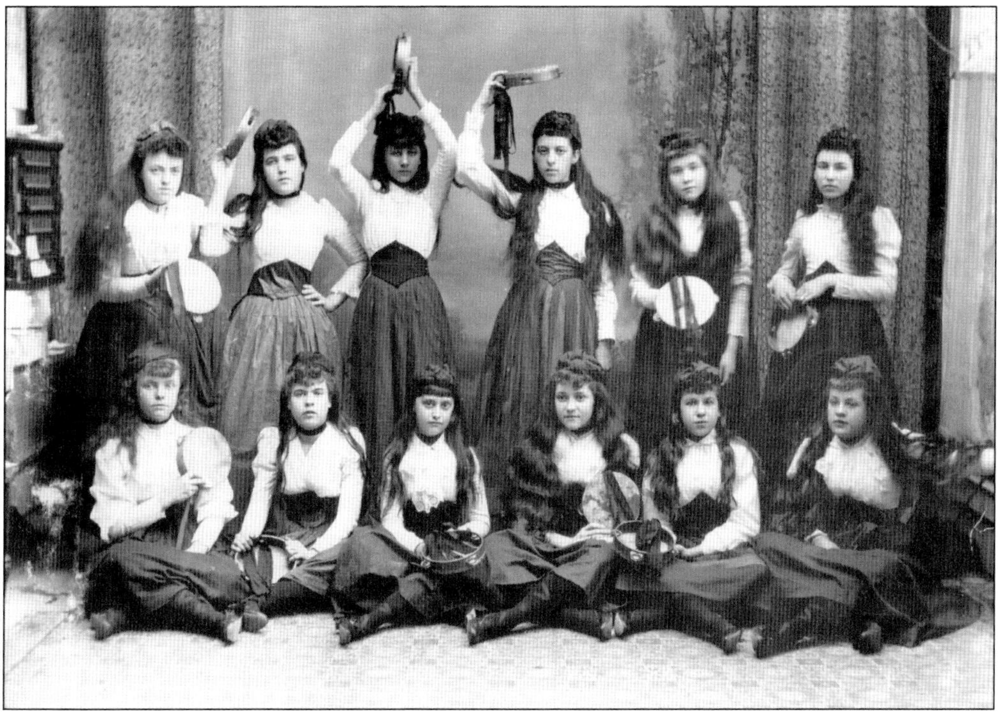

The 12-member Tambourine Drill Group poses in an undated photograph to be used for advertising its performances at the opera house. Small ensembles like the Tambourine Drill Group would perform during intermissions of larger works.

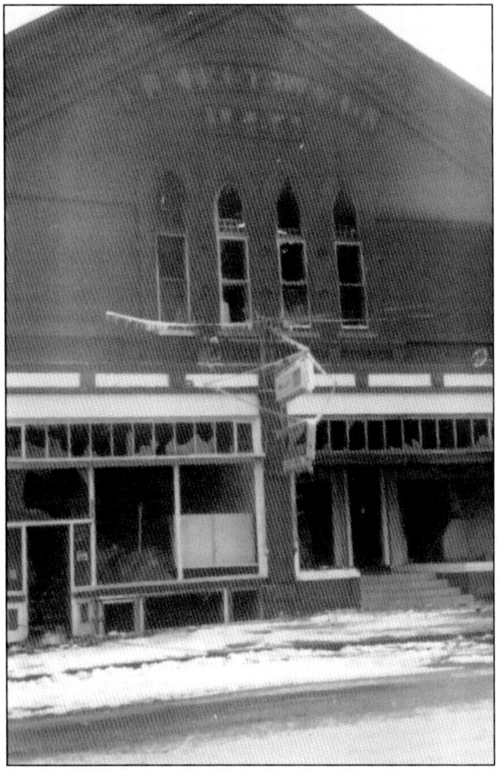

A series of photographs was taken in August 1970 showing the boarded remains of the once-glorious Kingsland Opera House. The growing popularity of the far less expensive movie houses shut down many of the old entertainment halls. Shortly after the photographs were taken, the opera house was torn down and removed. Many of the newer residents of Keeseville find it hard to believe that the town was the home of a grand opera house.

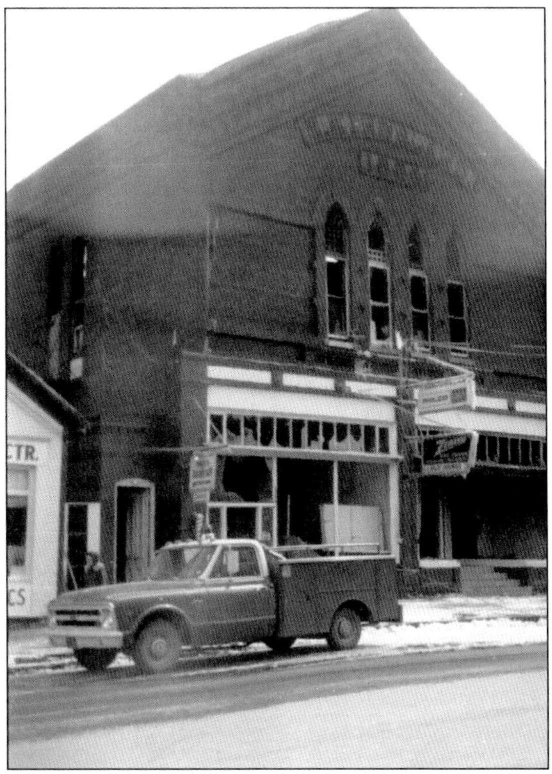

This photograph gives a final look at the Kingsland Opera House in 1970. Surprisingly few artifacts of the opera house beyond the photographs presented here remain, which has added to modern Keeseville's unawareness of the opera house's existence.

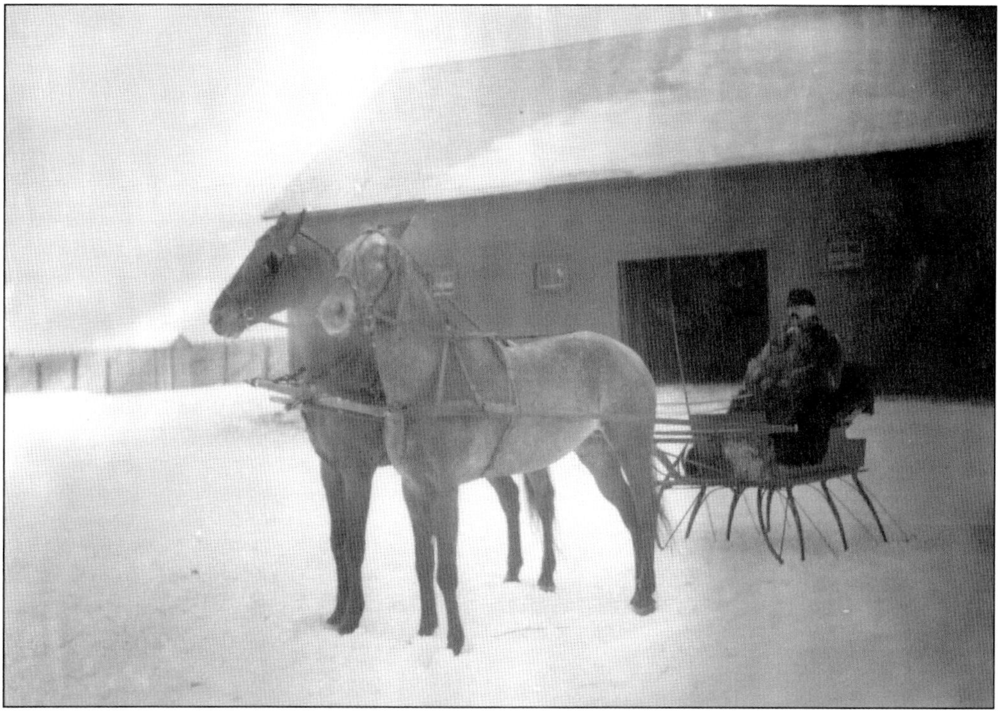

The normal mode of transportation for residents of Keeseville during the 1800s was horse and buggy. Dr. Mahlon Holcombe is sitting in 1900 in his buggy that he used to travel throughout the area to tend to his patients. Dr. Holcombe was the brother-in-law to Frank Hopkins, a prominent businessman who ran a drugstore.

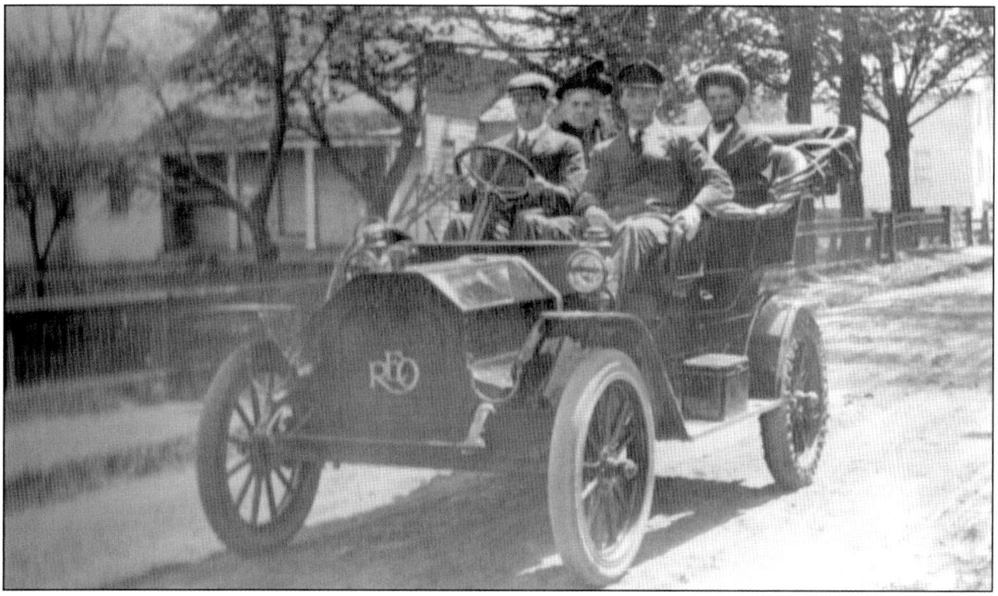

The age of the automobile brought about the end of Keeseville's glory days as more prominently located mills and factories across the country took over the demand for the materials produced in Keeseville. In this photograph are Willard and Mary Baber and two others in their new automobile driving through Keeseville.

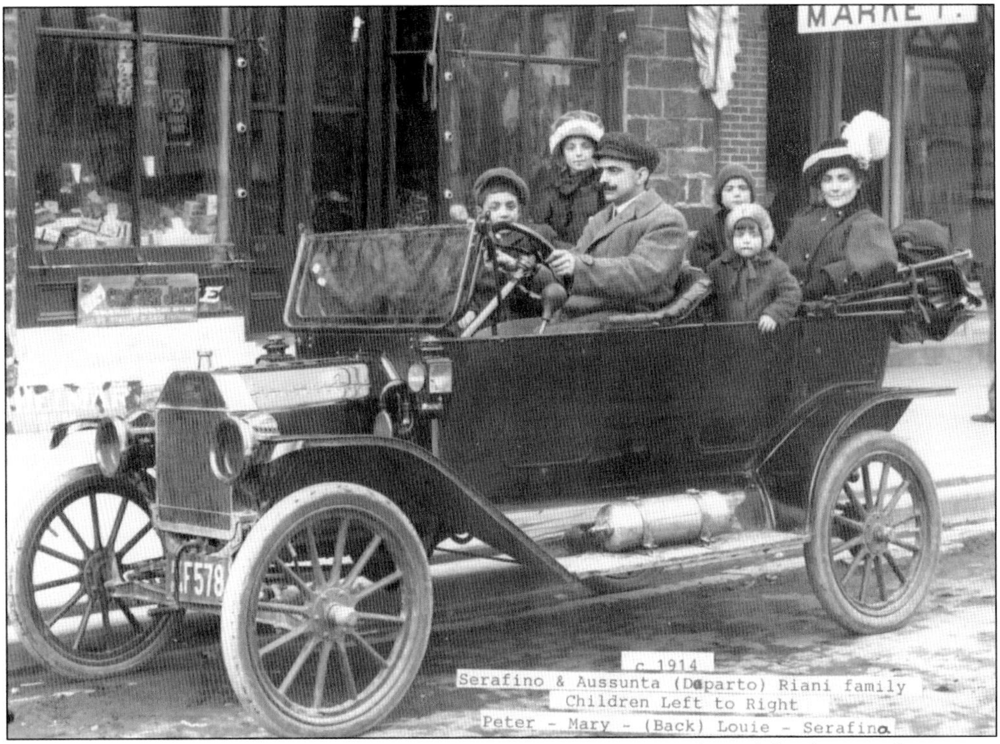

Another of the first residents to own an automobile was Serafino Riani, as shown here with his wife, Aussunta, and children, from left to right, Peter, Mary, Louie, and Serafina. This photograph was taken around 1914.

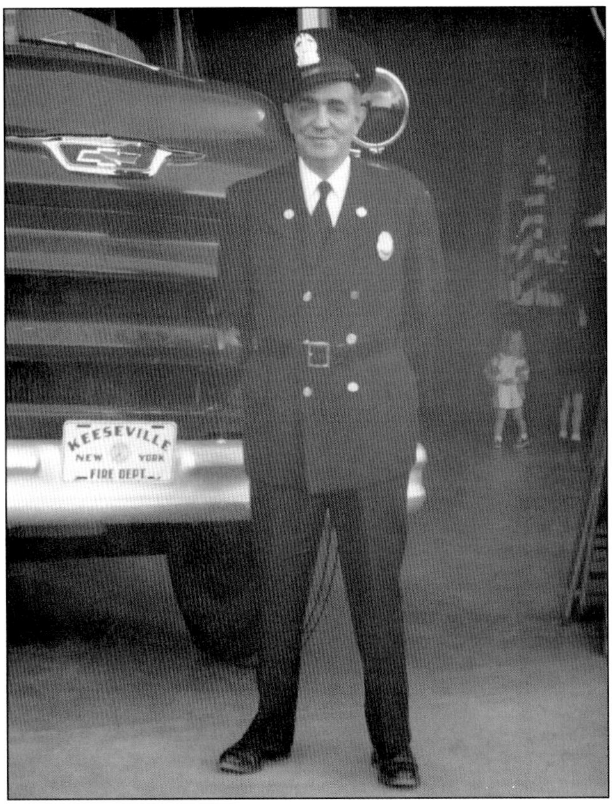

Peter Riani poses in front of a fire engine in the old fire station on River Street. Now a prominent member of the Keeseville Fire Department and Elks, he is almost 50 years older in 1962 than in the previous photograph in the car with his parents and siblings.

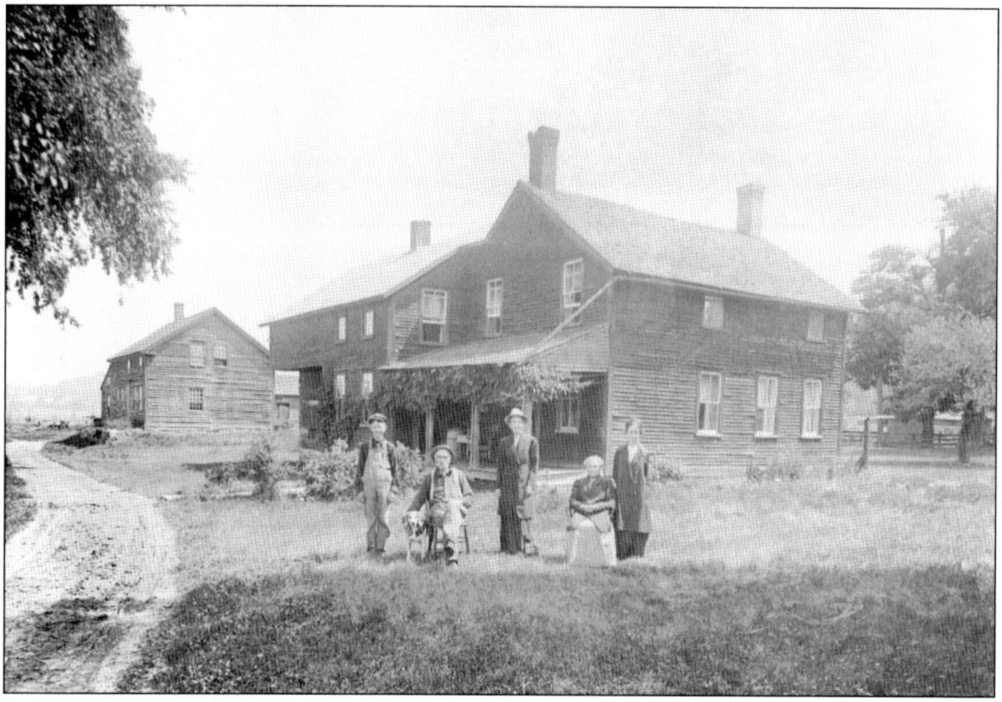

Located in the outskirts of the Keeseville community, the Doughty family poses before their homestead. Mr. and Mrs. Doughty are seated in chairs in this undated photograph with their three children and the family dog standing beside them.

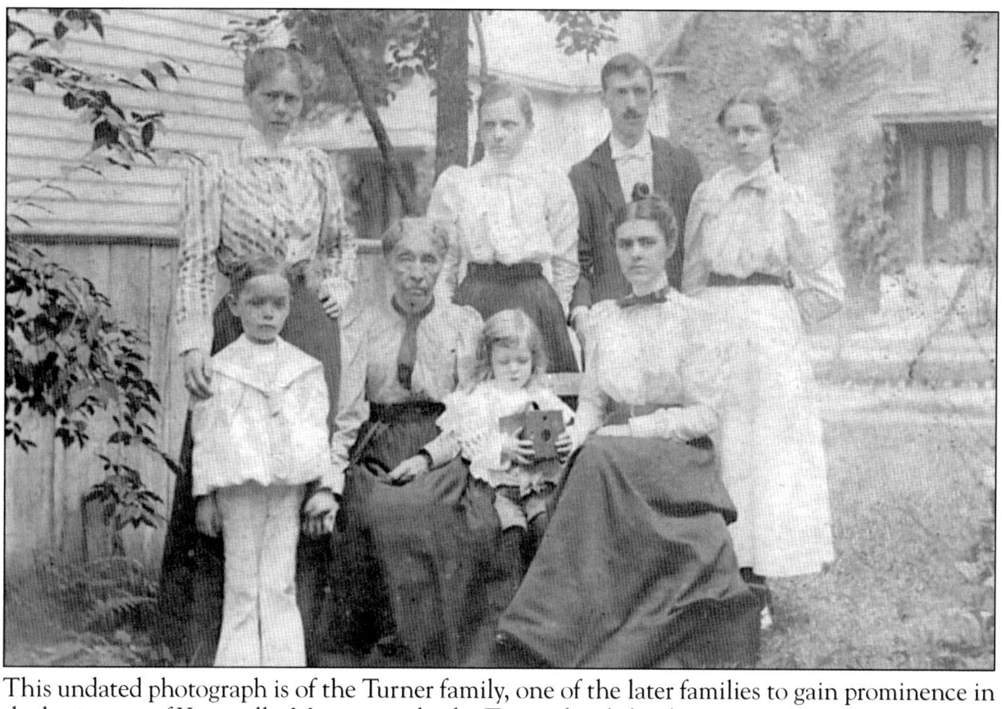

This undated photograph is of the Turner family, one of the later families to gain prominence in the businesses of Keeseville. More recently, the Turner family has been instrumental in preserving the history of Keeseville.

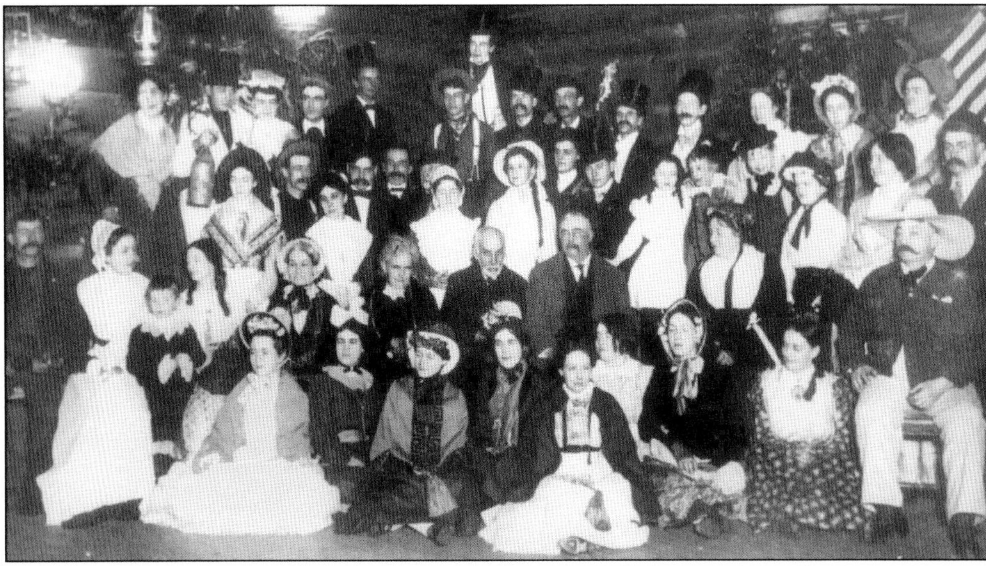

In 1898, revelers take a break from dancing for a photograph during a barn dance in Sweeney's Barn. Shortly after this, the barn burned down in a tremendous fire fueled by the many casings and supplies in the barn.

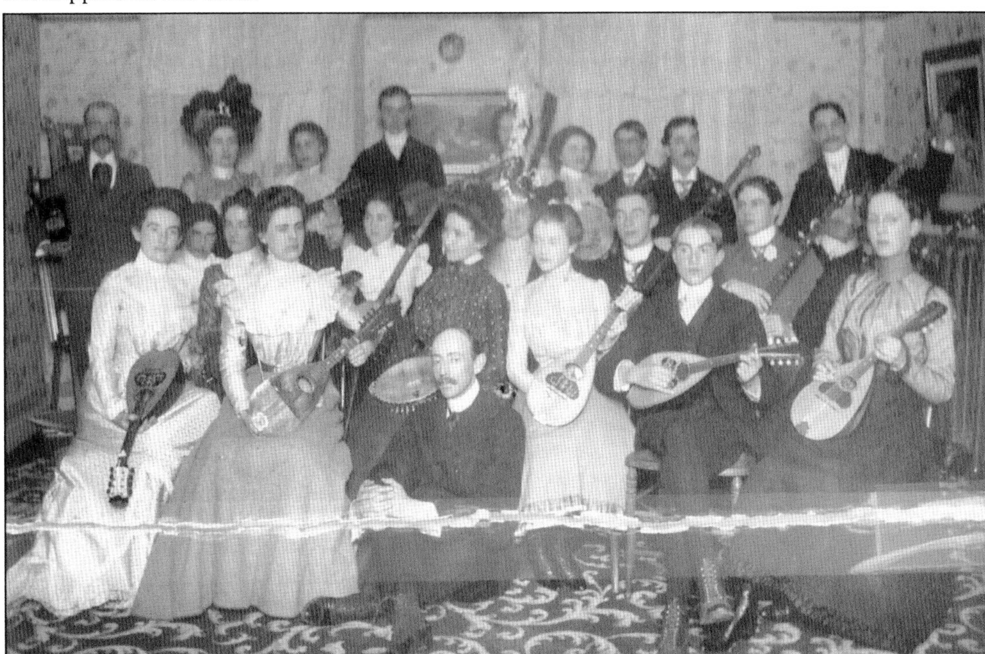

Members of Leonard's Mandolin Club pose in this undated photograph in the Boynton House, which is where the club met. Pictured here from left to right are (first row) Mrs. Fletcher, Anna Prince, Elizabeth Lecarre, Helen Pope, Bob Boynton, and Mary Rider; (second row) Leliah DeMoulin, Anne Thomas, Gertrude Leonndry, Mable Cook, Carl Bull, V. Dumolin, and Kim Kelly; (third row) Will Prince, Kitlee Prince, Jessica Baber, Lester Cord, Anna St. Louis, Eva Veer, John Dodge, George Robarge, and Napoleon St. Louis. Mr. Leonard, the instructor, is seated on the floor in front of his pupils.

This posed photograph shows Mrs. Dumollin in the middle of unidentified friends and family. The Dumollin family owned one of the well-known homes in Keeseville.

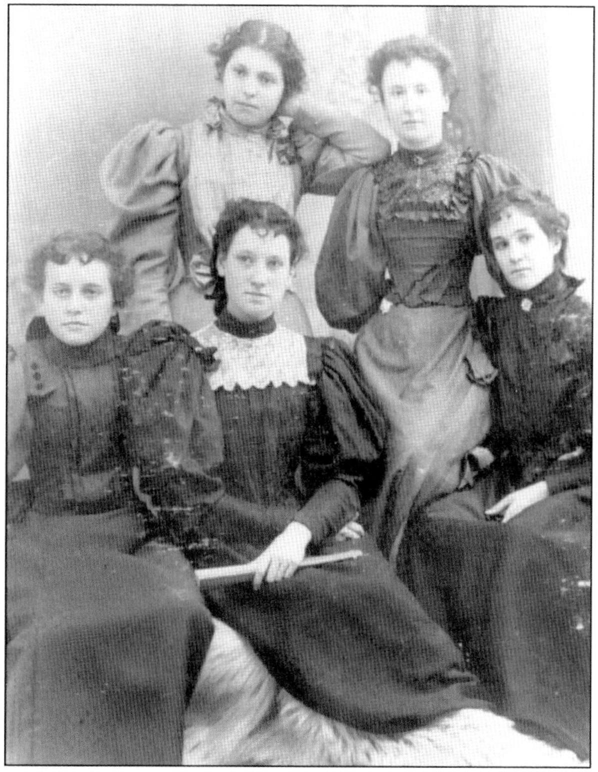

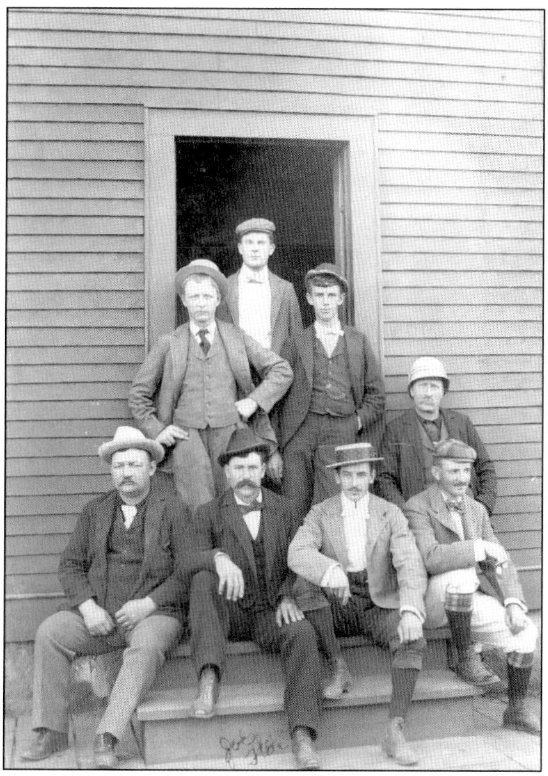

This undated photograph shows a group of Keeseville men standing in a doorway in their finest attire, all with ties and hats as well as higher-quality shoes and boots.

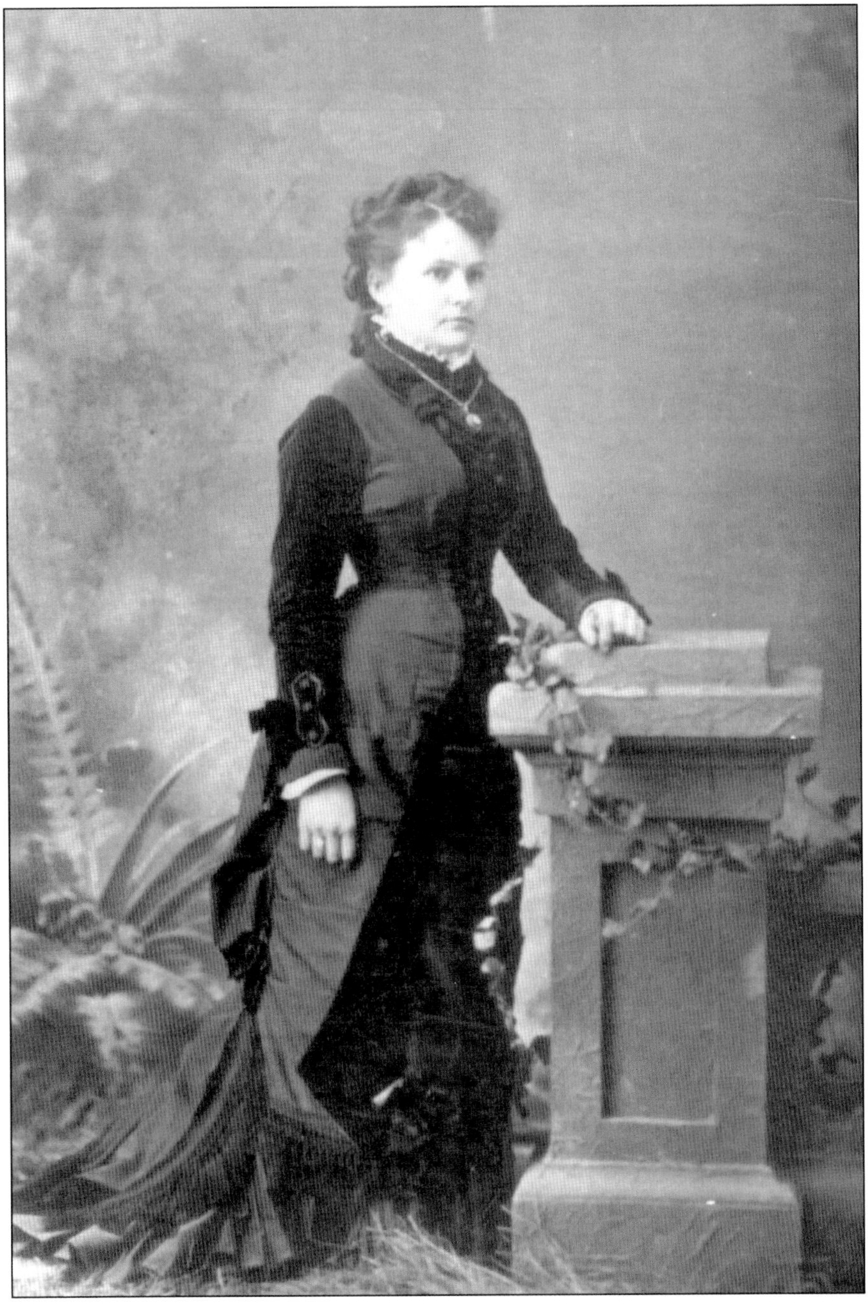

Adeline Turner poses for an undated portrait. The Turners were a prominent business family who owned one of the long-standing, successful drugstores in Keeseville. Through the years, many names have shone prominently in the history of Keeseville, starting with Anderson and Keese of the earlier settlers followed by Prescott, Mould, Kingsland, and Turner later. Two Keeseville residents gained fame on an international level, William Henry Jackson, the famous Civil War painter, and Eva Tanguay, the performer. As he left Keeseville at an early age, little to no material is available concerning Jackson during his time in Keeseville; however, plenty of material does exist on Tanguay.

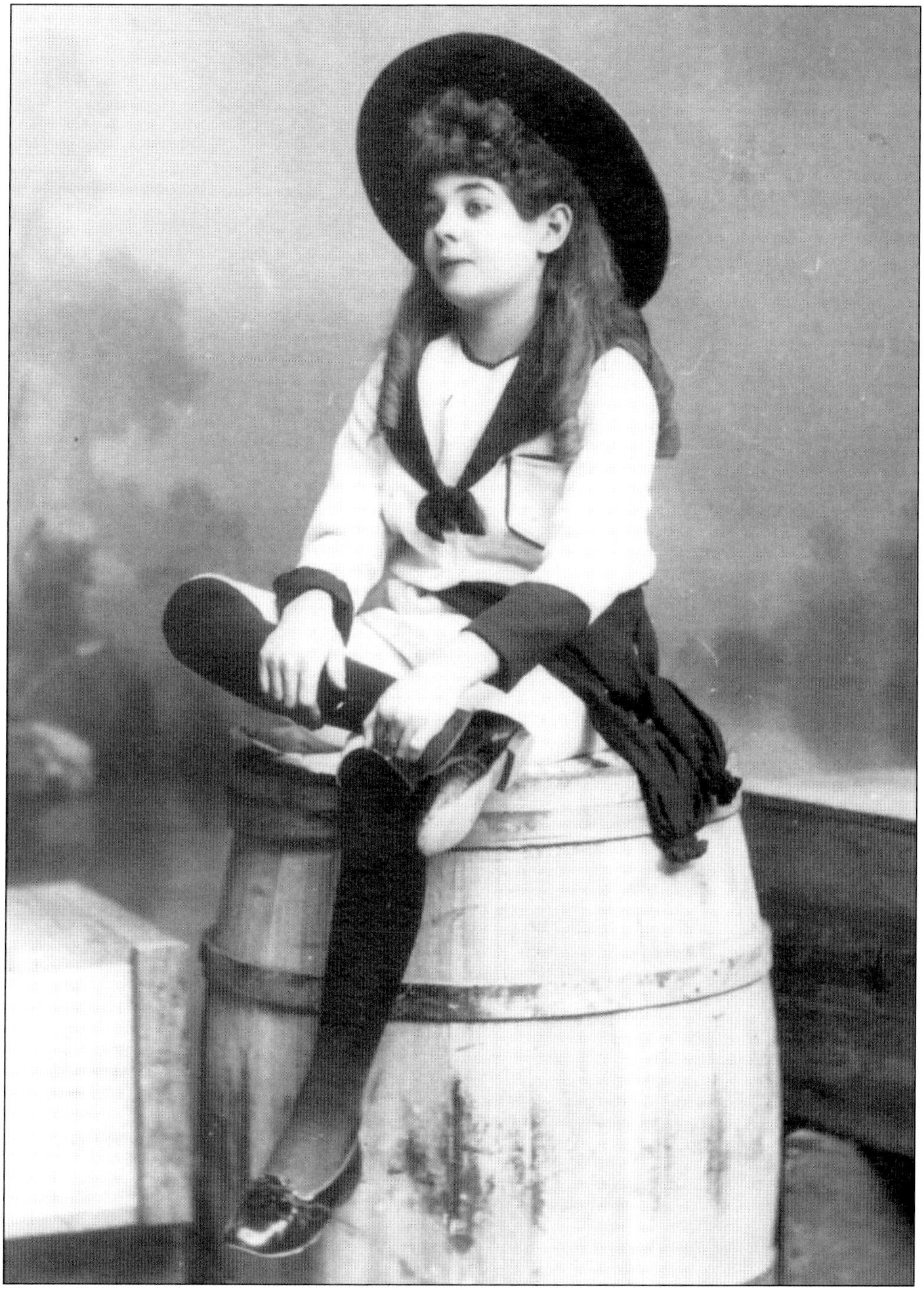

Arguably the most famous individual to come from Keeseville was Eva Tanguay. She was born in Marbleton, Quebec, in 1878. Her family moved to Keeseville, where her father died, leaving the family without means. Winning her first public appearance in an amateur night in Holyoke, Massachusetts, before she was eight years old, Tanguay was a natural for the stage. Soon she had the title role in an ongoing *Little Lord Fauntleroy* production.

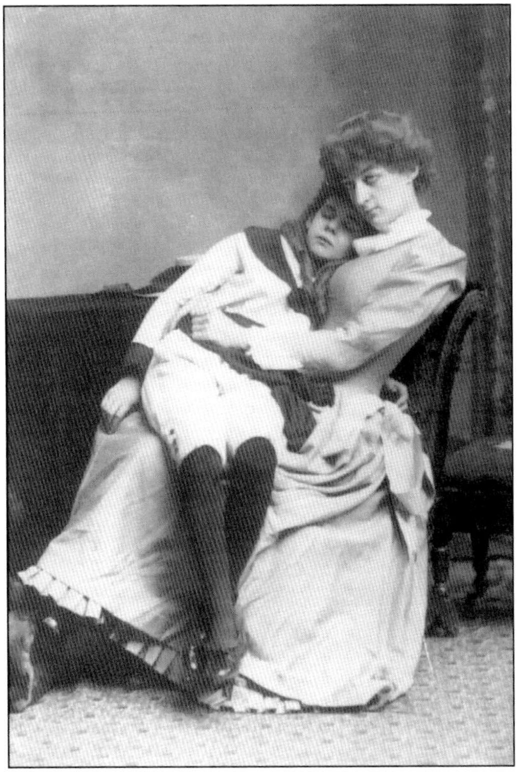

She gained stardom in 1904 singing "I Don't Care" on Broadway during her performance of *The Chaperons*. A Ziegfield Follies girl, Tanguay was earning $3,500 a week and known for her daring and provocative performances, including one as Salome.

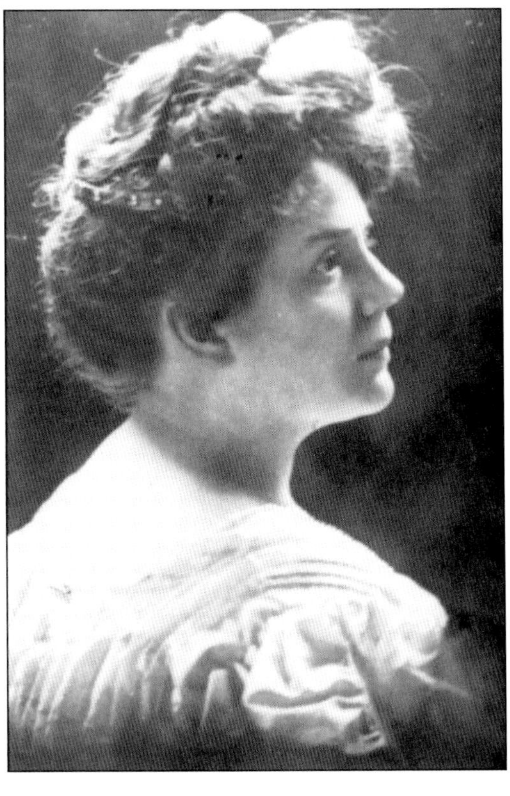

After losing her fortune in the crash of the 1920s, Tanguay went blind in 1933 due to illness and needed the help of friends to pay for operations that did restore her sight. Eva Tanguay died on January 11, 1946, in Hollywood, California.

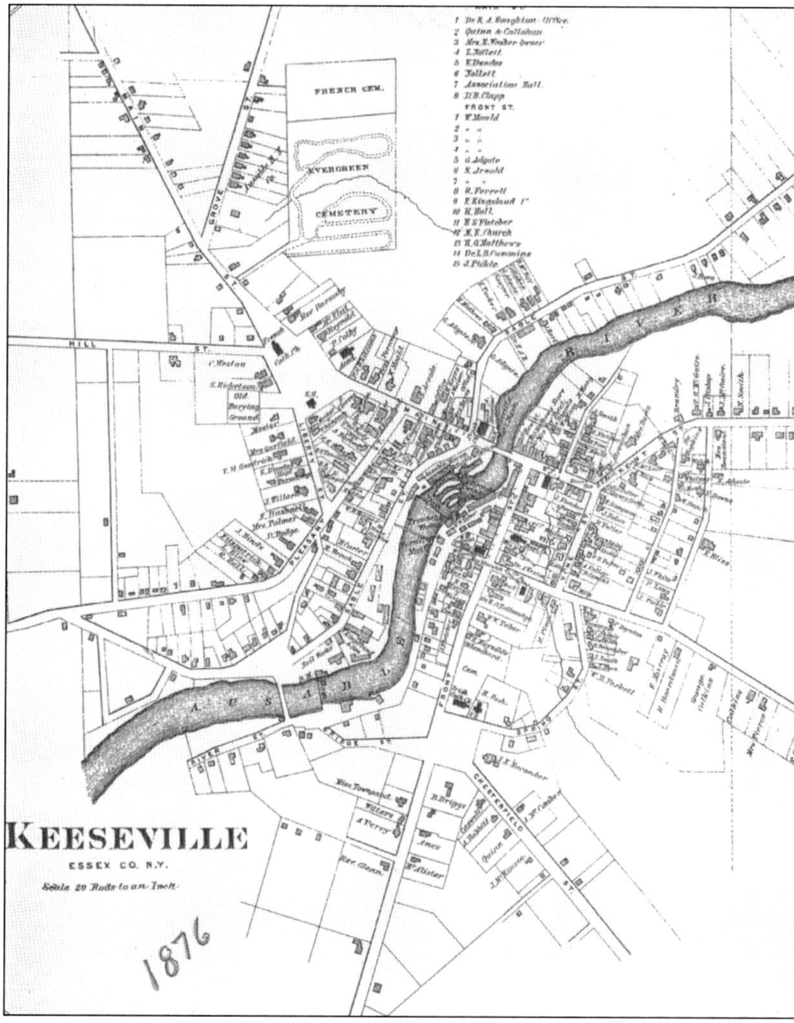

The 1876 map of Keeseville is one of the most popular reproduced maps of the area today, with copies still available to purchase to this day. The map represents the Keeseville community at its economic height.

1800	Keeseville is first settled and a tavern, gristmill, and some residences are soon built.
1810	The first bridge is built to connect the two sides of the Ausable River, and industries are starting to build.
1820	Schools and churches are established as industry continues to prosper.
1830	Iron and wood industries continue to build the community.
1840s	More businesses are established on both sides of the river as the population swells to over 2,000 residents.
1850s–1870s	These years were Keeseville's pinnacle as a commercial and industrial center.
1880s	The peanut railroad is established as businesses start to show a decline.
1890–1920	These decades saw the end of the industrial age for Keeseville.
1920–1950	Keeseville settles into a quiet existence in the region.
1950–1960	The creation of Interstate 87, the Northway, brings a small renewal in business for the community and stretches businesses out toward Exit 34.

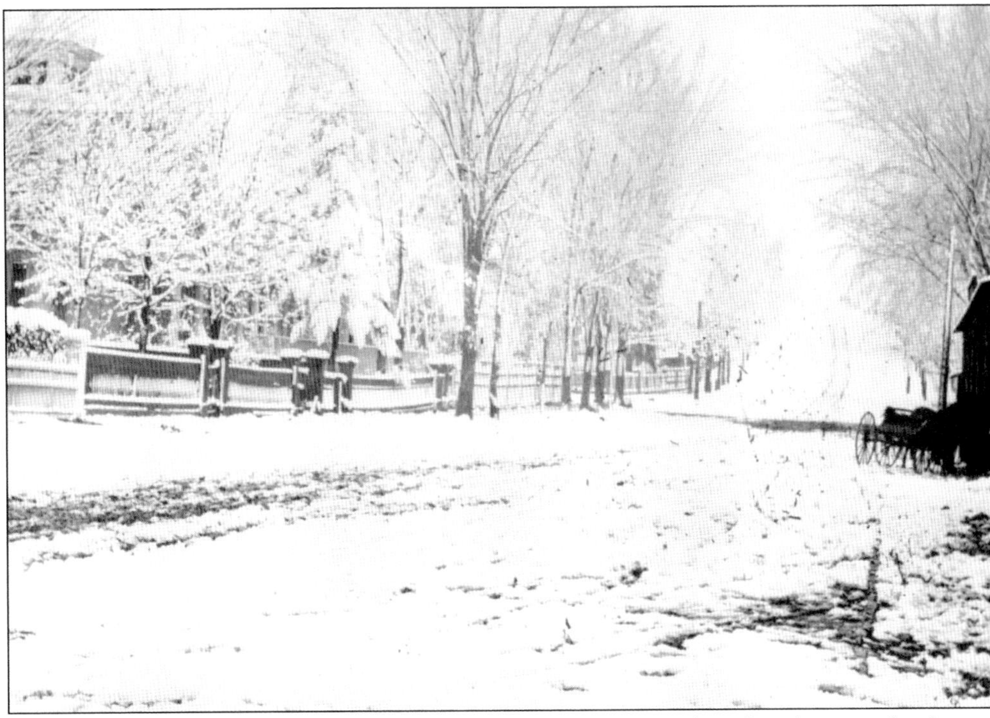

In 1860, the streets around Keeseville were still dirt, as illustrated in this photograph of upper Front Street after a small snowstorm.

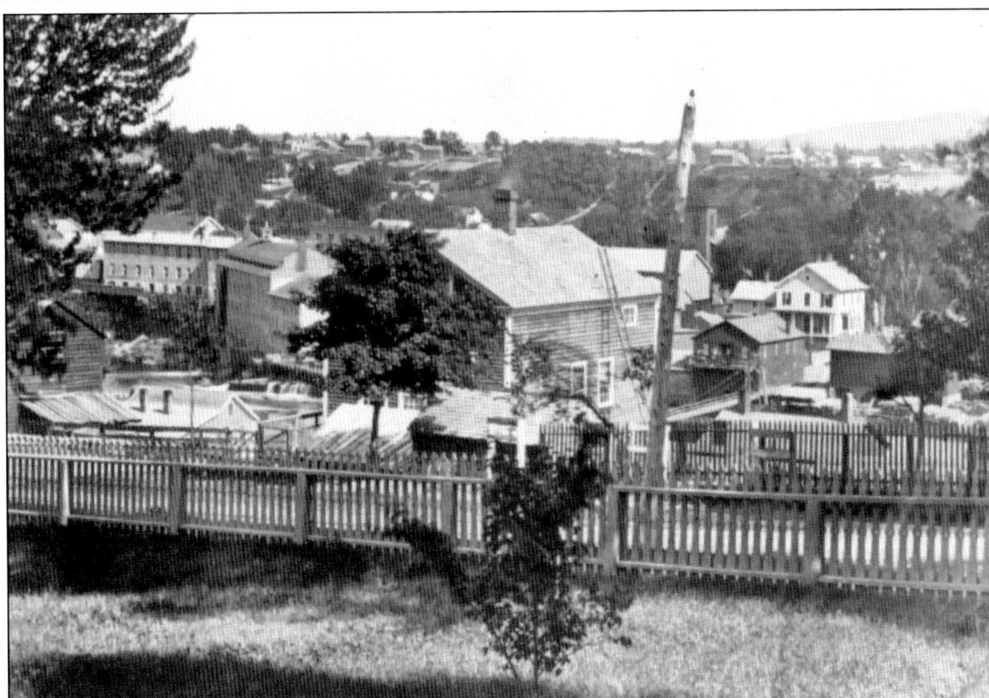

In 1876, Keeseville was prospering, and electricity, telephone, sidewalks, and paved streets were starting to develop. The houses grew closer together as more people moved into the community.

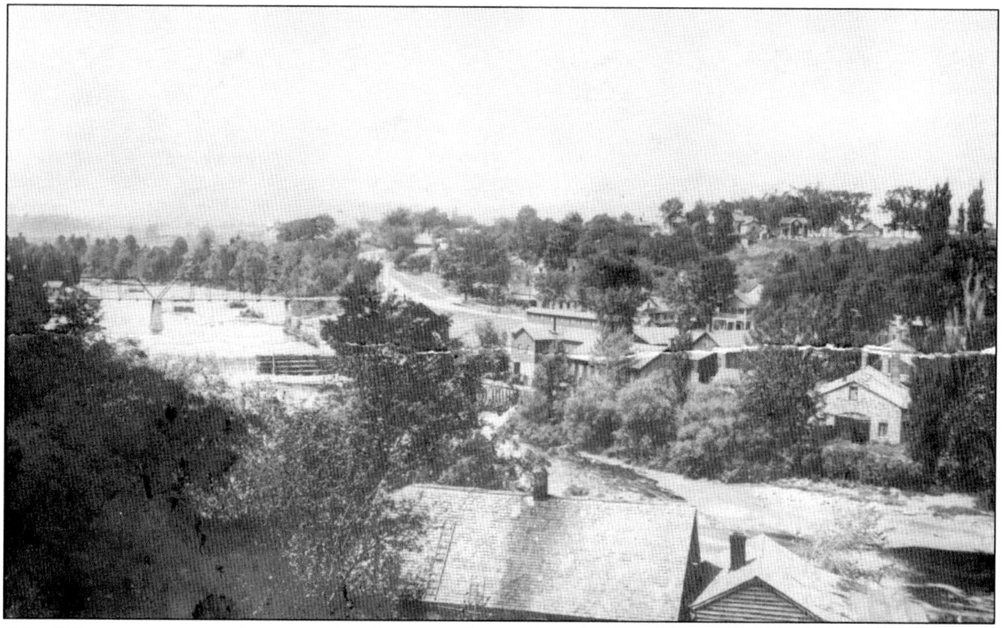

B.B. Witter took this photograph of Keeseville in the late 1800s. In the center background, the iron truss bridge stands with the upper dam beneath it. The image gives a good indication of how much forest grew around the residences that made up the outer edges of the townships of Ausable and Chesterfield and the village of Keeseville. More development was going on in the center of the village.

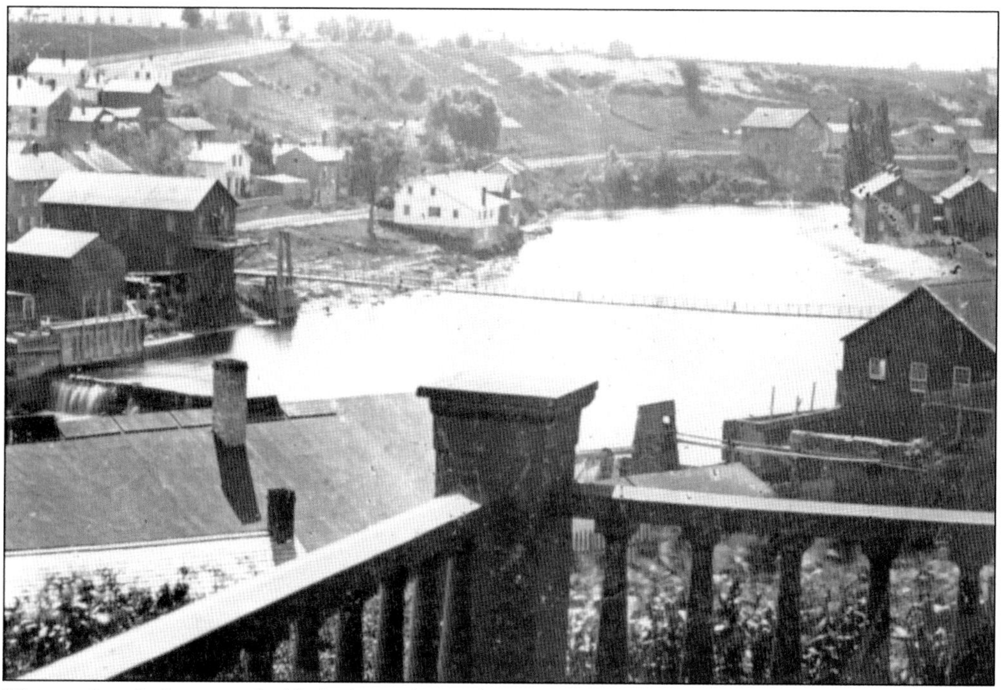

This undated photograph, likely from the early 1800s, gives a unique look at the Ausable River and Keeseville area around the river from the balcony of one of the residences. The lower dam is visible, as is an older version of the bridge that crossed the river at the time.

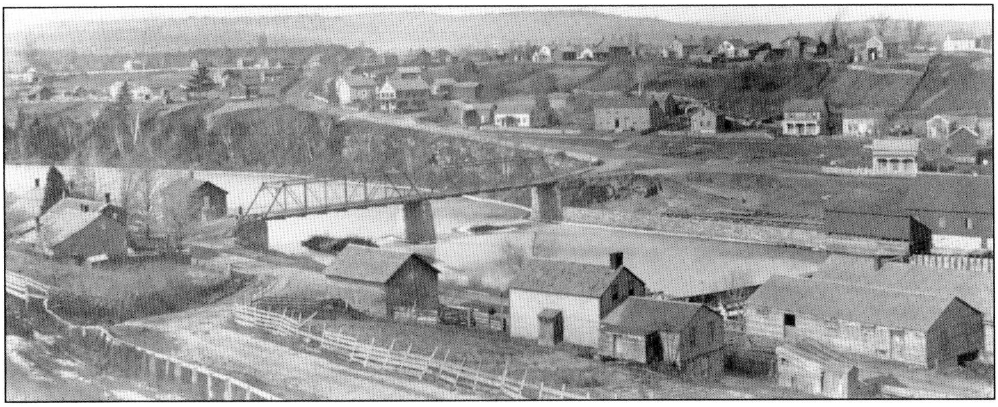

This photograph was taken 20 years after the image on page 19. Not much has really changed for the outskirts of Keeseville. Other than a change in the trees on the slopes in the background and some repairs to the fencing in the front of the photograph, the two images look identical. This similarity indicates the community's industry had already quieted in the late 1800s.

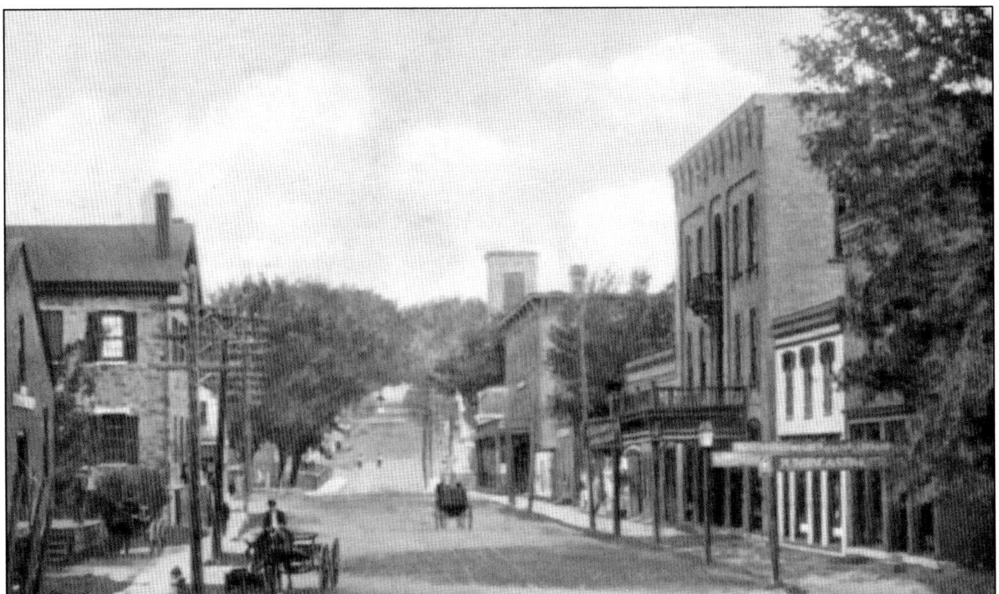

This postcard shows Main Street as it appeared in the late 1800s. While most of the trade businesses operated on Front Street, numerous small businesses did exist on either side of the Arch Bridge.

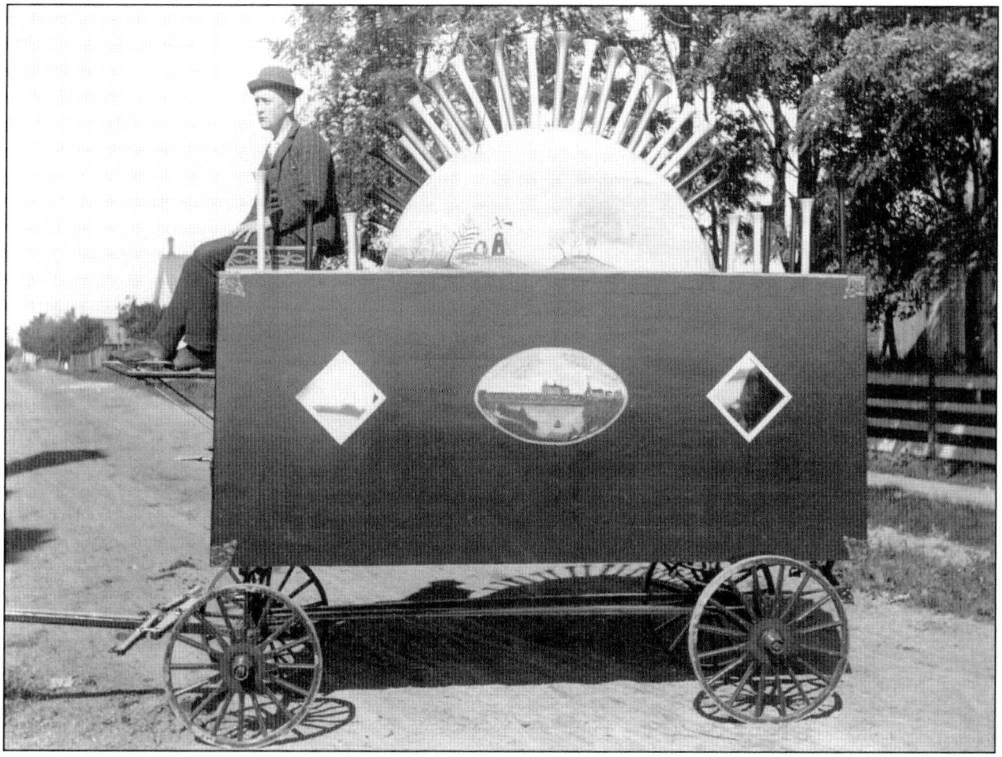

Circuses and other traveling entertainment groups were popular attractions in the mid-1800s and well into the 20th century. In 1920, while a circus was performing in Picotte's Field, this calliope wagon was photographed near the field.

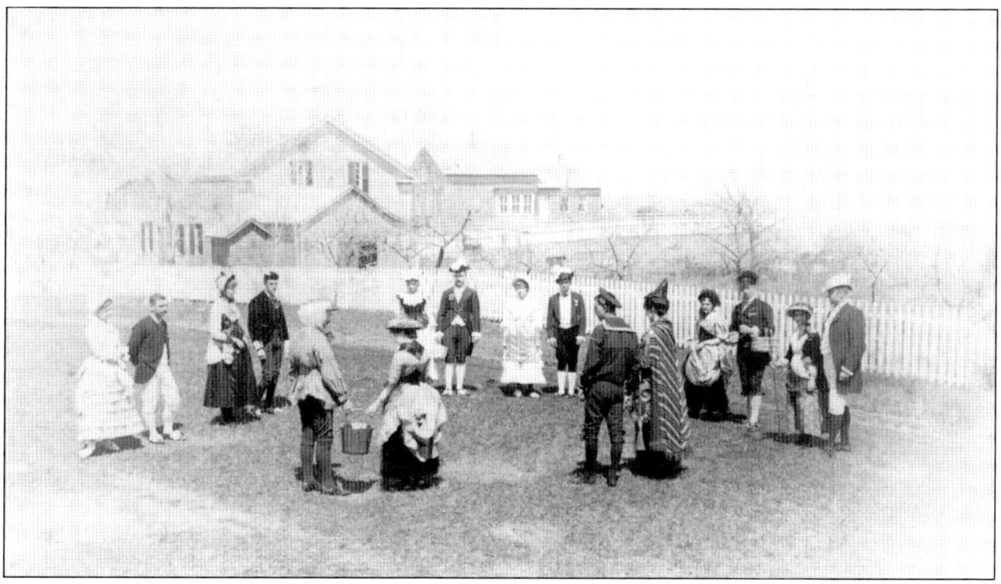

Eight couples show off their costumes to each other in this photograph from April 1883. The occasion is a Mother Goose party at the private residence known as Rembrandt Hall. Entertainments such as elaborately themed parties were a welcome break from the hard work of the industrial community.

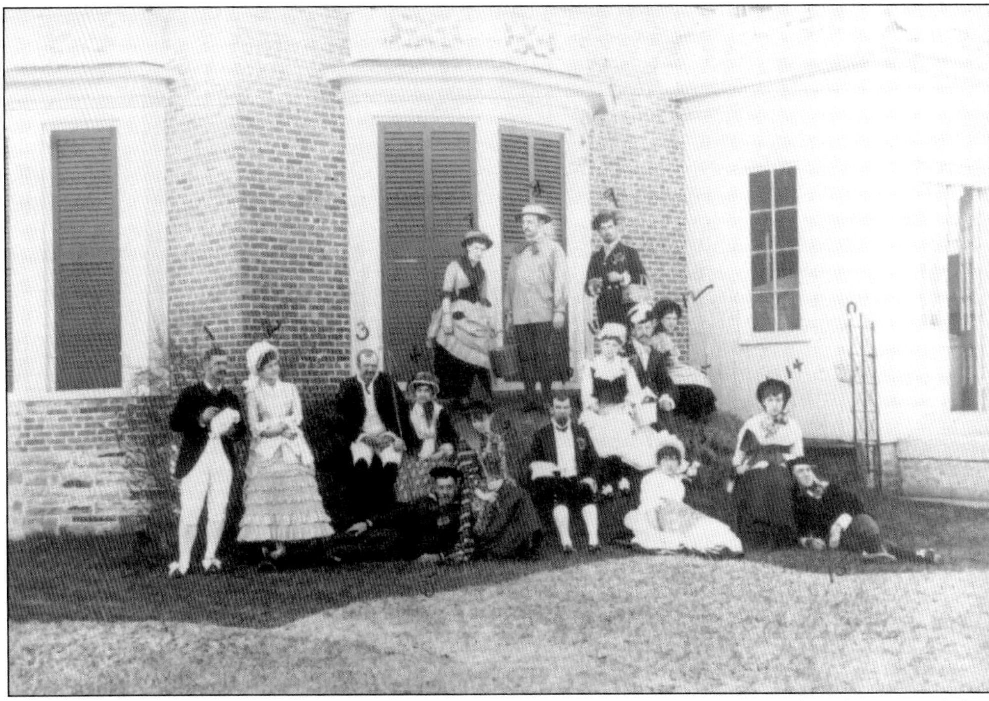

The Mother Goose party attendees rest against Rembrandt Hall. While the photograph has numbers written next to all 16 people, the identifying sheet has been lost, and it is unknown who was in attendance.

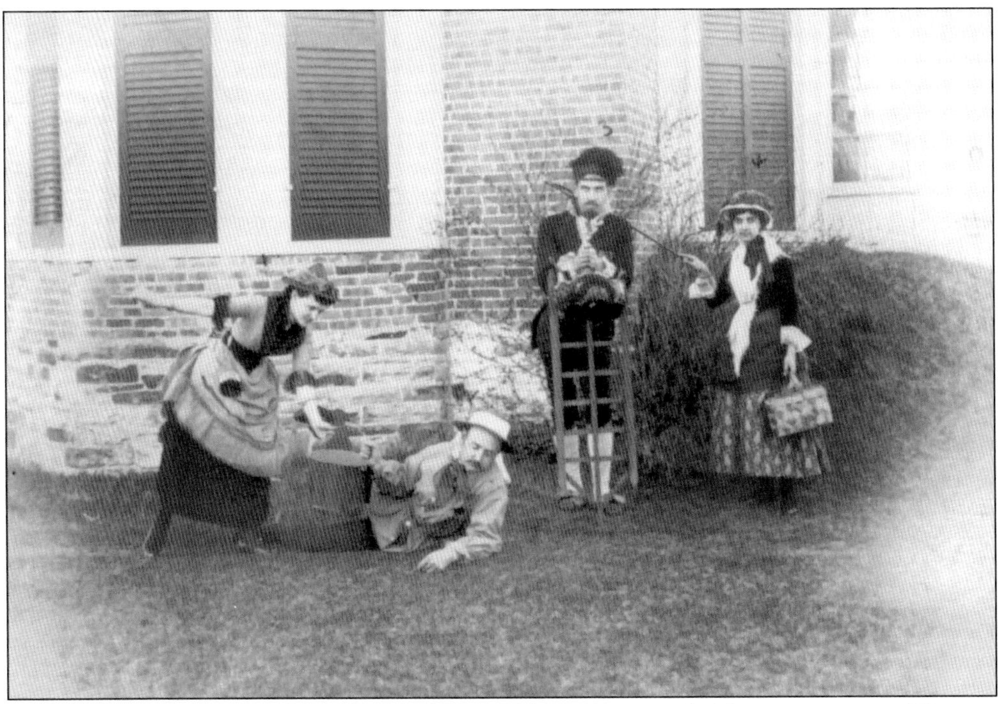

This photograph provides a closer view of some of the participants' elaborate costumes. The two couples depicted are portraying Jack and Jill as well as Little Bo Peep.

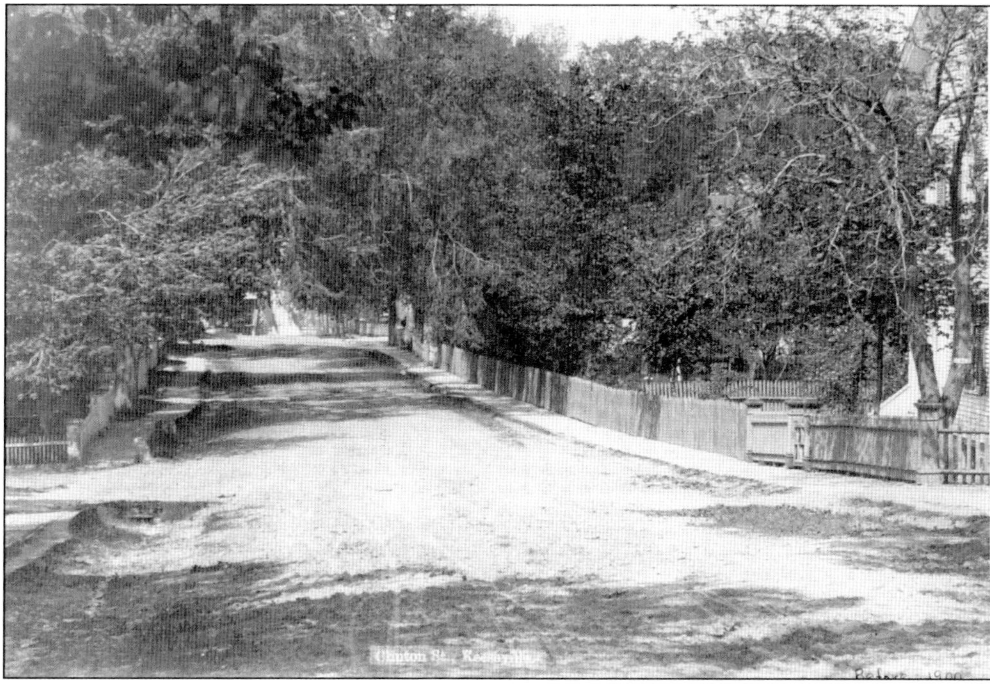

Before 1900, Clinton Street still had the overgrowth of trees that reminds residents that they are living in the Adirondacks, a very mountainous and tree-filled part of New York.

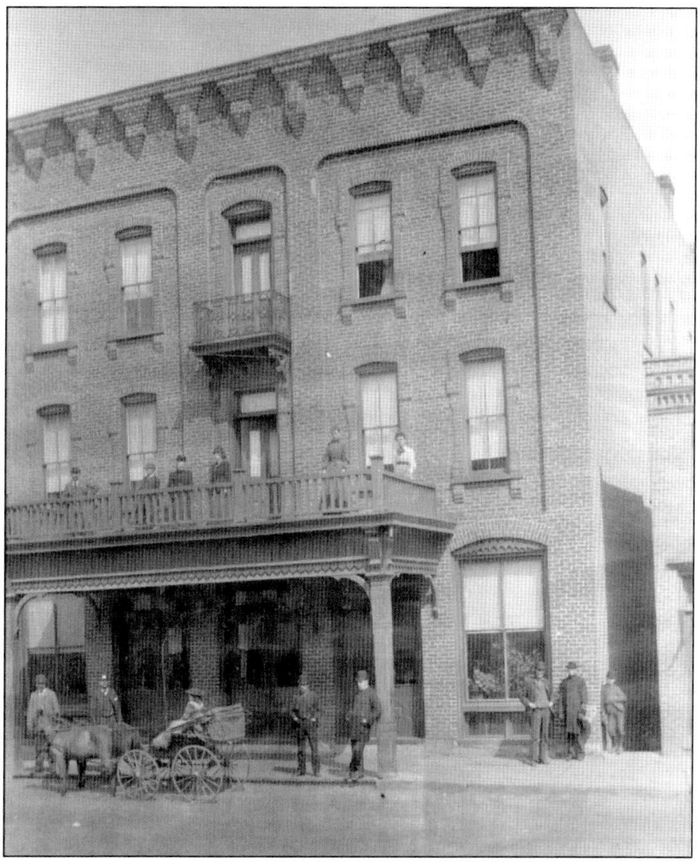

Another popular building on Main Street was the Delmont House, which was built by Louis N. Nollet. Damaged in a fire in 1892, this building would later be called the Adirondack.

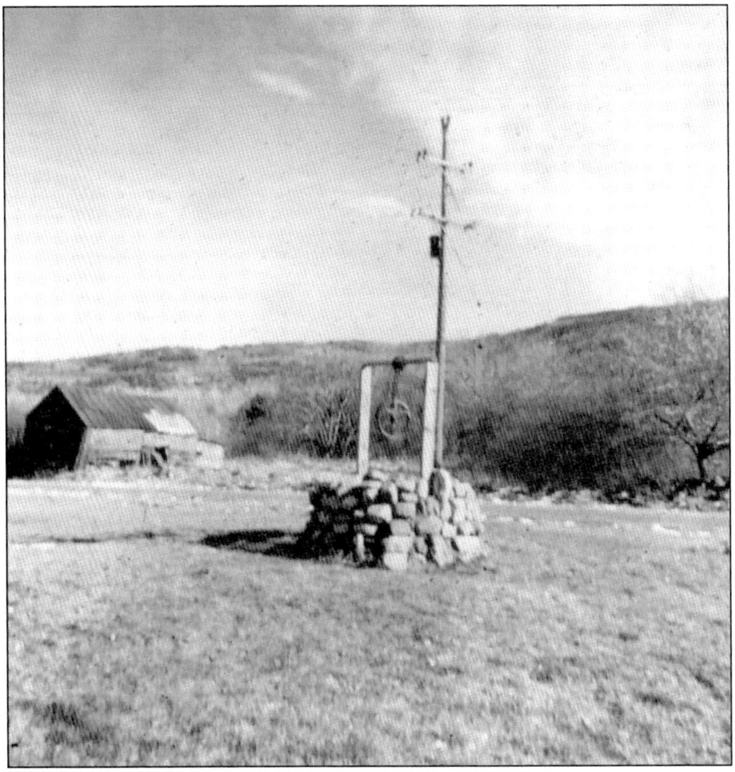

While dated from the 1880s, the subject of this photograph is far older. The well and Bosworth Tavern were the first constructions in the Keeseville area. Bosworth Tavern became the home of the first post office for the community.

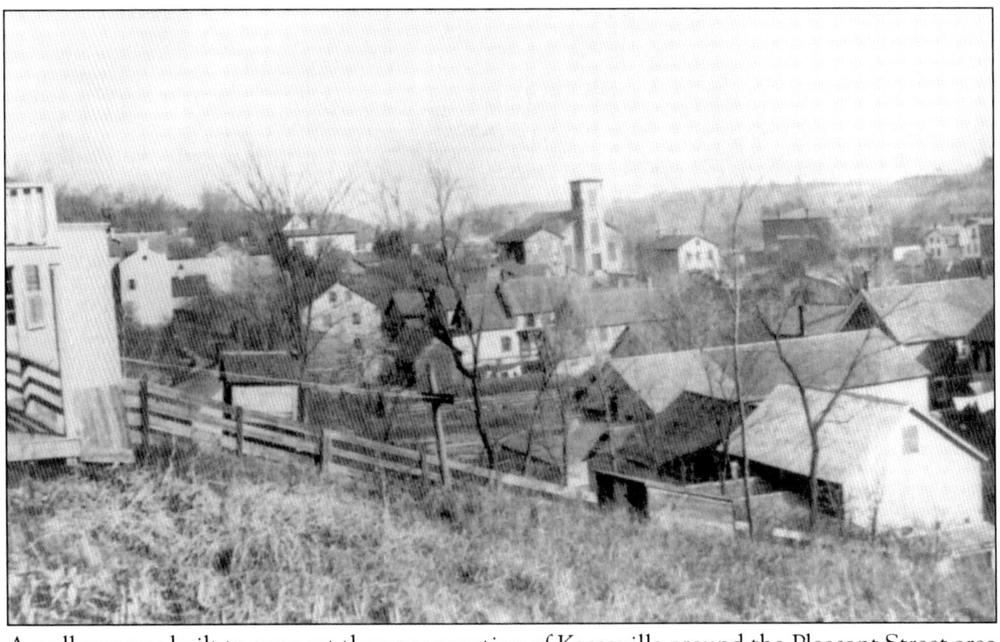

A walkway was built to connect the upper portion of Keeseville around the Pleasant Street area with the downtown community. Now a steep stairway brings pedestrians to an opening behind Riverside Tavern on Ausable Street directly across from the suspension bridge, which takes pedestrians across the river into the township of Chesterfield and Essex County, as well as the main business hub of Front Street.

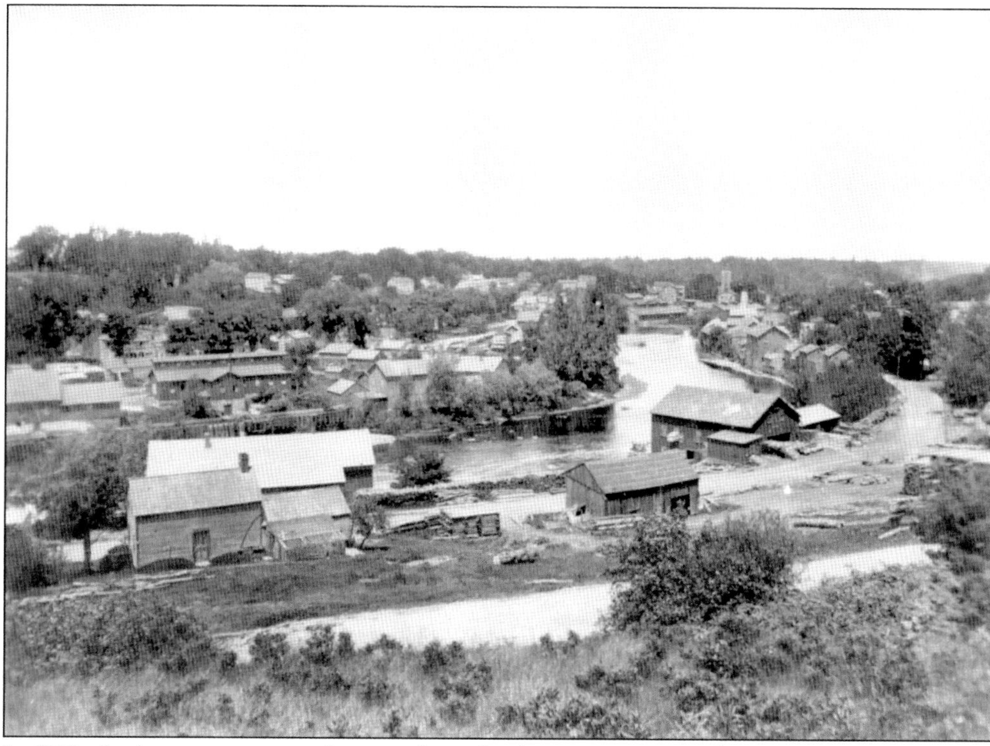

In 1903, the homes were spreading out from the downtown Keeseville area, which can be seen in the center of the photograph. The Congregational Presbyterian church can be seen above the village.

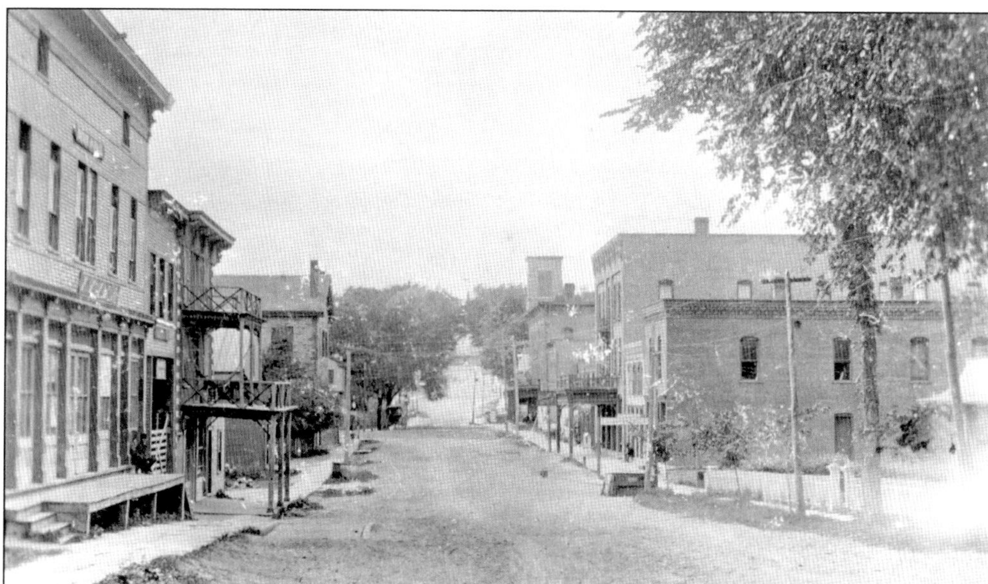

This undated photograph gives an earlier view of Main Street. Throughout modern Keeseville there are a few square concrete blocks near the side of the road. While no longer serving any purpose, in the 1800s, these blocks gave passengers the needed height to climb in and out of horse-drawn carriages.

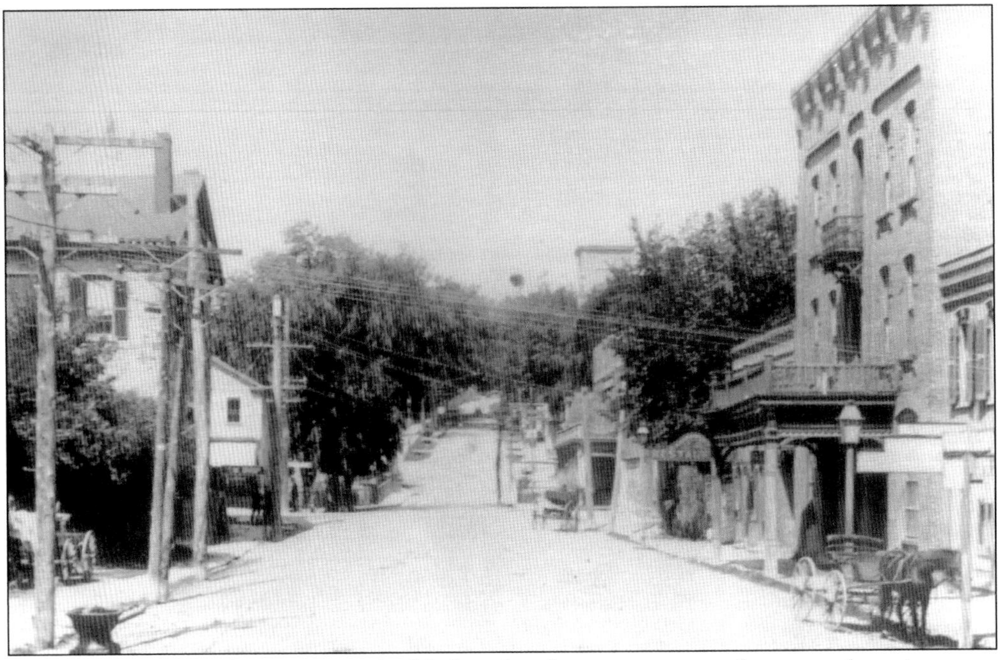

This undated view of Main Street highlights the changing times as horses and carriages are still prevalent, but utility poles are now running across the street. The popular Delmont House can be seen on the right side of the street near the bottom of the photograph with an unknown restaurant next to it.

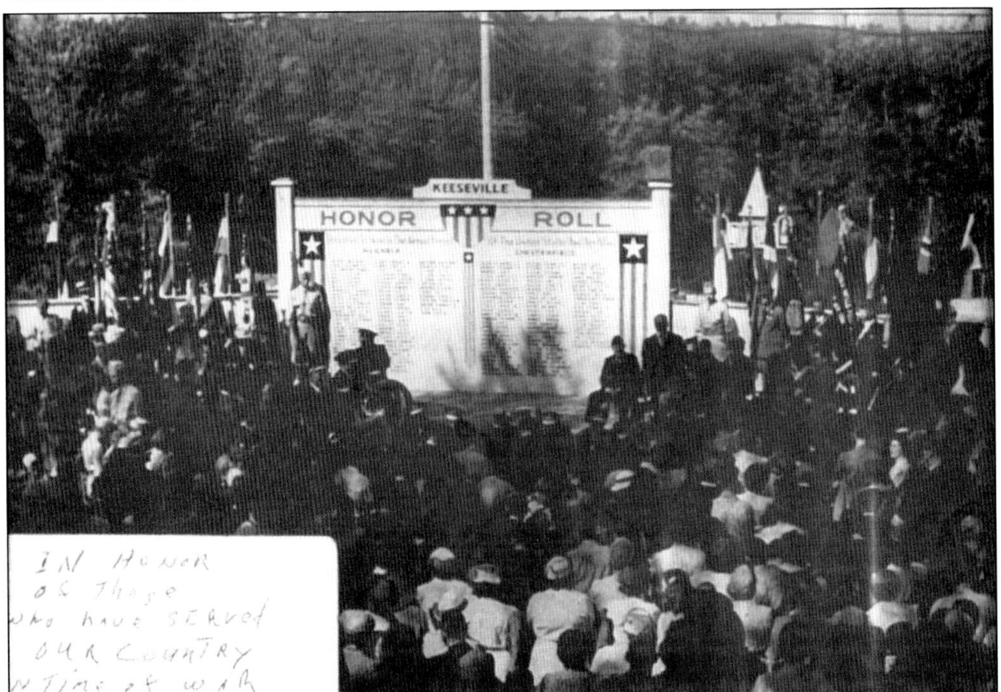

A veterans memorial park was built at the intersection of Main Street and Front Street next to the Arch Bridge. On Labor Day 1942, a Keeseville Honor Roll Memorial was dedicated and installed.

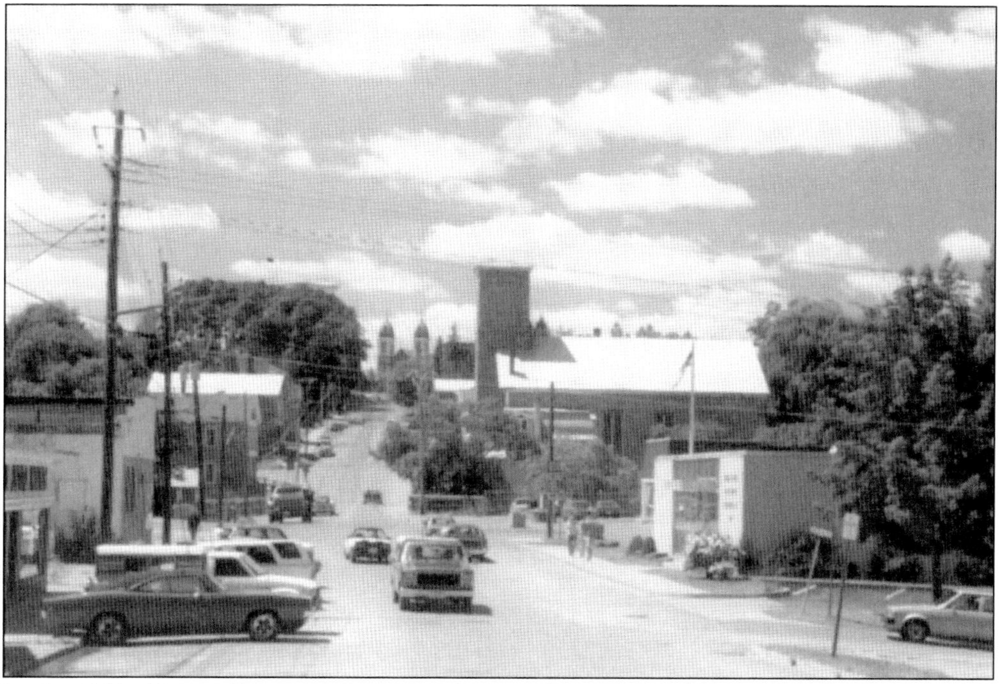

In the 1950s, Keeseville's Main Street was busy with traffic. In the center background can be seen St John the Baptist Church. The post office can be seen to the right, and there is no traffic light over the intersection between Main Street and Front Street.

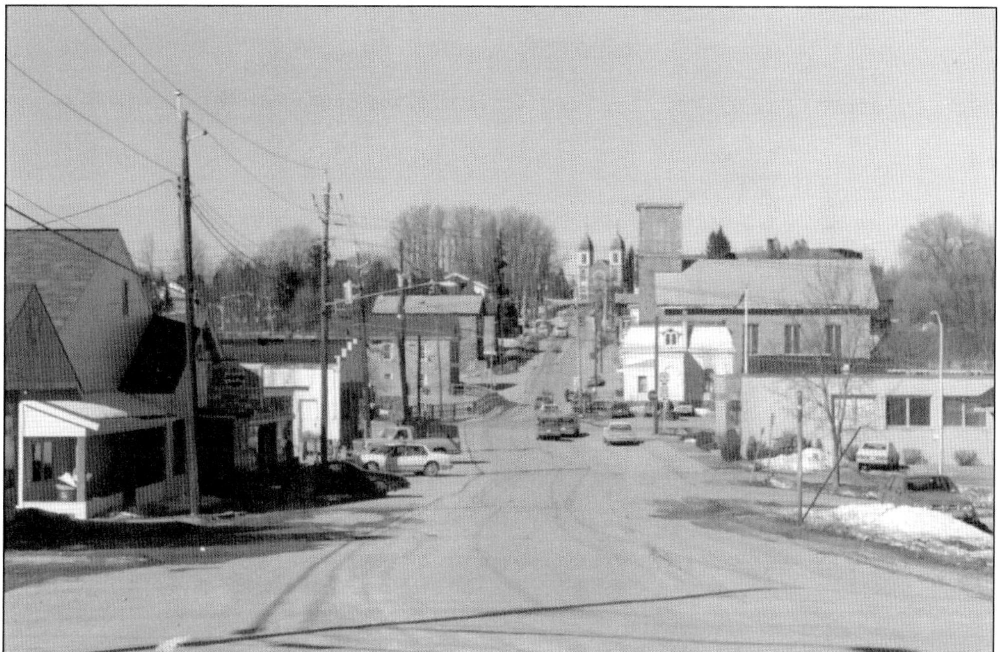

This image of Main Street in the 1960s was taken in the same location as the previous photograph. The biggest change is the season; the leaves have all fallen, giving the area a more wide-open look. The traffic light at the intersection still had not been installed by this point.

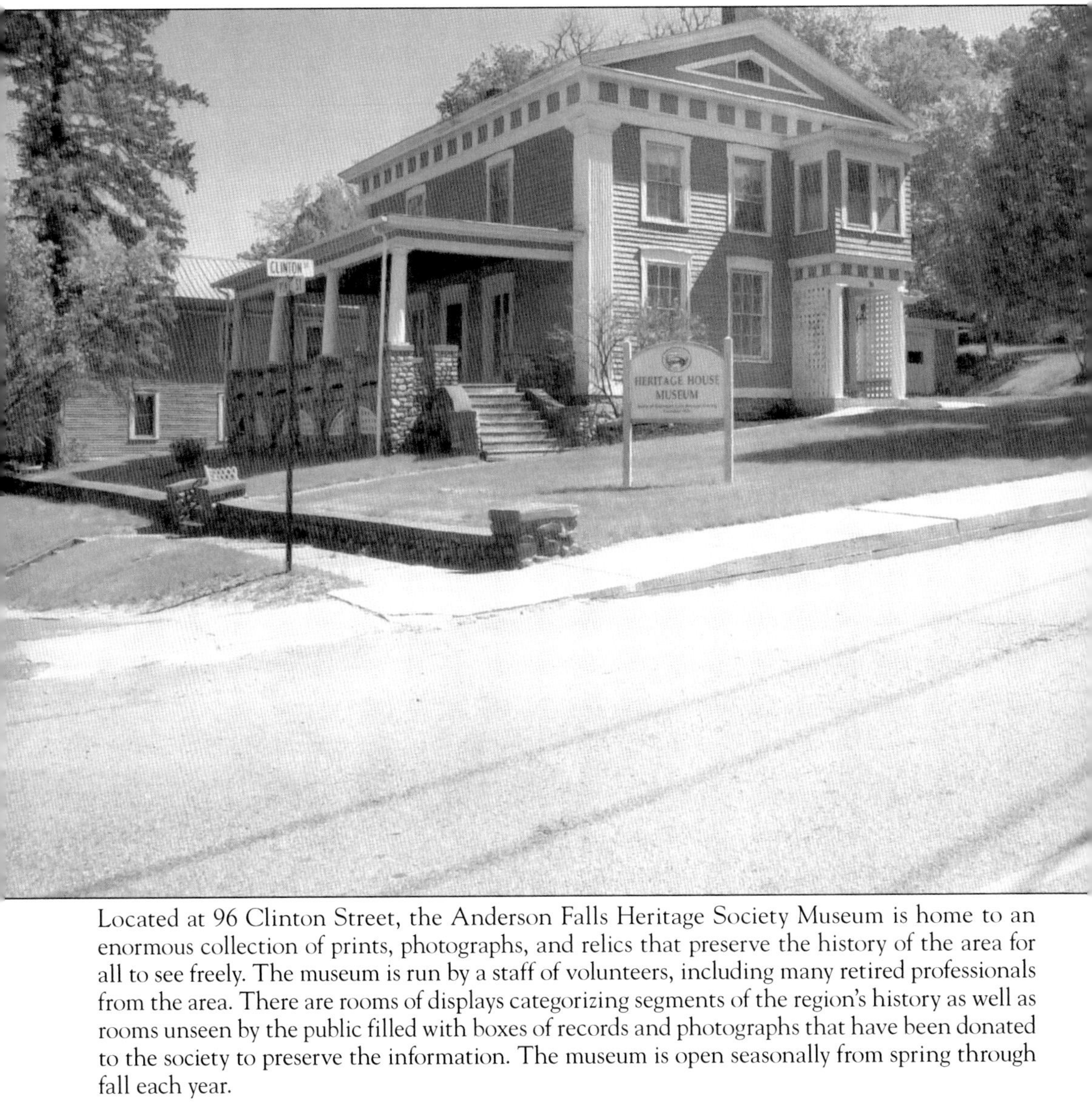

Located at 96 Clinton Street, the Anderson Falls Heritage Society Museum is home to an enormous collection of prints, photographs, and relics that preserve the history of the area for all to see freely. The museum is run by a staff of volunteers, including many retired professionals from the area. There are rooms of displays categorizing segments of the region's history as well as rooms unseen by the public filled with boxes of records and photographs that have been donated to the society to preserve the information. The museum is open seasonally from spring through fall each year.

Two

Port Kent

As Keeseville prospered, so did the neighboring community of Port Kent, located just 3.5 miles north on the banks of Lake Champlain. Port Kent was named after the chancellor of New York James Kent. With its picturesque view of the lake and its proximity to Ausable Chasm and the Adirondack Mountains, Port Kent soon boasted numerous hotels and a ferry system on the lake. The Canadian Pacific Railroad passed through the edge of Port Kent against the lake and made the community a hub for transportation. Eventually, Keeseville merchants would build a rail line connecting Keeseville with Port Kent, allowing the businessmen to ship their paper and iron goods out up to Montreal, across to Burlington, Vermont, downstate to Albany, and onward to New York City. In the midst of Port Kent, 862 acres were established as the Wickham Marsh Wildlife Management Area. Today, an Amtrak depot is a brief stop for the rail line, and a ferry runs seasonally from Port Kent to Burlington, Vermont, on an hour-long ferry ride.

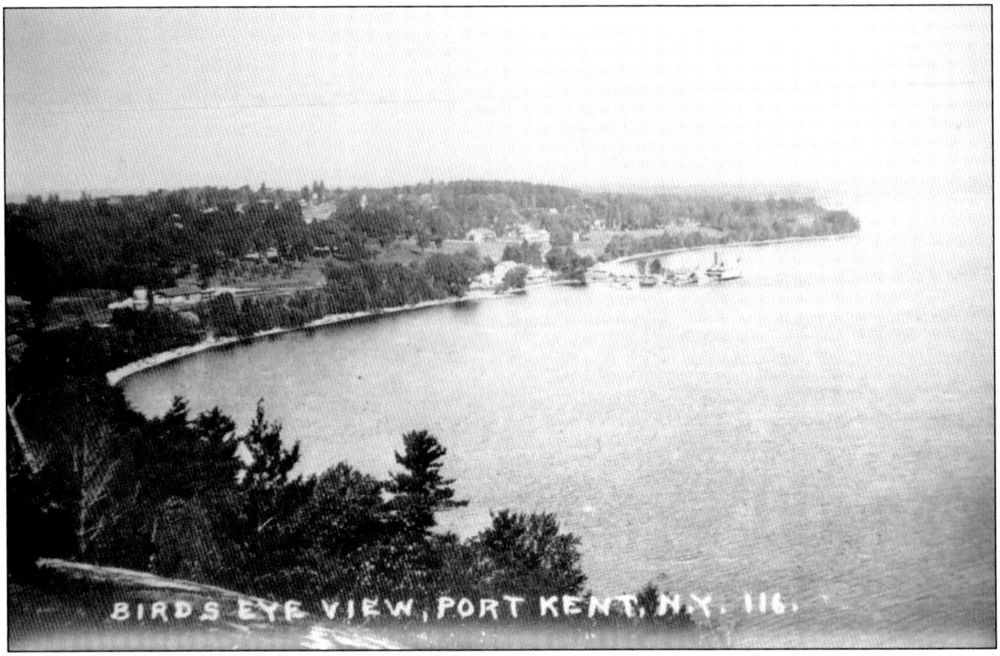

This postcard from 1910 to 1920 shows a bird's-eye view of Port Kent with the beach and ferry dock in the center and the hotels and houses rising up the slope from the lakefront. The white building closest to the left edge was the depot for the Canadian Pacific Railroad and the peanut railroad of Keeseville.

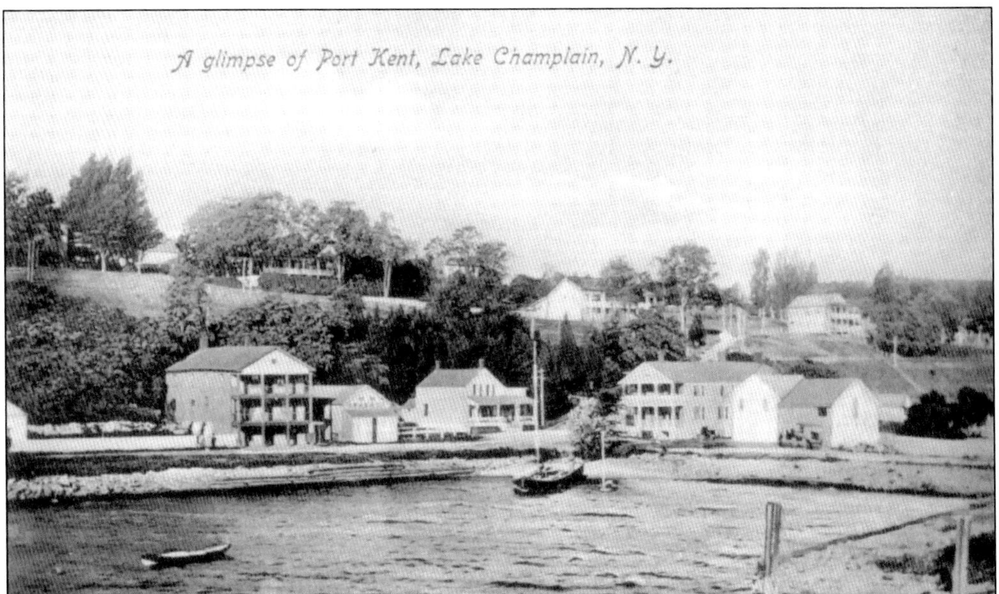

This 1910s view comes from a boat on the lake looking at the shoreline; Rennell's store is on the left along with several houses, hotels, and the boat dock, where passengers debarked to the Burlington to Port Kent ferry. While the buildings have changed, the ferry still runs on a seasonal basis.

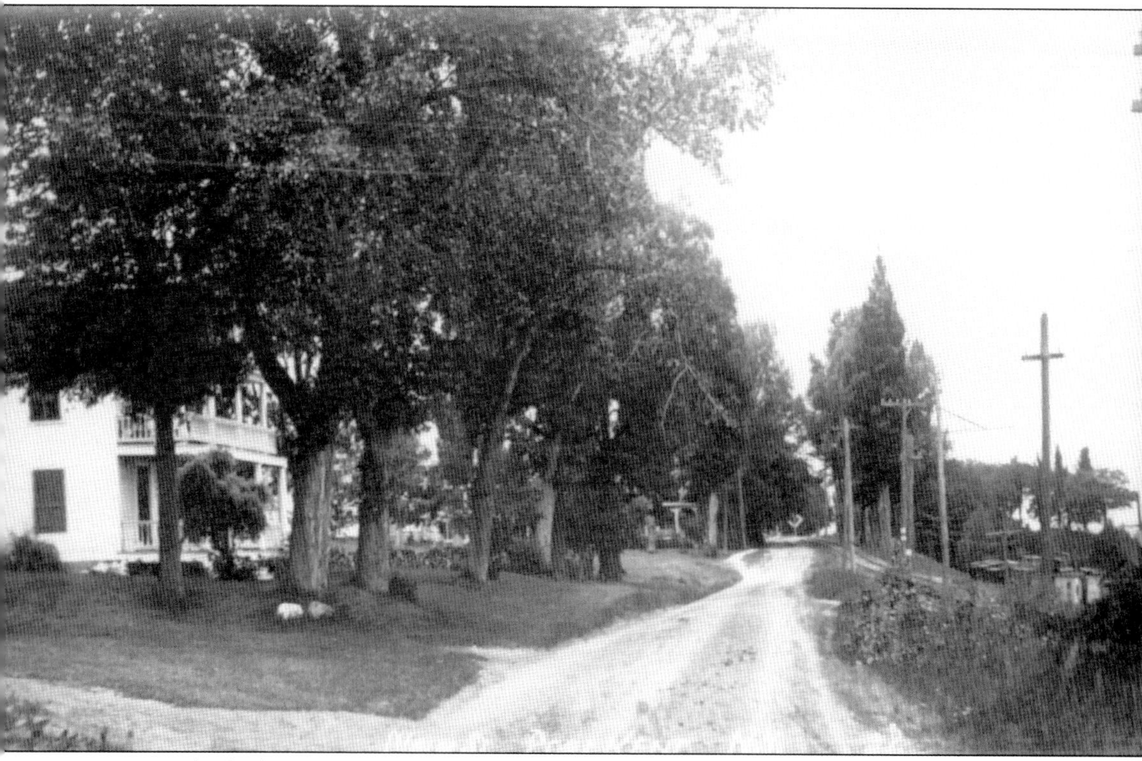

Houses were built along Lake Street, one of the main thoroughfares for Port Kent, which ran along the edge of Lake Champlain. The road runs parallel to the lake, connects to Ausable Chasm, and points south toward Plattsburgh and Montreal to the north. Hotels advertised daytrips to Lake Placid and Montreal as part of their offerings. This postcard view misidentifies Lake Street as Main Street in Port Kent, which ran above the slope with more hotels, cottages, and houses. The slope provided spectacular views of the lake. The rise also offered grounds for tennis and golf to the hotel patrons. Today, Lake Street travels around the edge of the popular nature preserve Wickham Marsh Wildlife Management Area.

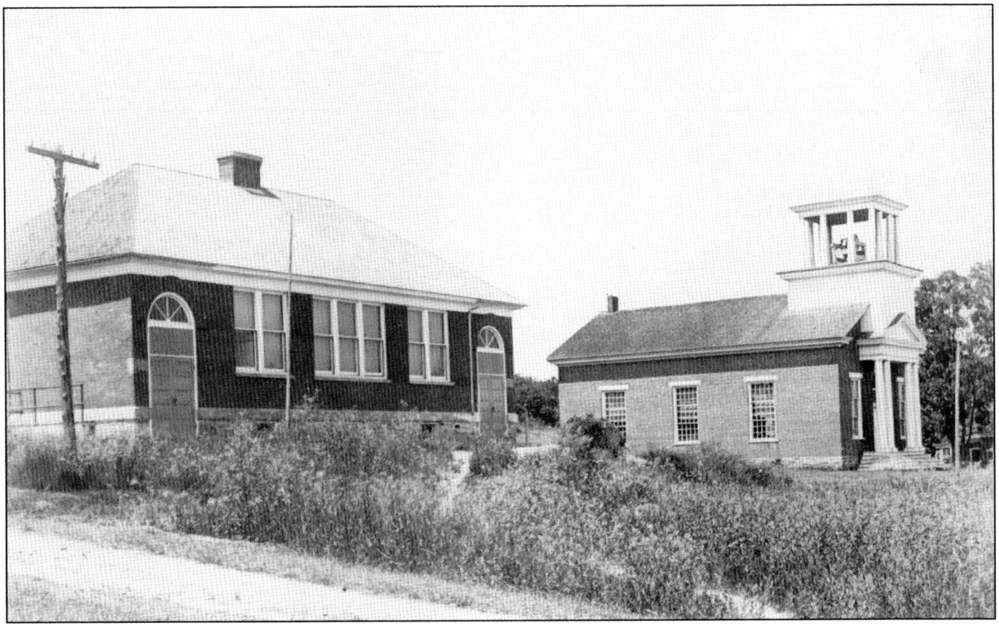

During its heyday from the mid-1800s to the mid-1900s, Port Kent had a steady population of between 150 to 200 residents, mostly for the seasonal hotel trade. For the local population, several churches and a school were in operation but have since closed as ready transportation allow residents to visit outlying larger communities regularly. This early 1900s photograph shows the Union Church and school.

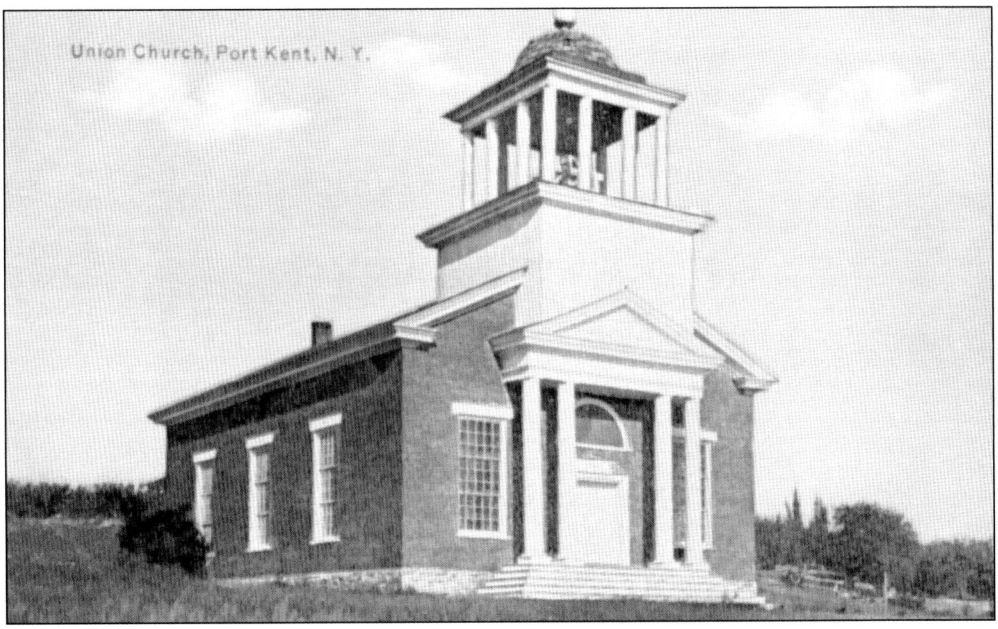

This photograph shows another view of the Union Church. The church was located up the slope in the middle of Port Kent and served approximately 100 parishioners during its operation. The local school was built to the left of the church.

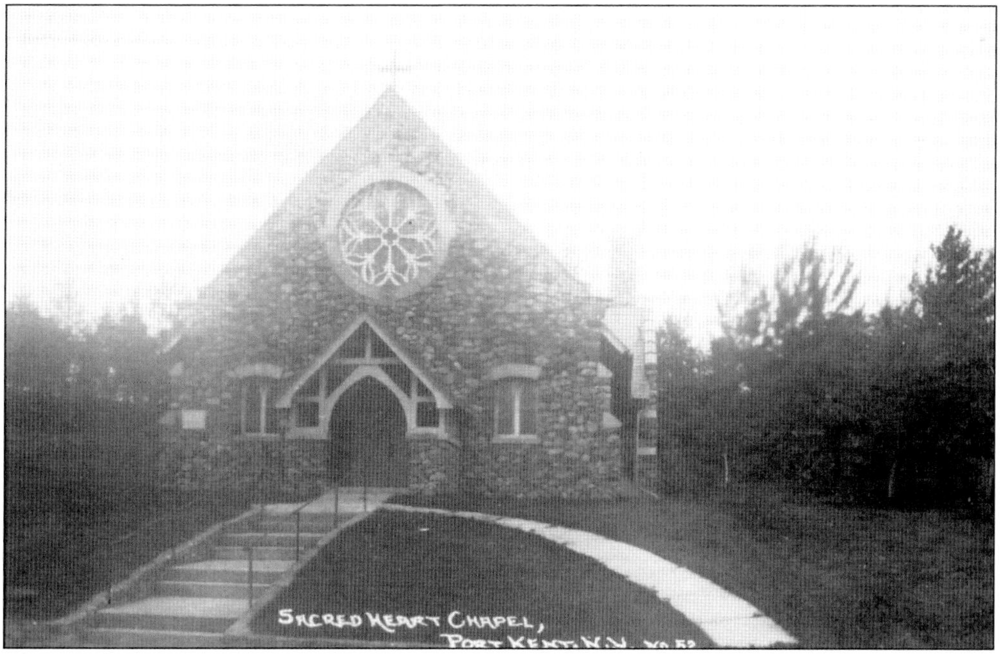

The North Country has a strong Catholic presence, which led to the Sacred Heart Chapel in Port Kent, a small stone church built in the 1800s to service the local population as well as all the vacationers from New York City and Burlington, Vermont. As the tourist trade waned in the early 1900s, the local churches faced a dwindling attendance as well.

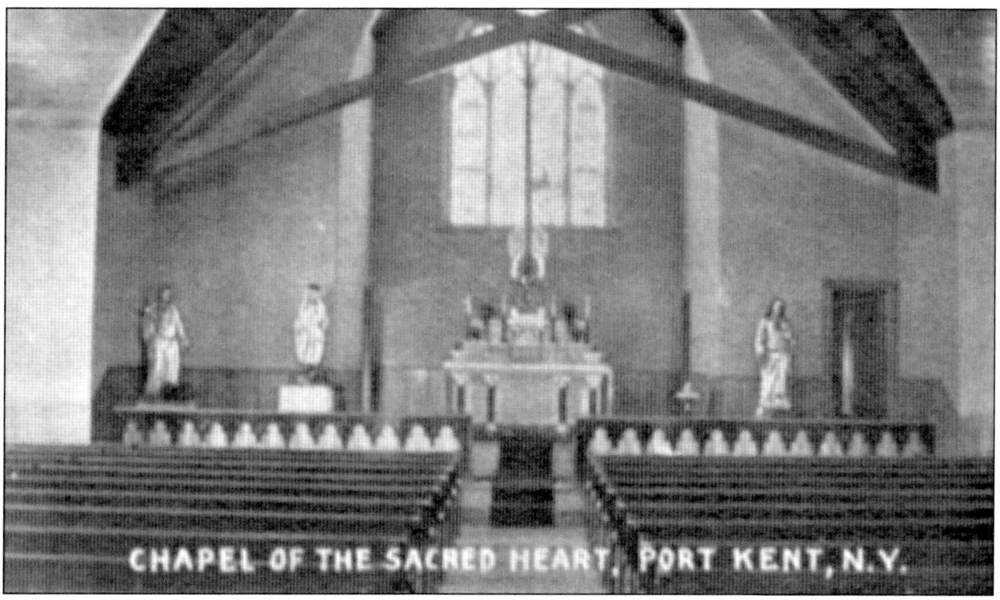

This postcard from the early 1900s shows the interior of the Sacred Heart Chapel from in back of the pews, highlighting the altar and statues of Mary, Joseph, and Jesus with his sacred heart. During the late spring, summer, and early fall, the church would meet the religious needs of the many tourists in the area.

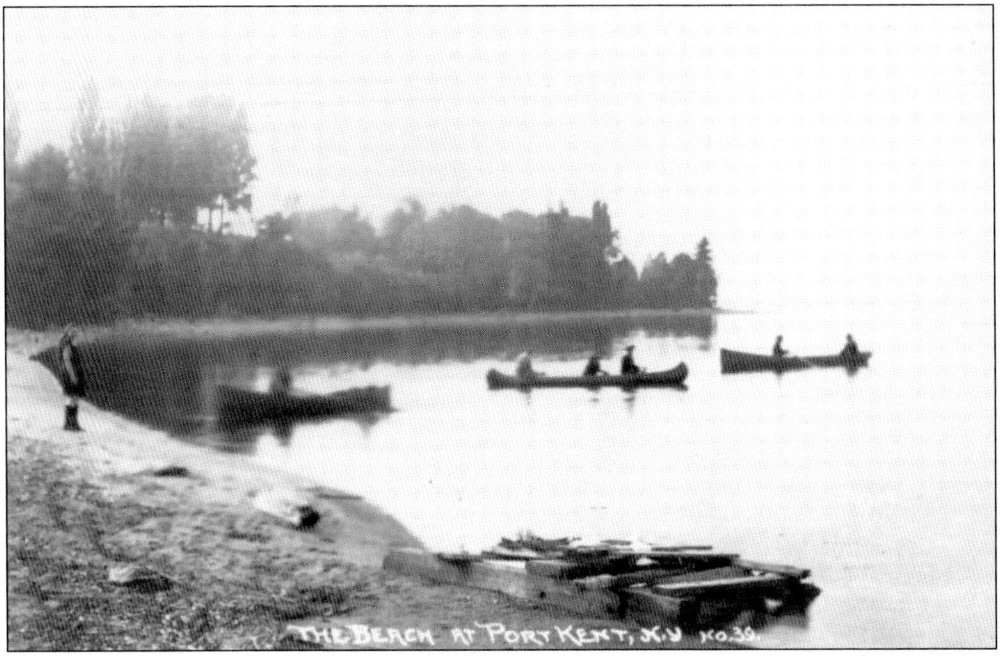

This postcard from the early 1900s shows the canoes and small boats available to vacationers to use as part of their stay at the local hotels. The long, fine sandy beach gave easy access to the lake a short distance from the active ferry dock. Canal boats were also very common on the lake with an active boat building operation across the lake in Shelburne, Vermont.

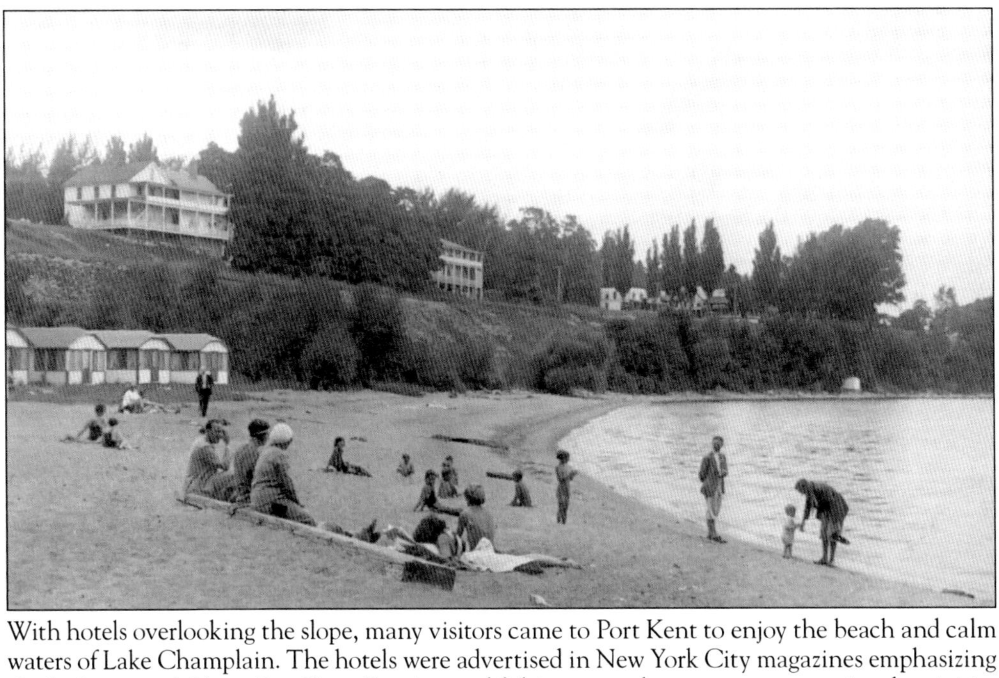

With hotels overlooking the slope, many visitors came to Port Kent to enjoy the beach and calm waters of Lake Champlain. The hotels were advertised in New York City magazines emphasizing the bathing available in Port Kent. Boating and fishing were also common recreational activities in the water.

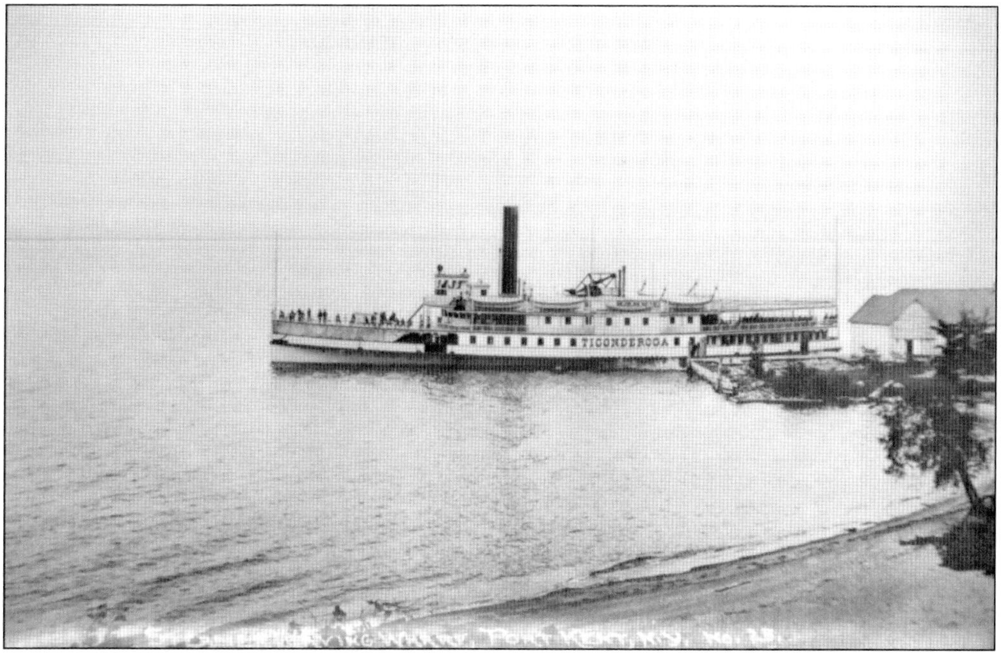

The steamboat *Ticonderoga* was the most famous of the ferries between Burlington, Vermont, and Port Kent, New York. During its career, the *Ticonderoga* served many lines for the Lake Champlain Transportation Company and briefly worked as a floating casino. When retired in the 1950s, the *Ticonderoga* was docked at the Maritime Museum in Shelburne, Vermont.

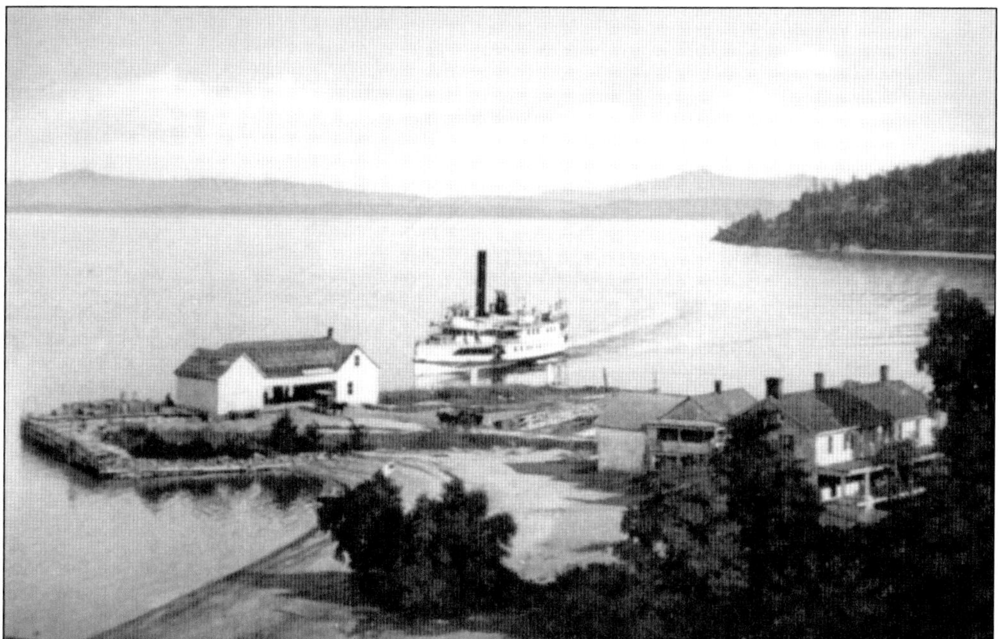

This undated postcard view is of a ferry from the Lake Champlain Transportation Company pulling into the dock at Port Kent. Today, as during the heyday of Port Kent, the run is seasonal, starting in June and running until October, offering an hour-long scenic ride across the lake between Port Kent and Burlington, Vermont.

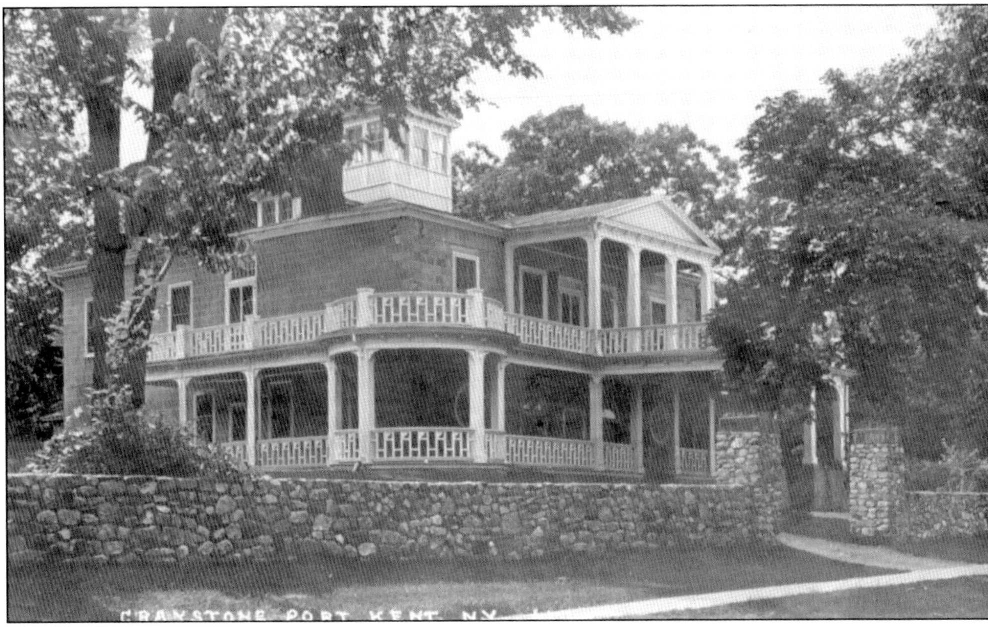

Many gorgeous houses were built in Port Kent, including the Elkanah Watson Manor with its widow's peak and large circular windows revealing views of the scenic Lake Champlain. Most famous of the local houses, it has been occupied since 1828 and was designated a National Historic Landmark in 1968.

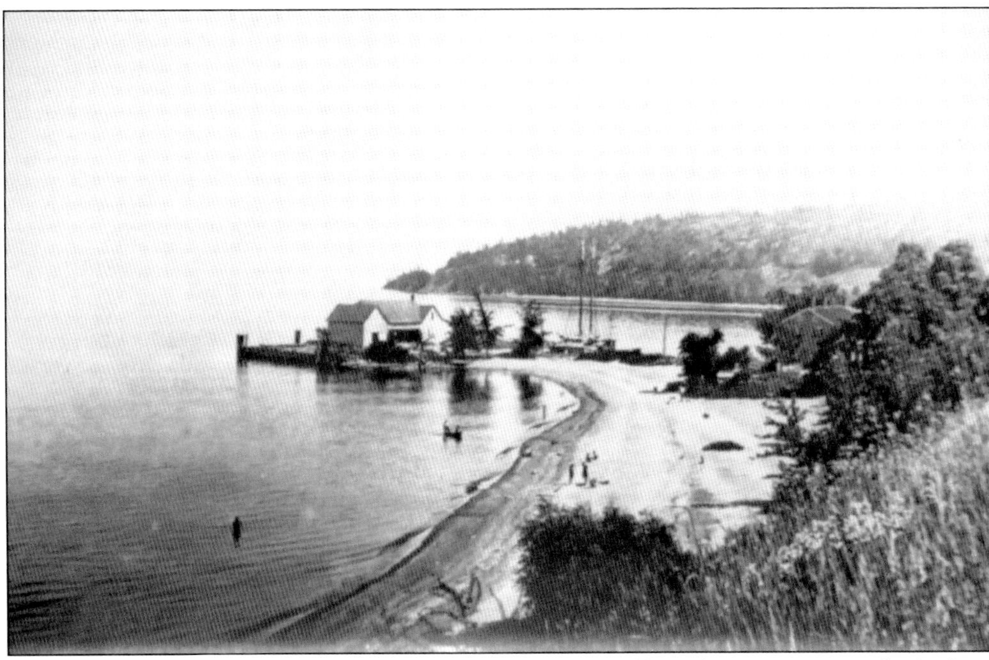

While tourism was the main trade for Port Kent, the Rennell Brothers' Store near the bathing beach offered a general store for the residents as well as visitors disembarking from the ferry. Today, a small gift shop operated by the Lake Champlain Transportation Company is located on the ferry dock.

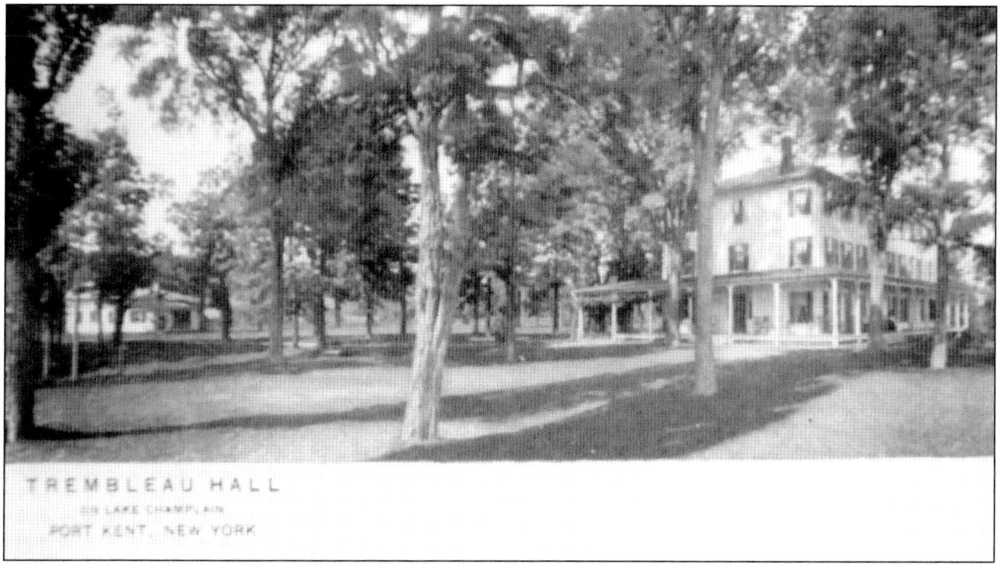

One of the most popular of Port Kent's numerous hotels was Trembleau Hall. It was opened seasonally and originally operated by Farrell and Adgate. Later, it would be owned by Martin Rennell and sons. The house proper had room for 20 guests with additional housing in guest cottages on the property.

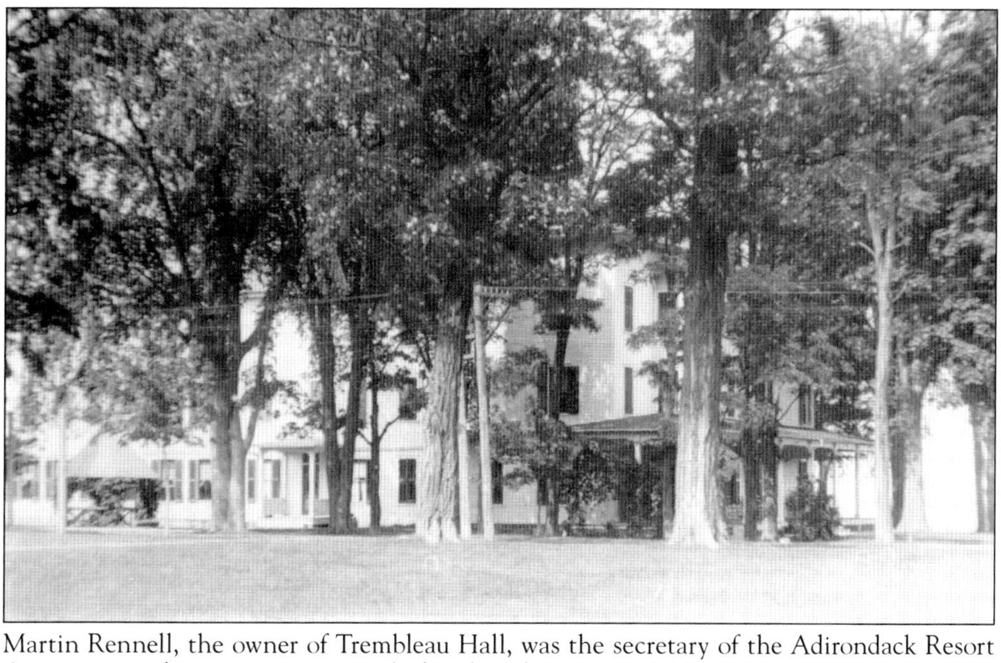

Martin Rennell, the owner of Trembleau Hall, was the secretary of the Adirondack Resort Association and active in promoting the hotels and resorts available in the Adirondacks. Rennell owned several hotels besides Trembleau Hall in the Port Kent area during the peak of the tourist industry.

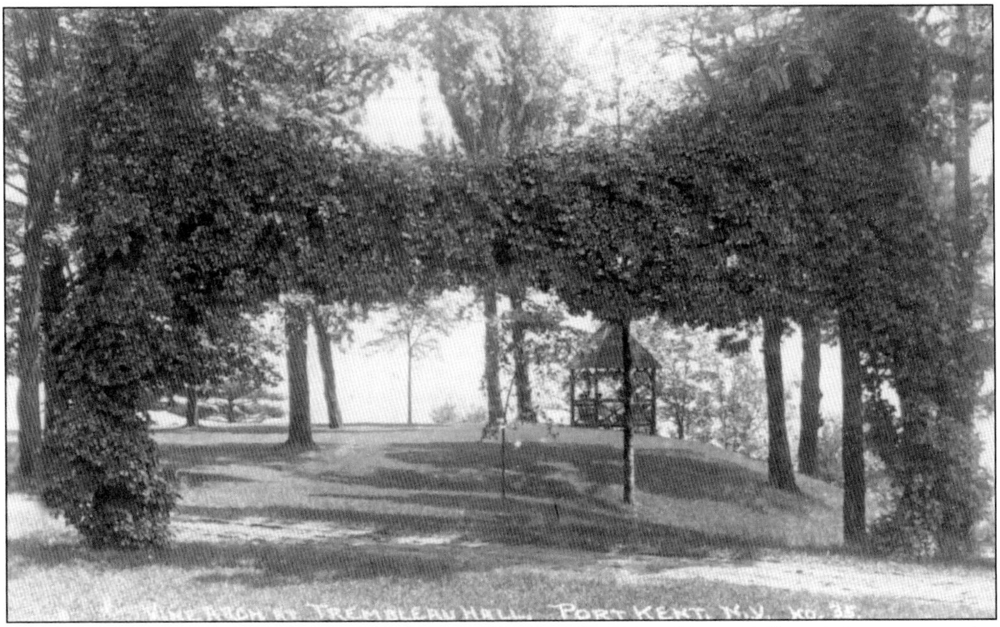

A 1928 advertisement in a New York City paper advertised Trembleau Hall and Cottages in the Adirondacks as a modern hotel with shady lawns, a clean, sandy beach, refined atmosphere, fishing, and tennis, ideally located three miles from Ausable Chasm. Daylong sightseeing trips to Lake Placid and Montreal were also available.

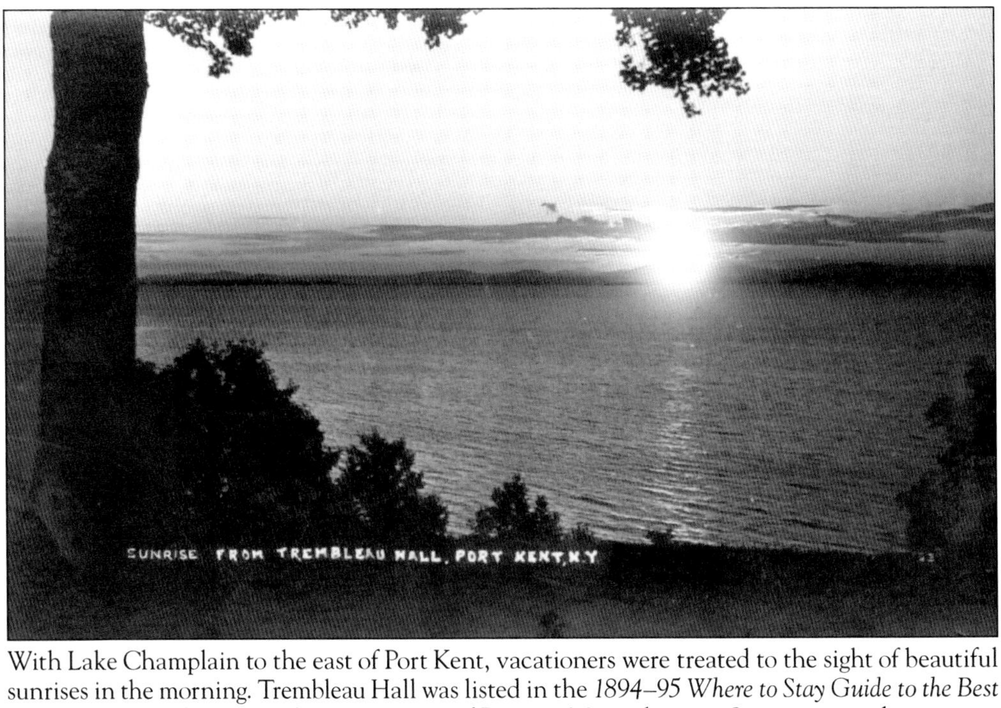

With Lake Champlain to the east of Port Kent, vacationers were treated to the sight of beautiful sunrises in the morning. Trembleau Hall was listed in the *1894–95 Where to Stay Guide to the Best Hotels in the World*, put out by Moses King of Boston, Massachusetts. It was reported as costing $2.50 a day with a scenic view of Lake Champlain.

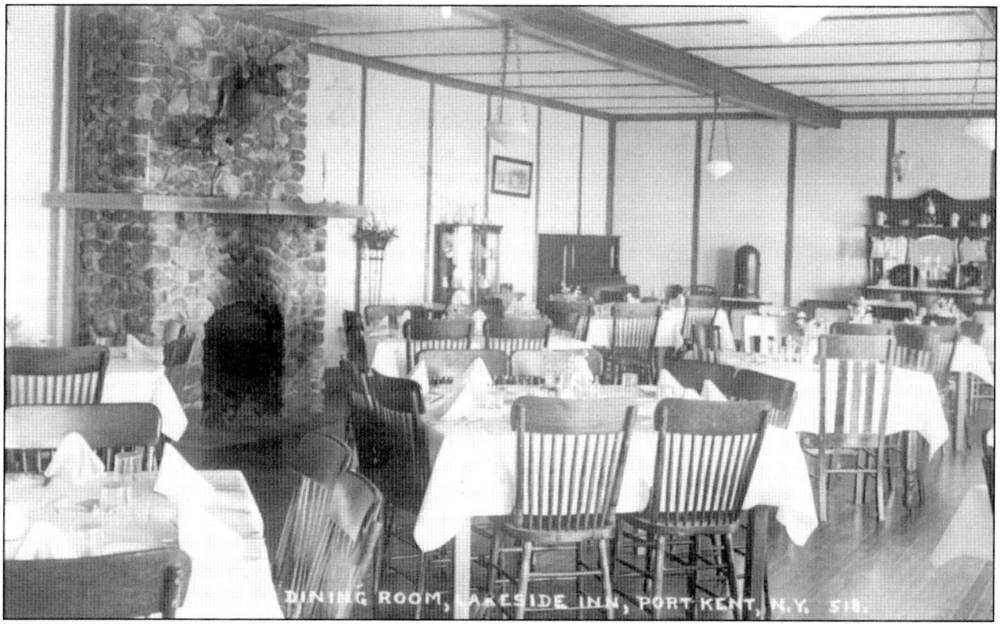

Another extremely popular vacation hotel in Port Kent was the Lakeside Inn, nestled on the shore of Lake Champlain. In 1928, the *New York Sun* reported the seasonal opening of the hotel and the fine home cooking. Dancing was also promoted as an activity available to tourists.

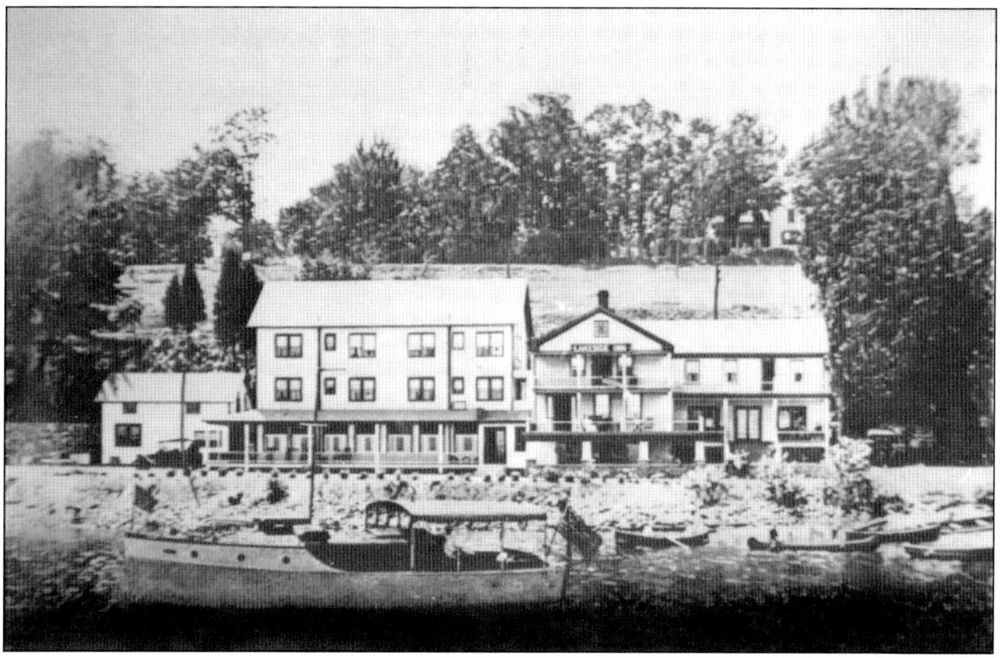

The Lakeside Hotel was located on the lake with boat launches in front of it. This early 1900 postcard shows one of the unique canal boats that were popular on the lake from the 1900s to the 1940s. The Shelburne Maritime Museum and the Plattsburgh Transportation Museum both feature canal boats in their exhibits.

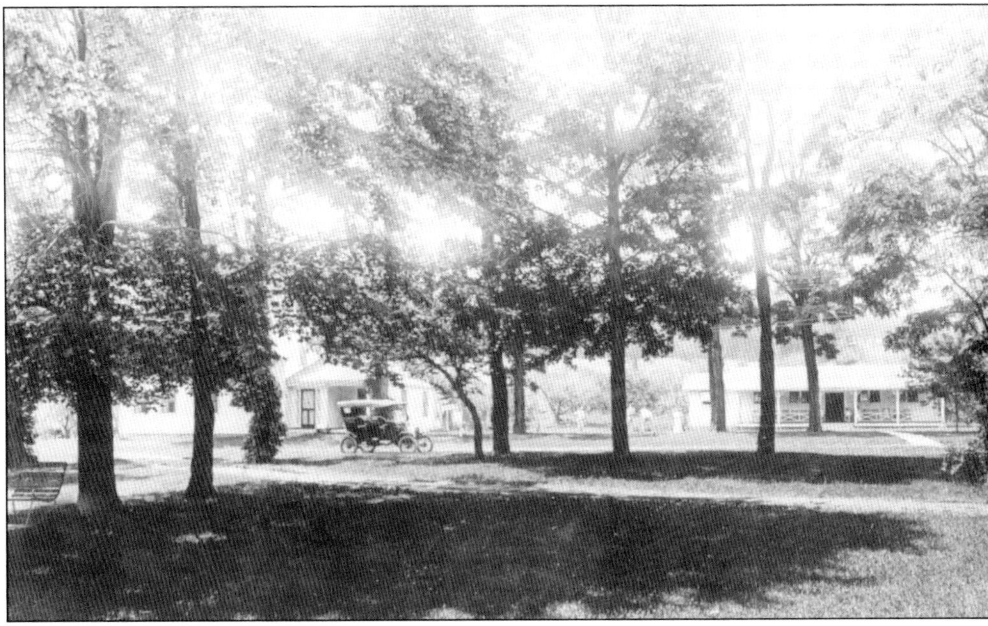

The Lakeside Hotel was owned and operated by Martin Rennell and Sons, who also operated Trembleau Hall. As secretary of the Adirondack Resort Association, Rennell actively promoted the hotels in the entire Adirondack region, primarily through paid advertisements in New York newspapers and magazines. Lakeside Inn had rooms for 125 guests, with rooms with and without running water and en suite private baths.

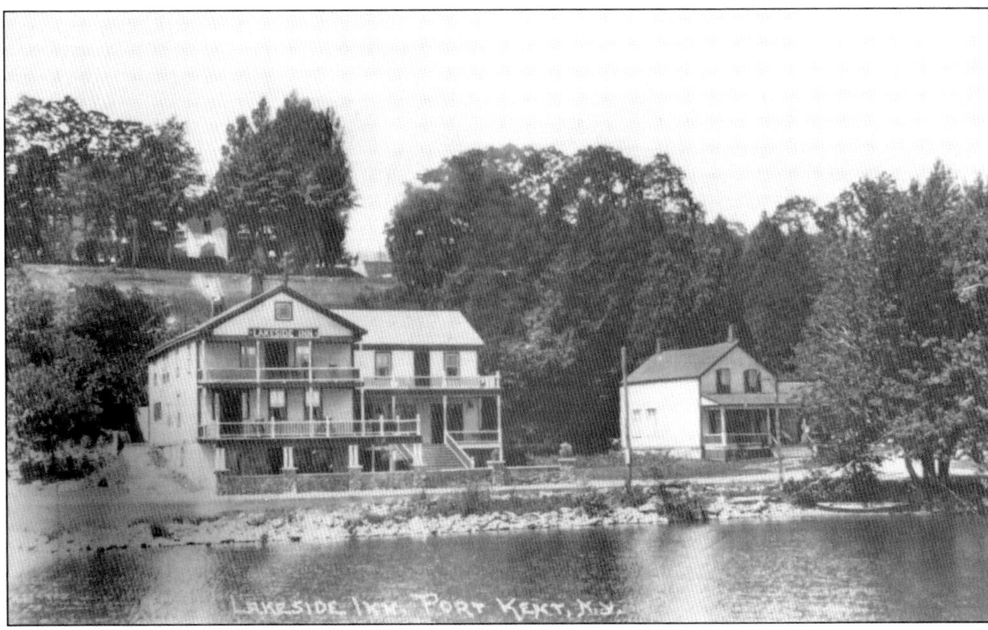

The Lakeside Inn promoted itself as an ideal location with Ausable Chasm three miles away, as well as a short drive to Lake Placid and Montreal. Among the many activities available at the inn were dancing, bathing, boating, tennis, and home-cooked meals.

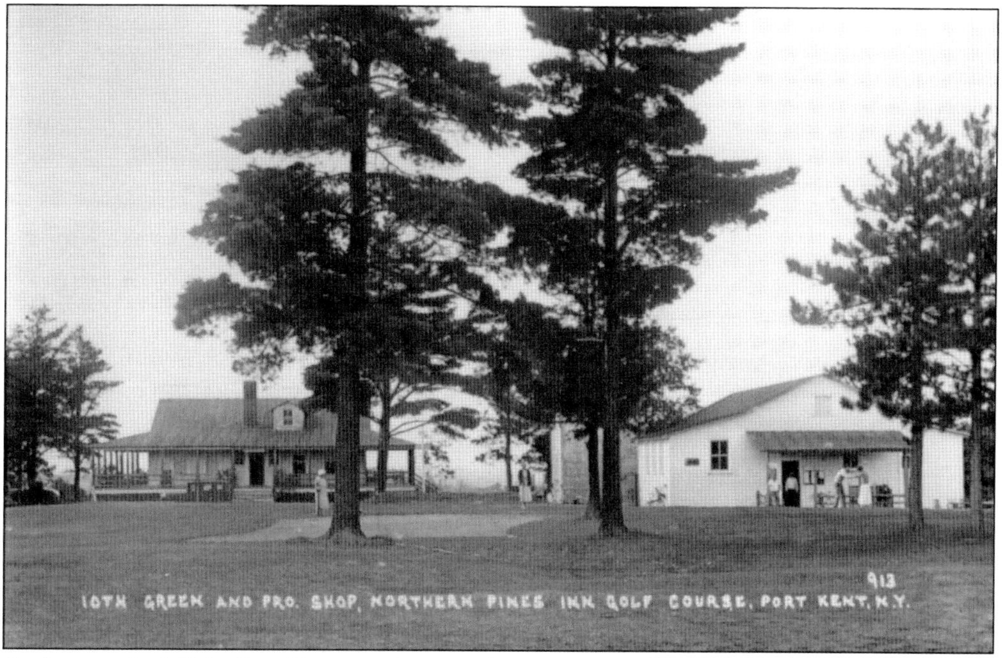

Farther up the hill in Port Kent another popular inn operated called the Northern Pines Inn. The flat location was ideal for a full-sized golf course as well as the nearby marshlands, which offered wonderful nature hikes. While none of the old hotels remain in operation today, Harmony Golf Course and Resort still operates on the site of Northern Pines Inn as well as a single-lot building development.

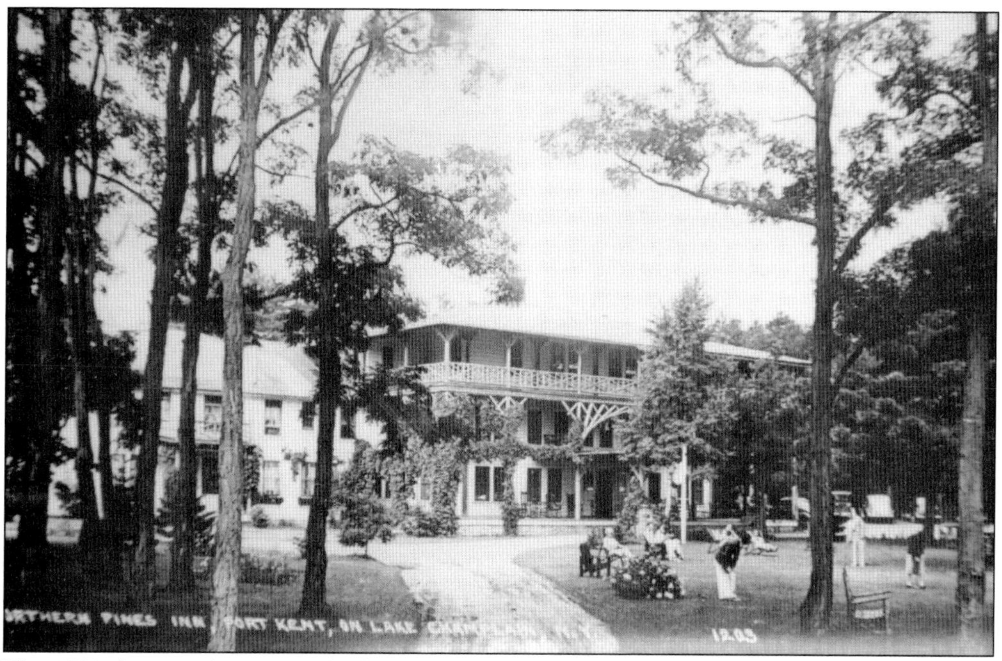

This 1938 photograph captures the front lawns of the Northern Pines Inn. True to its name, the inn was surrounded by a lush pine forest that was home to deer, turkeys, ospreys, chipmunks, and other wildlife. The local wildlife is now protected in the nearby Wickham Marsh Wildlife Preserve.

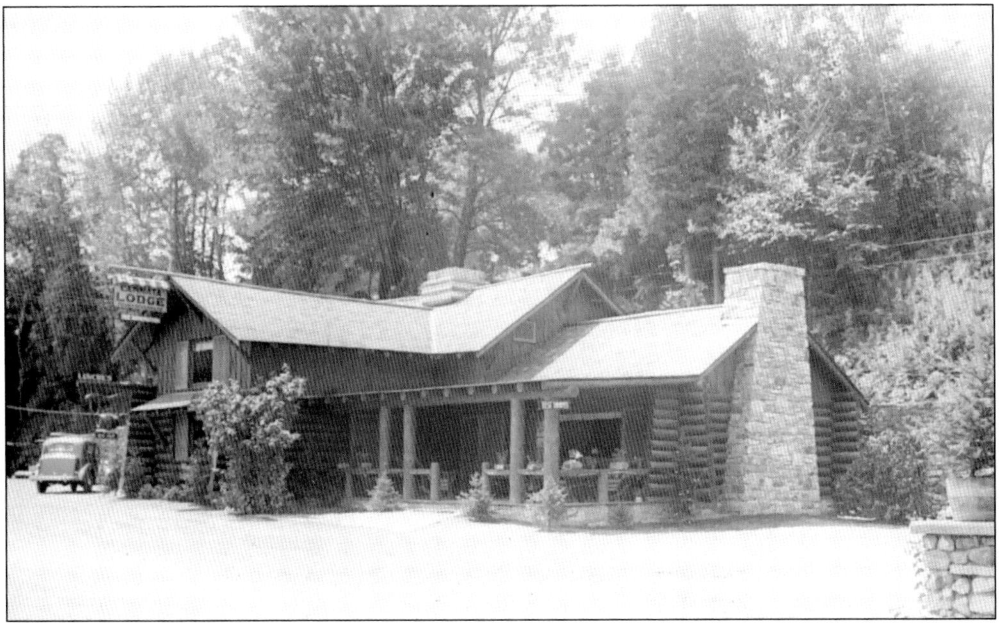

The Cannata Lodge capitalized on the rustic wilderness of the Adirondacks in Port Kent, as seen in this mid-1900s photograph. The lodge offered food and beverages, including a popular grill. The Cannata Lodge was a popular eatery located on the lake next to the ferry dock. At this time, after docking in Port Kent, more people were interested in stopping for food before continuing on towards Plattsburgh, Montreal, Lake Placid, Albany, and other points in New York.

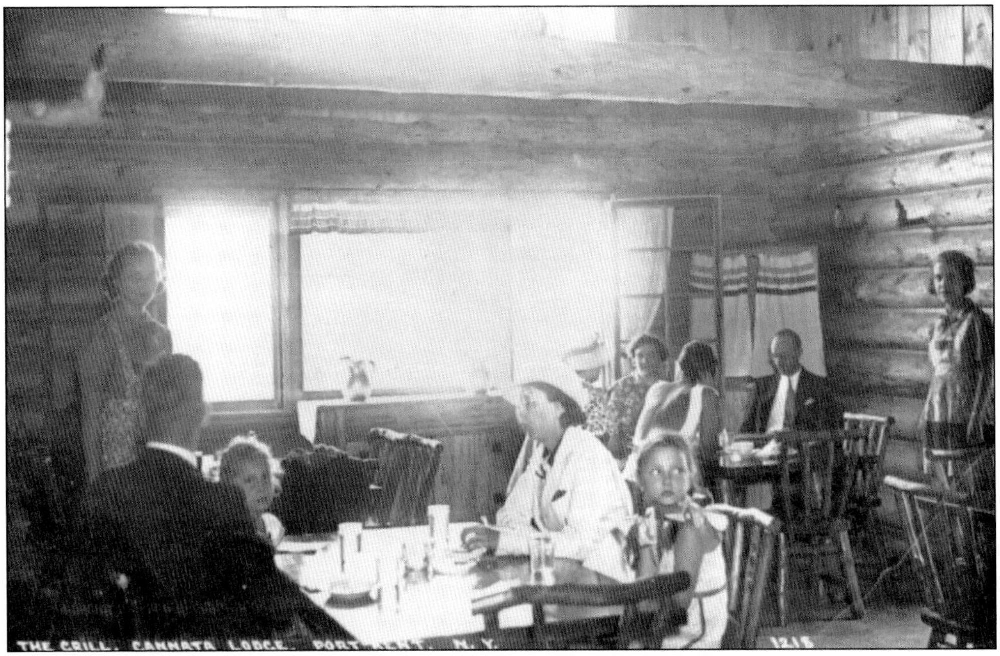

In this undated photograph of the interior of the Cannata Lodge, the décor readily evokes the Adirondack feel of the timber building. From its conception in the 1890s, the Cannata Lodge was a popular spot for drinks and live entertainment until it closed its doors in the 1980s, almost 100 years later.

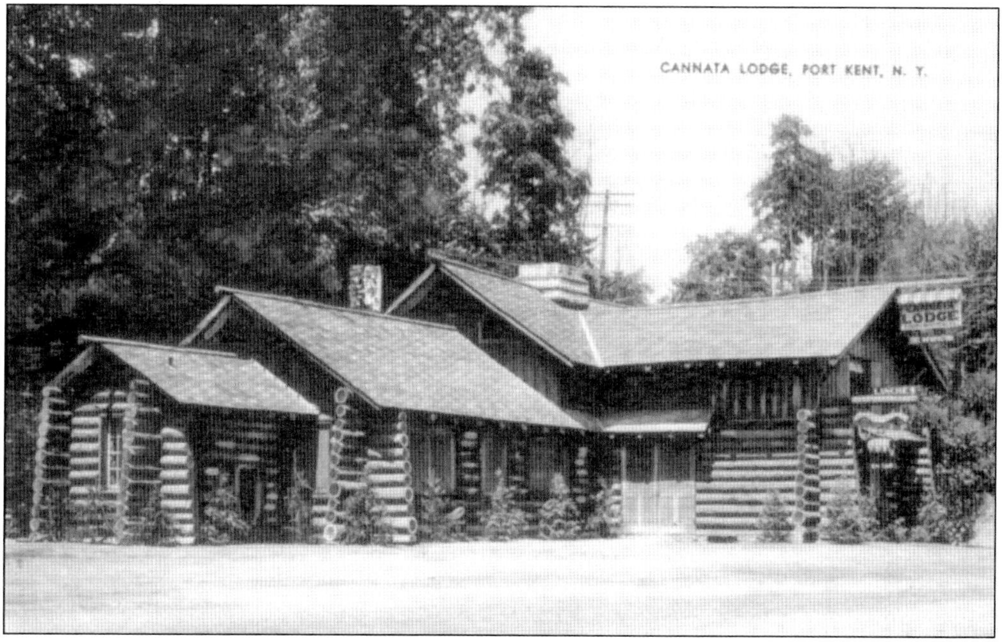

The Cannata Lodge was demolished in the 1980s. Only the small cabin on the left side of this undated postcard exists today. The tall chimney, which was a highlight of the lodge's lounge, can be seen in the back.

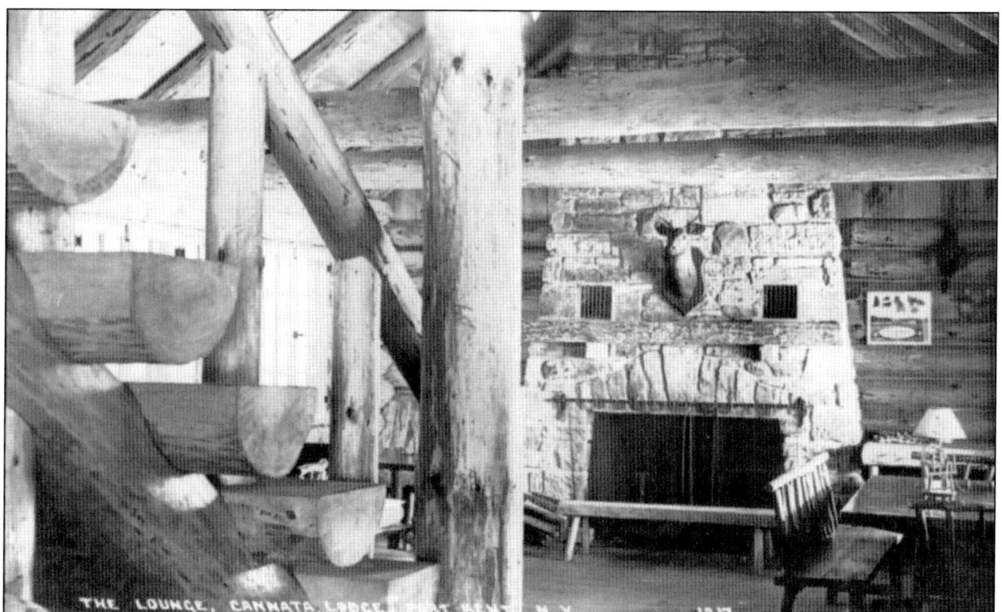

Advertising legal drinks, the Cannata Lodge became known more as a bar with popular local entertainment. Tourist memorabilia such as postcards, glasses, matchbook covers, and posters featuring live entertainment exist today, the only memories of the once-popular lodge, bar, grill, and lounge.

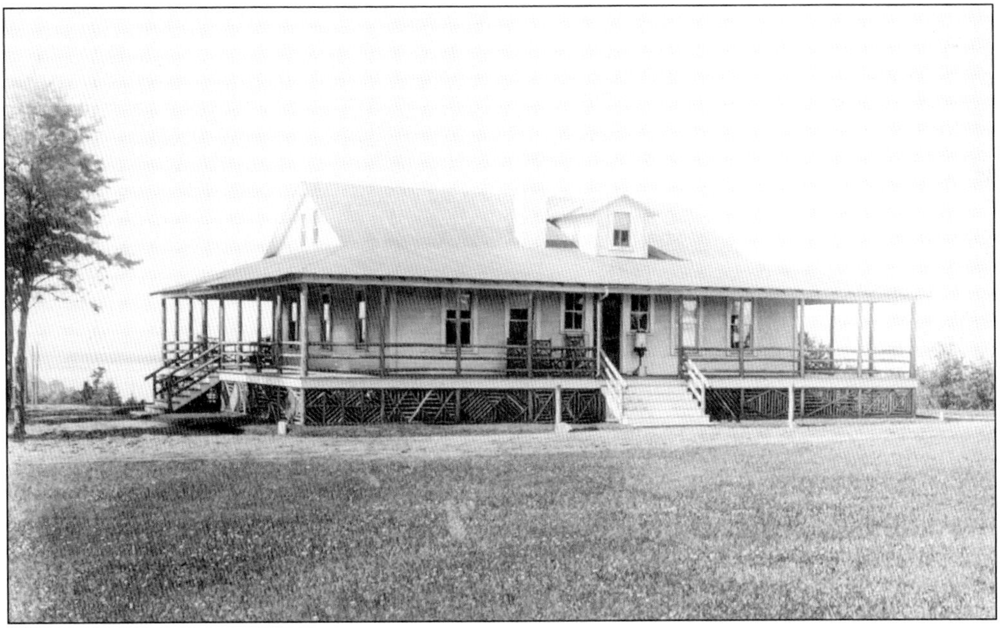

Champlain Country Club, as seen in this 1920s photograph, was another of the many hotels and entertainment spots in Port Kent capitalizing on the tourist trade. It also promoted tennis, golfing, and sporting activities.

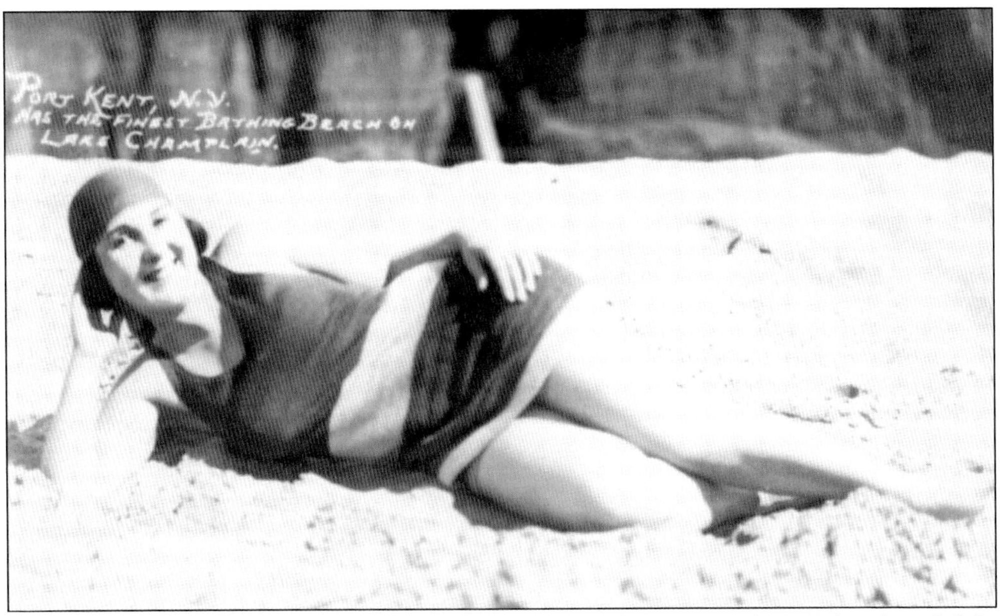

Port Kent was largely a tourist area from the 1880s through the 1930s, with many hotels and clubs opening and closing on the shore of Lake Champlain. Numerous professional postcard companies came to the area promoting Port Kent in series of postcards, such as this one of a bathing beauty in the 1910s.

Three

Clintonville

The history of Clintonville is connected to the mining of iron ore in the community. According to Dr. Gordon Pollard of SUNY Plattsburgh's Anthropology Department, George Griswold built a dam, a pair of forges, and a gristmill in 1810. Next came a store, a house for bloomery, and furnaces used for smelting iron. In 1824, the Peru Iron Company was organized, and mining began the next year. By 1842, Clintonville boasted 750 inhabitants. The ironworks consisted of a forge of 18 fires, which manufactured 1,600 tons of iron annually, a rolling mill, nail factory, chain cable factory, pocket furnace, machine shop, gristmill, and sawmill. Business boomed until the iron industry declined in the 1870s and ceased in the 1890s.

In 1876, George Baldwin of Keeseville took a series of stereo views of the Peru Steel and Iron Company. These are the only photographs known to have been taken of Clintonville's ironworks. In 2009, Dr. Gordon Pollard extensively researched the photographs and operations of the ironworks. His findings are on display at the Anderson Falls Heritage Museum, of which he is a member.

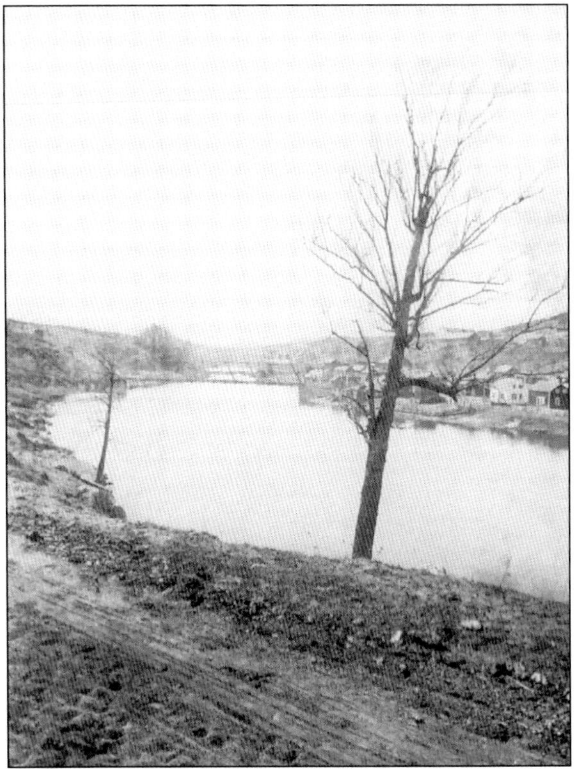

Off in the distance beyond the bridge is the upper dam and millworks. The upper dam was the site of the first dam built by George Griswold in 1810, marking the start of the iron business in Clintonville. In the foreground is the Ausable River, which first drew Griswold to the location. (Photograph and description used and provided with the permission of Dr. Gordon Pollard. Original Stereogram owned by Ronald C. Allen.)

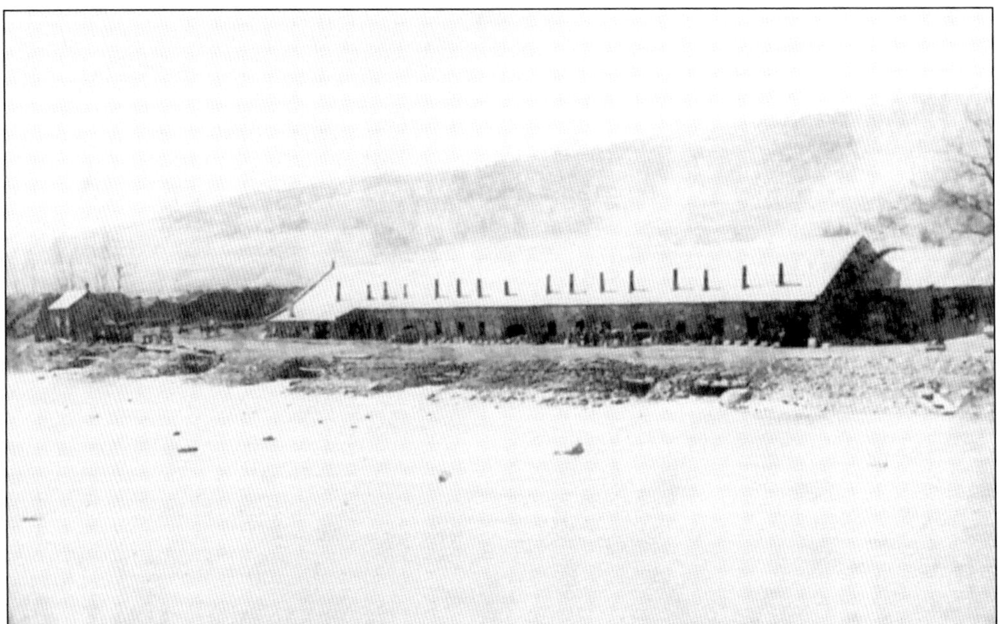

This photograph shows the Peru Steel and Iron Company lower forge of 16 fires. This was located a half mile below the Clintonville Bridge. At this time, the population of Clintonville was approaching over 800. The forge was capable of running 20 forge fires. (Photograph and description used and provided with the permission of Dr. Gordon Pollard.)

This photograph shows the upper dam mills area as it operated in 1856. The sawmill is located in the center of the photograph, and the rolling mill is at the center right. In 1856, a spring swell of water swept away the upper dam, sawmill, part of the rolling mill, and numerous other buildings, which were all rebuilt. (Photograph and description used and provided with the permission of Dr. Gordon Pollard.)

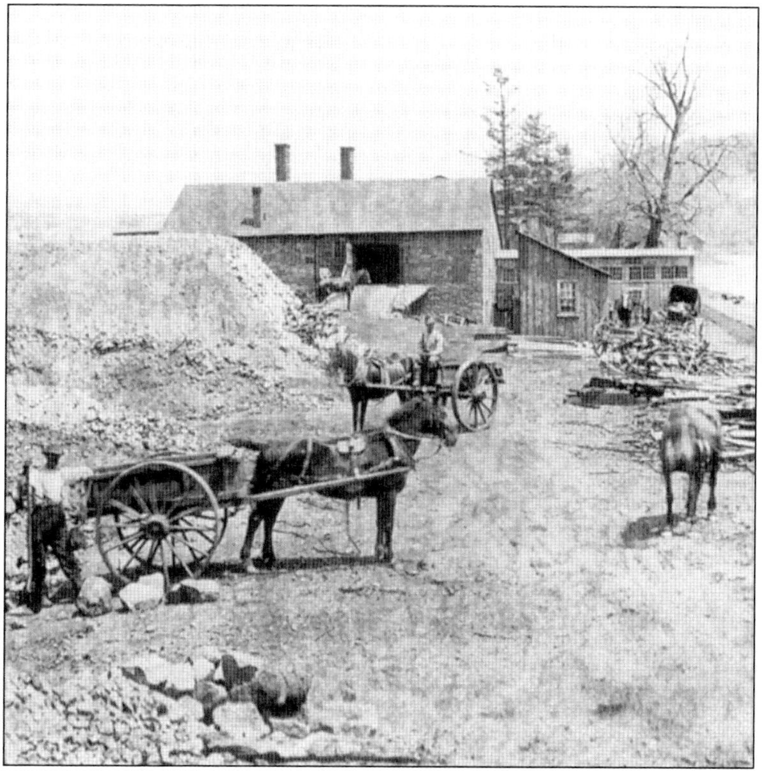

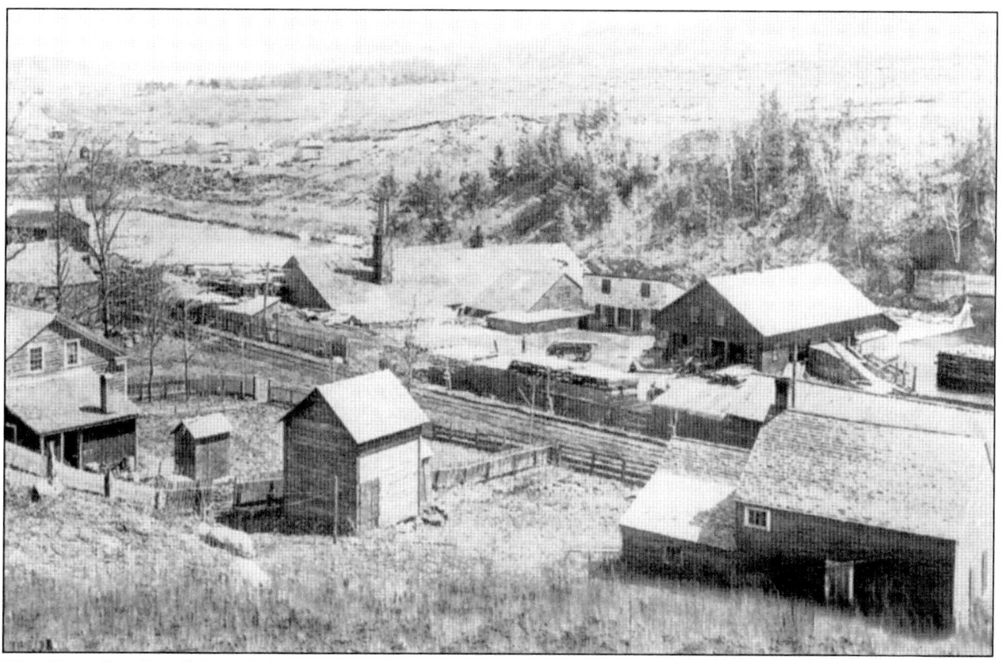

The Peru Steel and Iron Company used carts to transport the iron in its various stages of completion. These carts are located near the ore roasting pits. In the center, the separator building can be seen halfway between the Clintonville Bridge and lower forge. (Photograph and description used and provided with the permission of Dr. Gordon Pollard.)

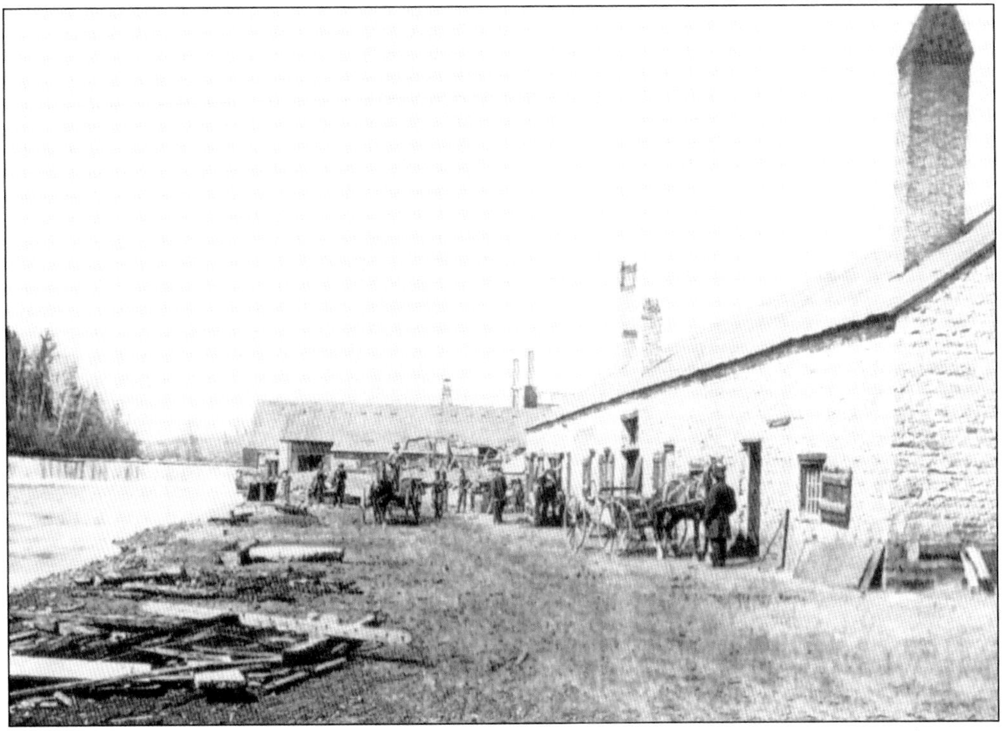

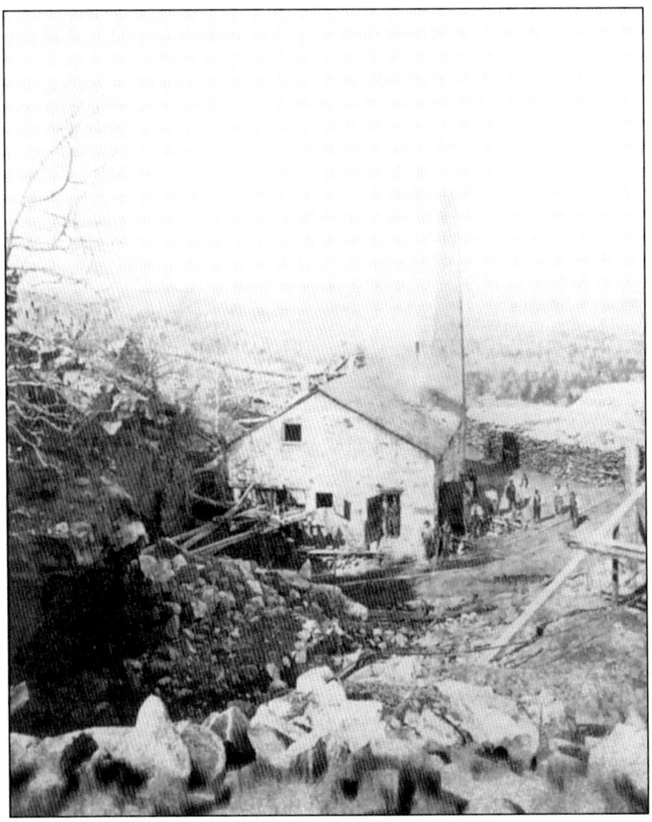

The Ausable River is shown on the left after it has come over the upper dams. The upper dam mill area had the stone-walled foundry and blacksmith shop, which can be seen on the right. Through its history, the operation had four company names, Peru Iron Company, and then Saltus and Company, followed by Peru Steel and Iron Company, and finally Peru Steel Ore Company. (Photograph and description used and provided with the permission of Dr. Gordon Pollard.)

The large stack of wood on the right-hand side of the image was used to fire the steam engine. The photograph also features a side-end view of the Palmer Hill engine house. (Photograph and description used and provided with the permission of Dr. Gordon Pollard.).

Four

Ausable Chasm

Now a popular, internationally known tourist attraction, Ausable Chasm was a land feature that first drew the attention of the early settlers, who realized the enormous power that the chasm generated. One of the first features named by the early settlers was Rainbow Falls, on the south end of the chasm. Ausable Chasm is a sandstone gorge approximately two miles in length, with Rainbow Falls feeding it on the south end.

In the 1880s, a cantilever bridge was erected spanning the deep gorge and allowing a small railroad to transport goods from Keeseville to Port Kent. This bridge was dismantled after the rail line closed in the 1920s. A new steel arch bridge now spans the chasm in the same location, 70 feet above the gorge bottom.

Today, Ausable Chasm is a year-round tourist attraction with trails around and through the caverns and gorge as well as white-water rafting and rock climbing in season. Recently, the chasm became home to the North Country Underground Railroad Museum.

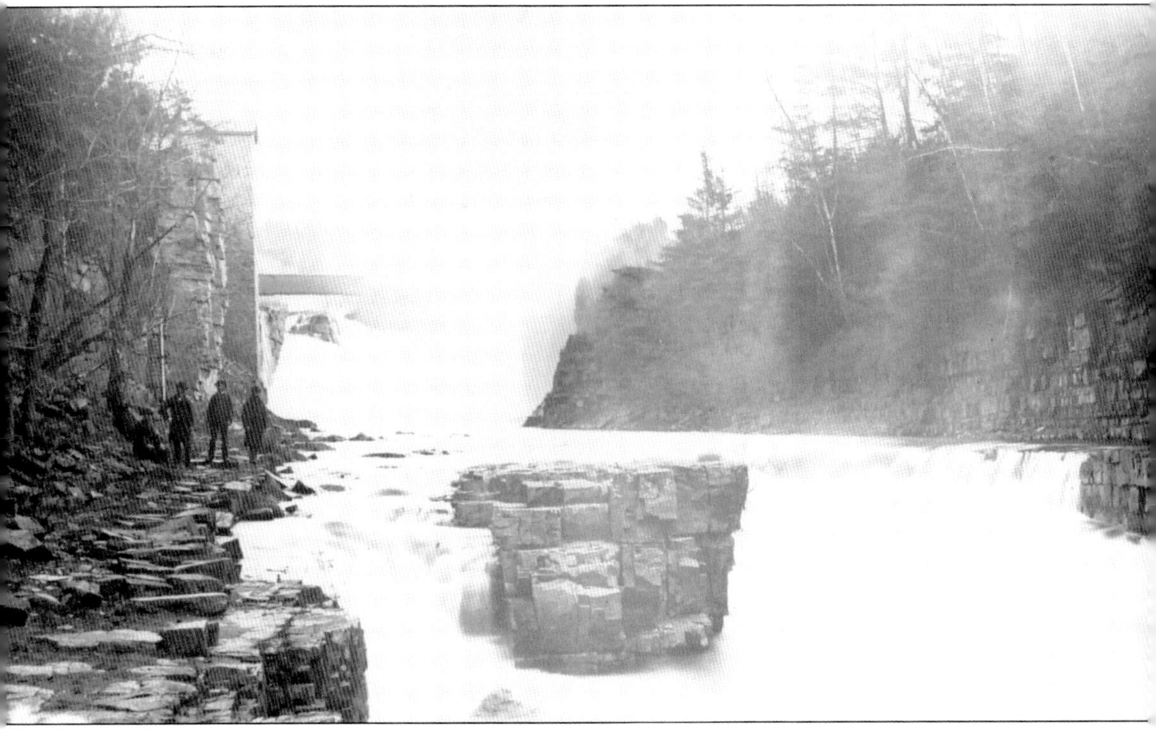

In the 1880s, a group of men are standing inside the chasm near the falls. The history of Keeseville and the surrounding area truly starts with the chasm. William Gilliland was the first European to document the chasm, which he wrote about in the 1786 journal of his exploratory travels. In 1806, John W. Anderson and John Keese both came into the area. At first, the name Anderson Falls reflected the fledgling community. Keese bought up much of the land and began businesses in lumber. Anderson partnered with Robert Hoyle, the first settler to the area, and they also entered the lumber business, but with connections to the Quebec market. Eventually the name of the community would change to reflect the predominant businessman, Keese, and the chasm would be known by the Ausable River that feeds through the chasm. The river was named by French explorers; *au sable* means "of sand."

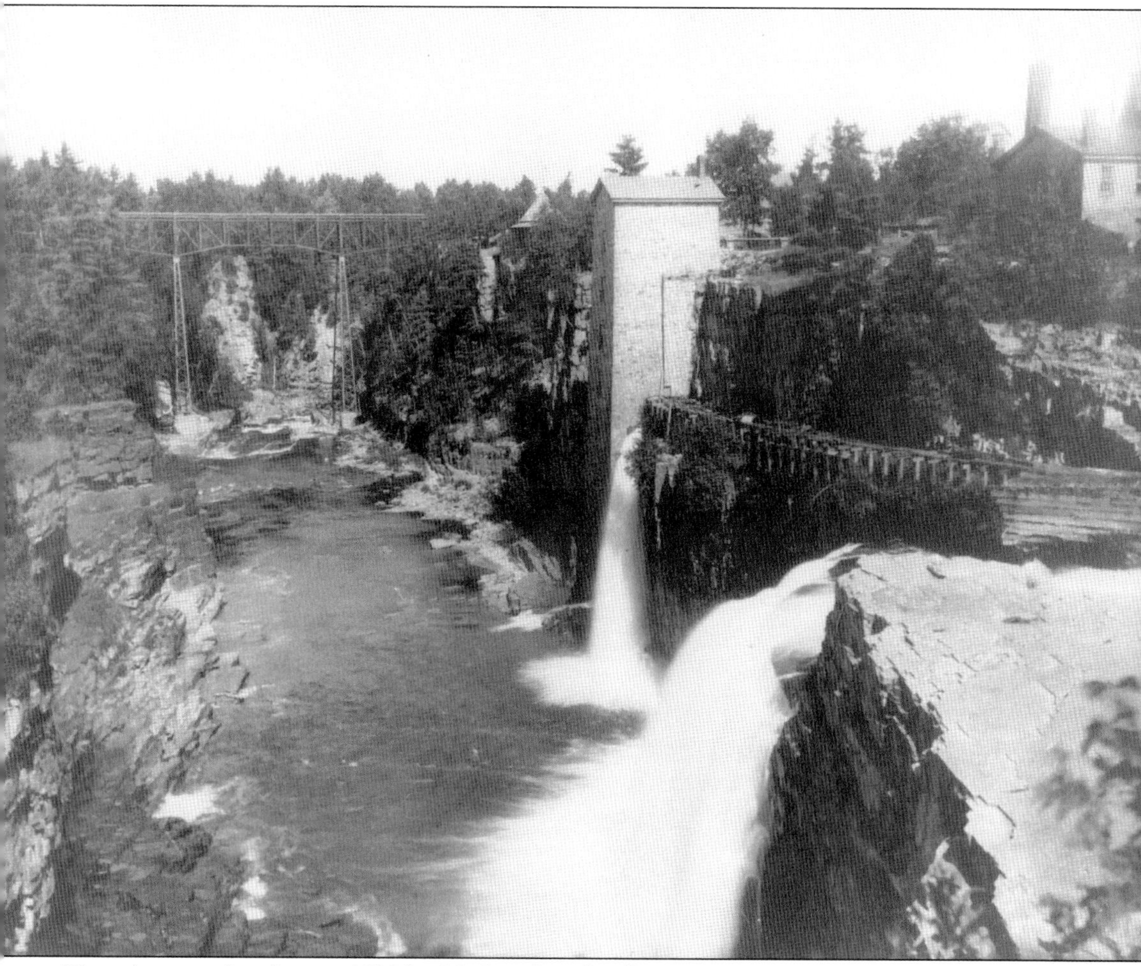

This photograph taken in 1890 highlights the wheelhouse (right) that powered the Ausable Chasm Horse Nail Works. In the background, the cantilever Keeseville railroad trestle bridge that operated until 1927 can be seen. The octagonal building just left of the wheelhouse is the first chasm entrance. To the left of the wheelhouse is Mooney's Mills. A cantilever bridge was built because the engineers feared the weight of the train constantly crossing the span would collapse the rough shale on either side of the gap.

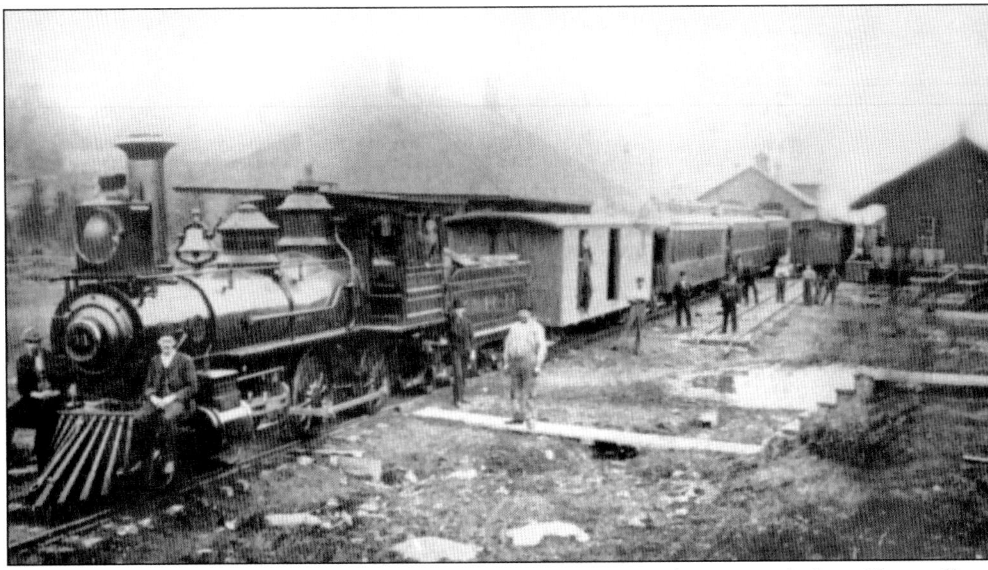

The peanut railroad was built by local businessmen to transport heavy goods from Keeseville to Port Kent, and it passed through the Ausable Chasm. The train ran seven trips daily during the week and three trips on Sundays, transporting goods and passengers on the 5.6-mile trip. As a cost-saving move, the builders did not add extra track for a turnaround or a roundabout, so the train ran one way—pulling the cars to Port Kent and pushing them back to Keeseville.

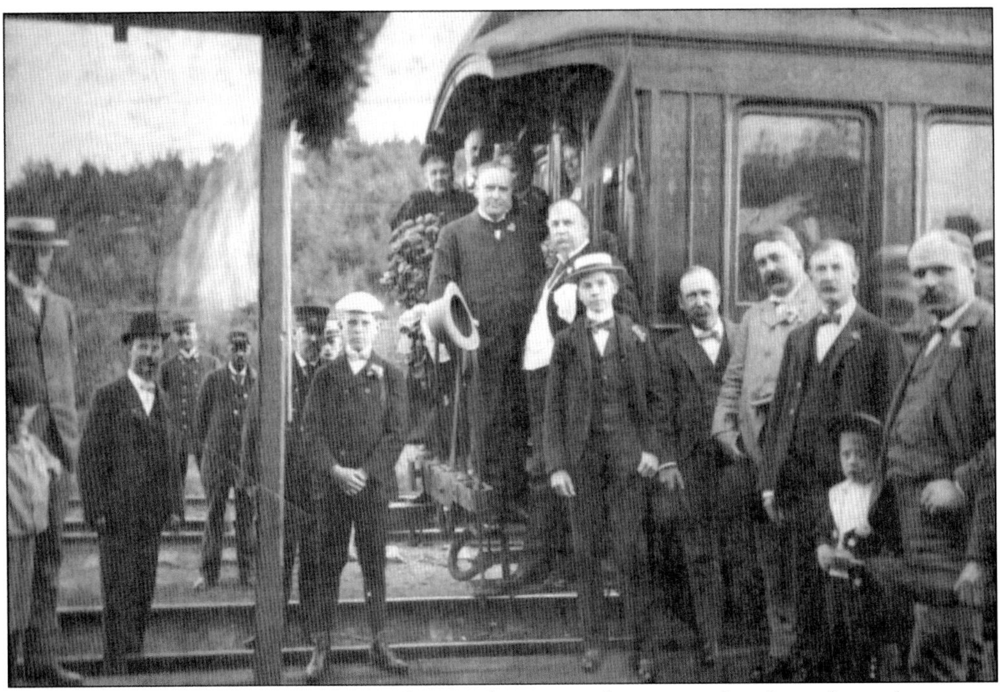

During his term, Pres. Warren G. Harding paid a visit to the area and took a ride on the peanut railroad through Ausable Chasm. He can be seen standing on the train in the center. Sadly, it was not long after this that the railroad closed down and was dismantled, leaving only a few rails in some backyards, a rusted water tower on a golf course, and the depot-turned-restaurant.

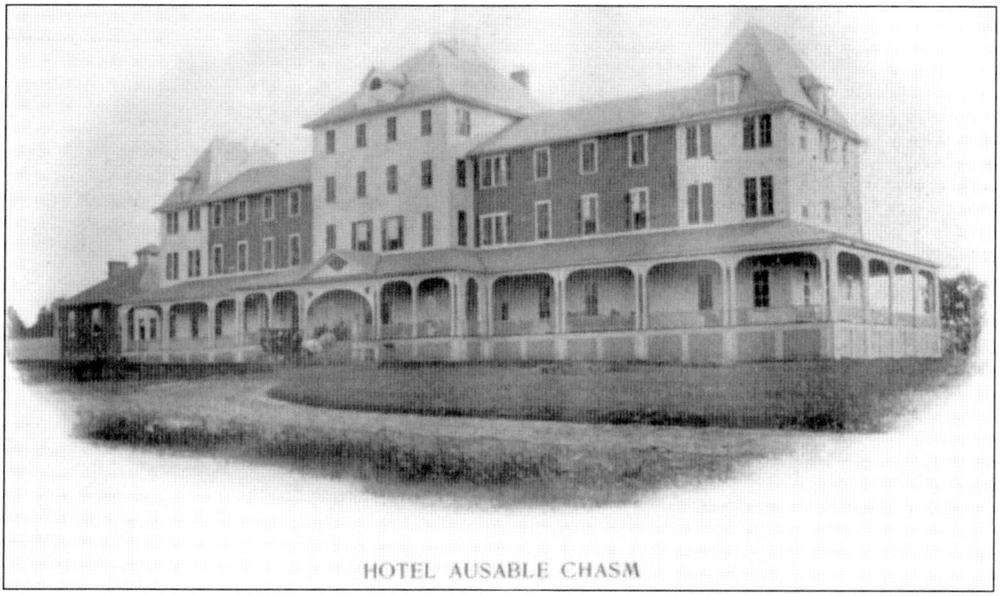

The grand Hotel Ausable Chasm was a popular tourist stop right on the edge of the chasm. From the 1880s through early 1900s, guests could stay at the hotel for $4 a night, but they also had to pay a 75¢ fee to enter the chasm and a 50¢ fee for a boat ride. For a nominal fee, visitors could also enjoy a round-trip ride on the peanut railroad, which passed the hotel on its round trip from Keeseville to Port Kent seven times a day during the week.

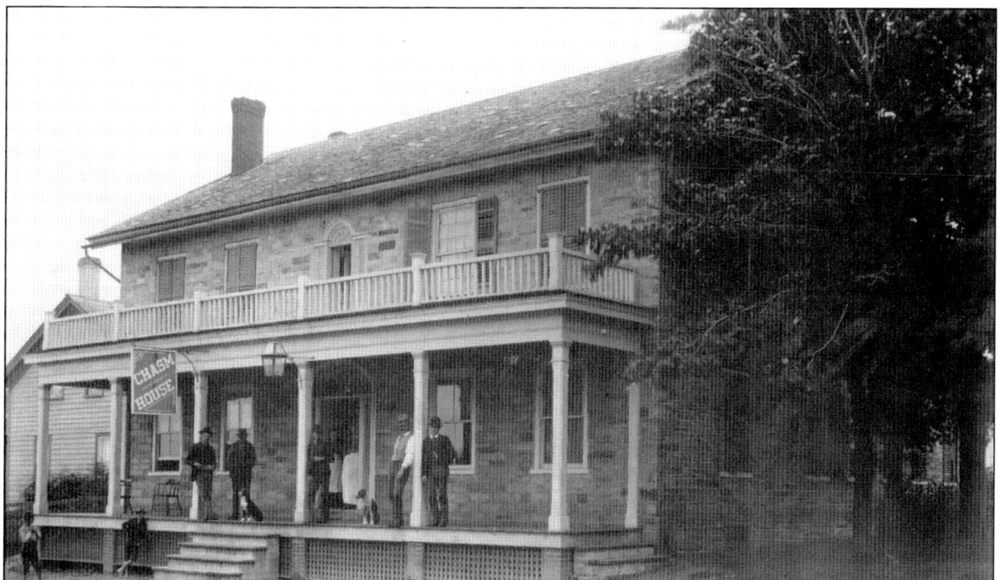

Constructed from sandstone from the chasm, the Chasm House, later known as the Chasm Inn, would become George Grames's Second Hand Furniture Store, as locally crafted furniture was plentiful with the production of Prescott's Furniture Factory in nearby Keeseville.

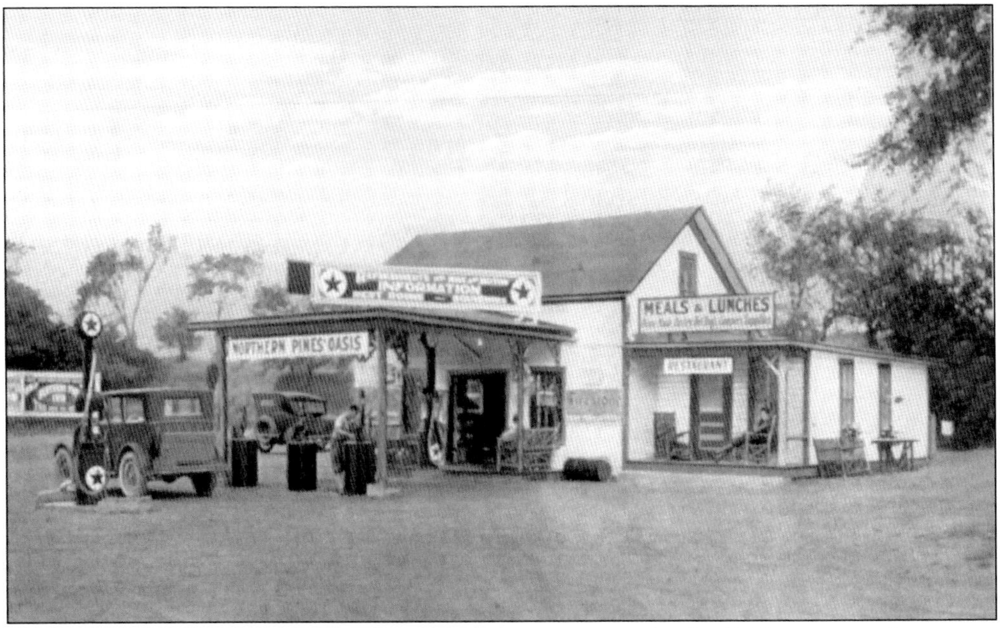

As the 1900s progressed, automobile travel became more common, and Ausable Chasm gained popularity as an easy trip with a remarkable natural wonder as the destination. Gas stations such as Northern Pines Oasis sprang up, offering gasoline as well as food and information to the numerous travelers.

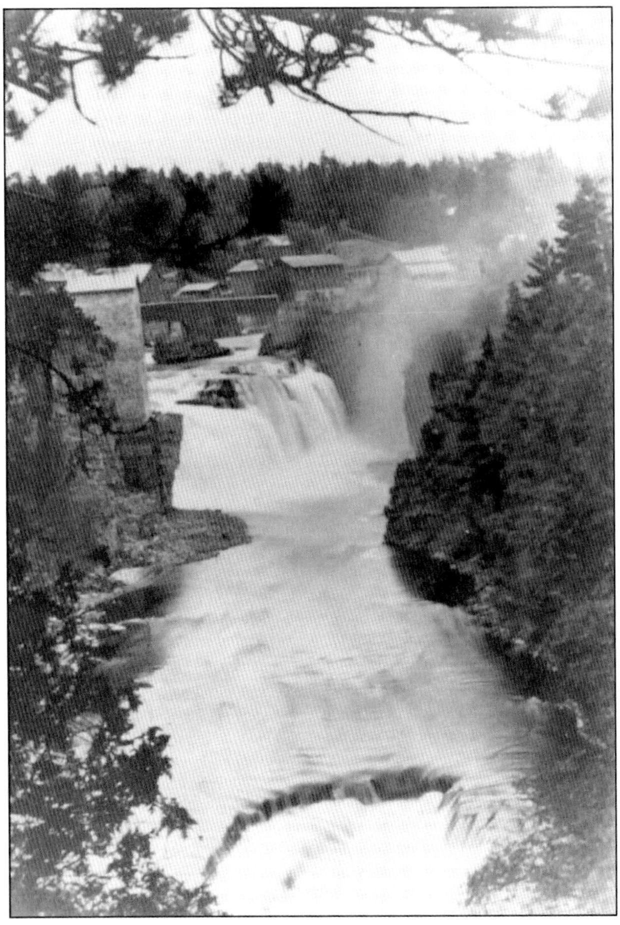

This photograph from 1870 highlights the strength of the falls that poured into the gorge. The name "Rainbow Falls" came largely from the constant rainbow visible in the mists that sprang up from the main falls. During the winter months, this spray would freeze into spectacular ice formations that often crashed with powerful force during fast thaws caused by abrupt temperature changes.

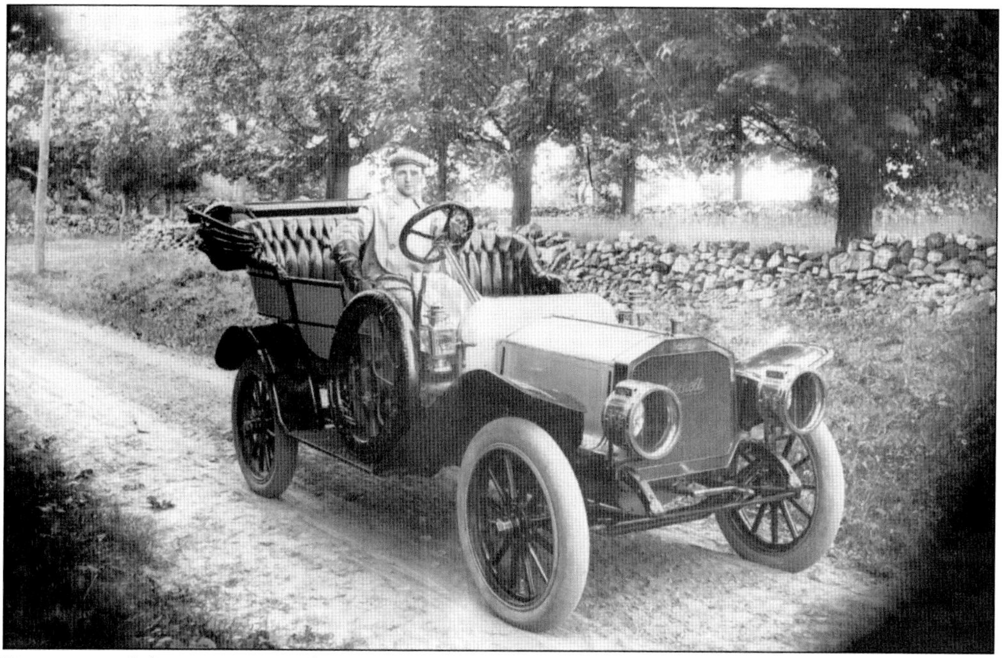

For many of the tourists to the region, the local hotels offered many daytrips and outings to faraway places such as Montreal, Canada, and Lake Placid, New York. While the hotel ran buses, originally drawn by teams of horses, bringing automobiles became common among the travelers, as is seen in this undated photograph of a visitor in his automobile near the Chasm Inn.

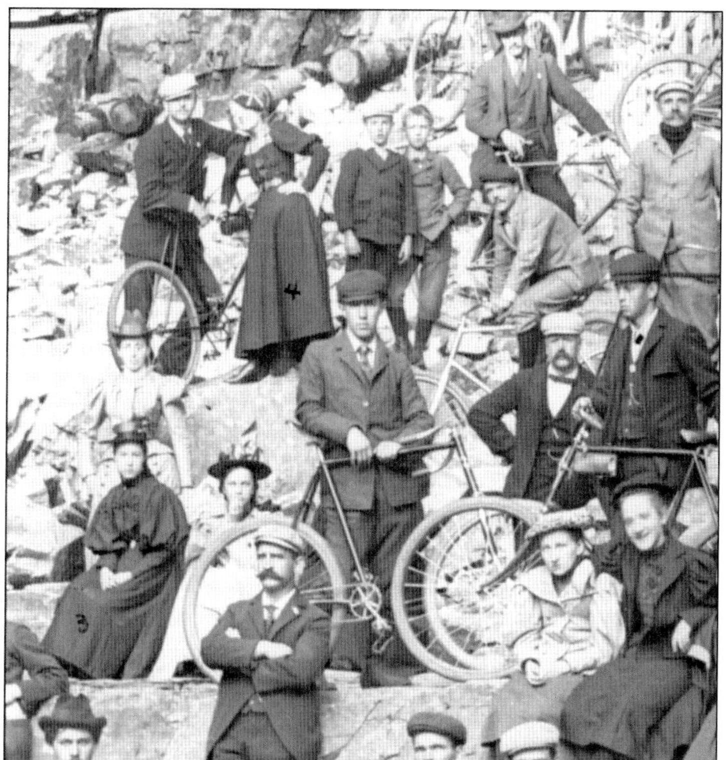

This undated photograph shows members of the Keeseville Bicycle Club taking a break after traveling the two miles from Keeseville to Ausable Chasm. With the numerous trails and paths connecting the many communities and businesses of the area, bicycles quickly became a popular mode of transportation for men and women of all ages. The activity grew into a popular club in Keeseville.

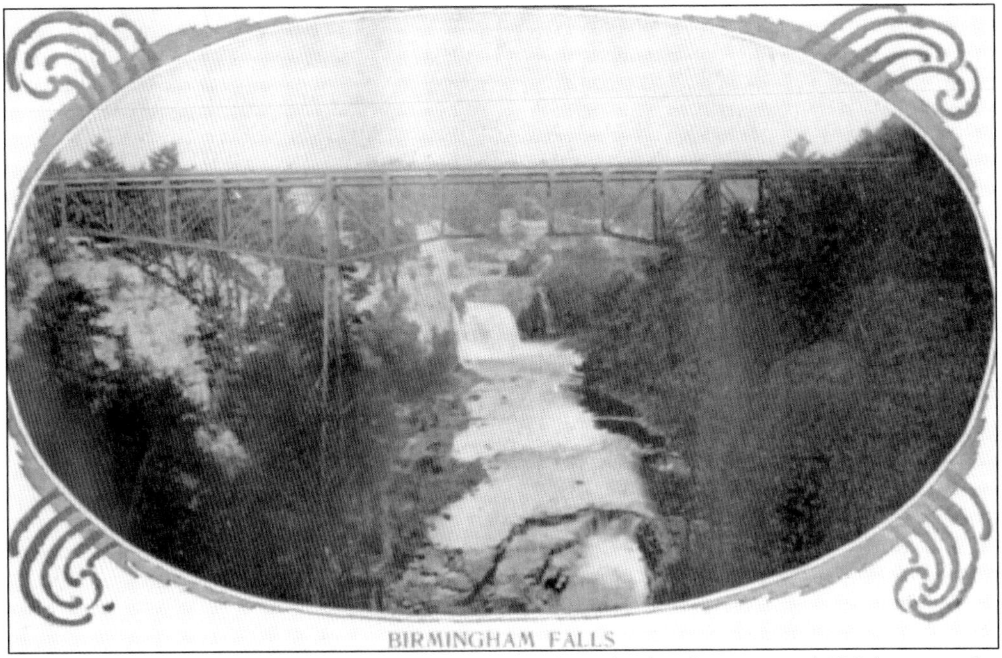

This photograph from the late 1880s shows the cantilever bridge that spanned 130 feet over the gorge. With the two-mile-wide chasm lying directly between Keeseville and Port Kent, throughout the years numerous bridges were built to allow access to both areas. The fear that the weight of any bridge would cause the sandstone chasm walls to collapse led to the use of cantilever bridges, which are bridges that gain more anchorage from vertical supports jutting out to balance the structure. The heavy peanut railroad relied on a cantilever bridge for its crossing of the chasm.

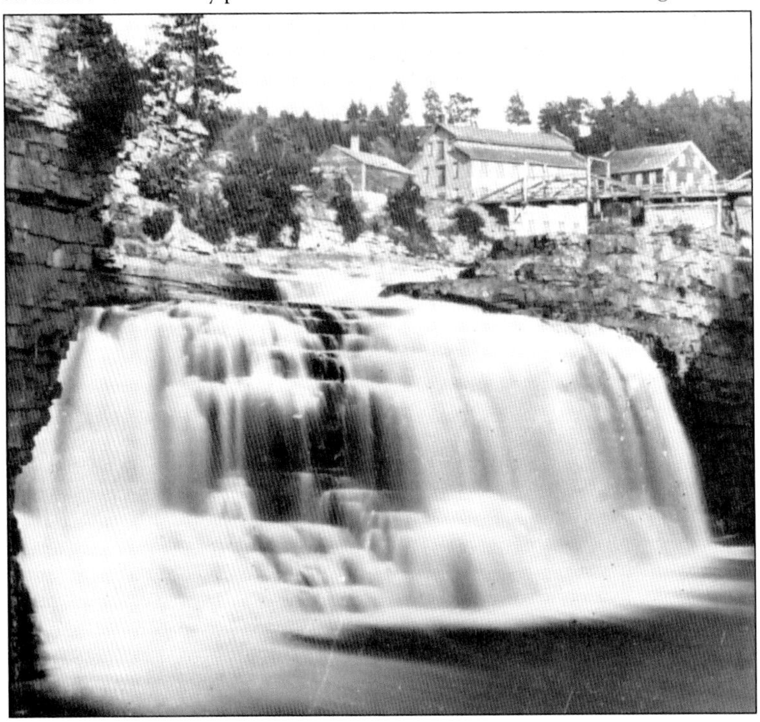

By 1870, the pulp mill operations were well underway at Rainbow Falls. The tourist business was also developing, and it took over in 1876, bringing thousands of visitors to the popular attraction every year.

Five

Harkness

As the pioneers settled and defined the areas of upstate New York, a group of Quakers settled on the northern edge of Keeseville and the town of Ausable on Hallock Hill, just south of Peru, New York. Among the first settlers were Daniel, David, and Nehemiah Harkness, and the growing community took their name for the settlement. Soon, two taverns, two blacksmith shops, two stores, an academy, and two Quaker meetinghouses grew from the community of approximately 50 families. Peter Keese built his manor house in this area also. Today, not much remains of the Quaker settlers' community, other than several stone dwellings, the Arnold Home, and the Harkness place, which is still home to the Harkness family.

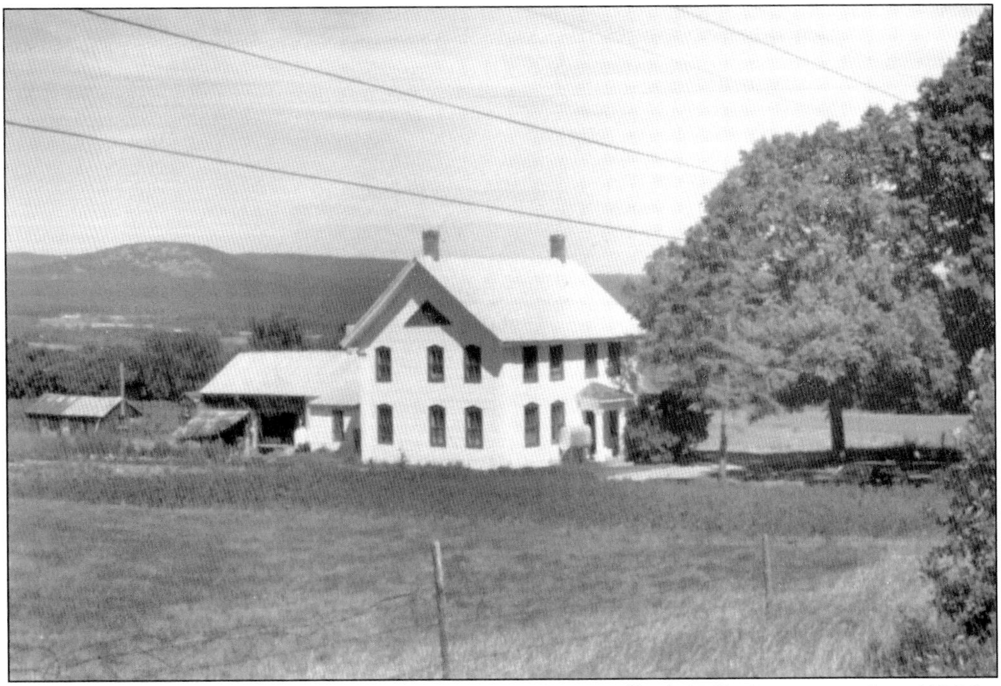

Pictured here in 1976 is the Harkness Homestead on Hallock Hill, first erected in 1820 by Daniel Harkness. Today, the house is still inhabited by the Harkness family. (Courtesy of George "Speedy" Arnold.)

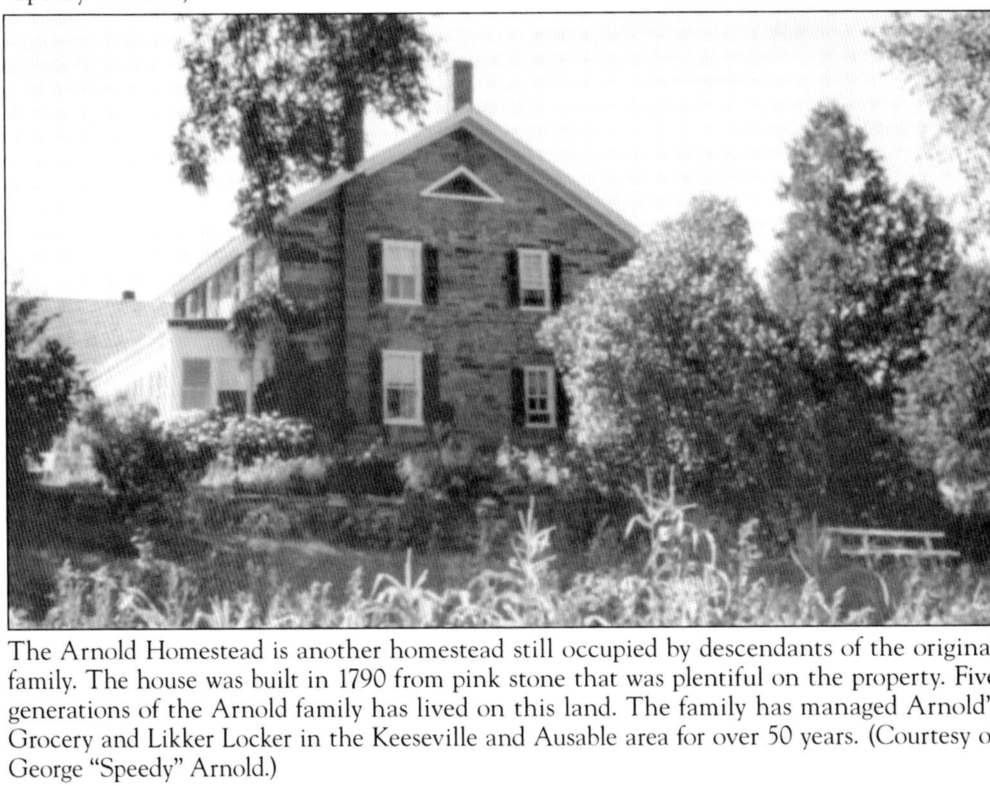

The Arnold Homestead is another homestead still occupied by descendants of the original family. The house was built in 1790 from pink stone that was plentiful on the property. Five generations of the Arnold family has lived on this land. The family has managed Arnold's Grocery and Likker Locker in the Keeseville and Ausable area for over 50 years. (Courtesy of George "Speedy" Arnold.)

Six

Port Douglass

Located in the middle of an inward sweep of Lake Champlain, Port Douglass lies in the town of Chesterfield and is a portion of Essex County. Port Douglass grew more as a vacation spot and tourist site rather than a hub for transportation like its neighbor three miles away, Port Kent. Port Douglass sits on the shore of Corlear Bay near Schuyler Island. Hotels and restaurants grew up in the small community, which is home to beautiful beaches on the shore of Lake Champlain.

Today, the community is still best known as a vacation location, with many Adirondack cabins on the lakeshore available for rental and amenities such as hot tubs and kayaks available for entertainment.

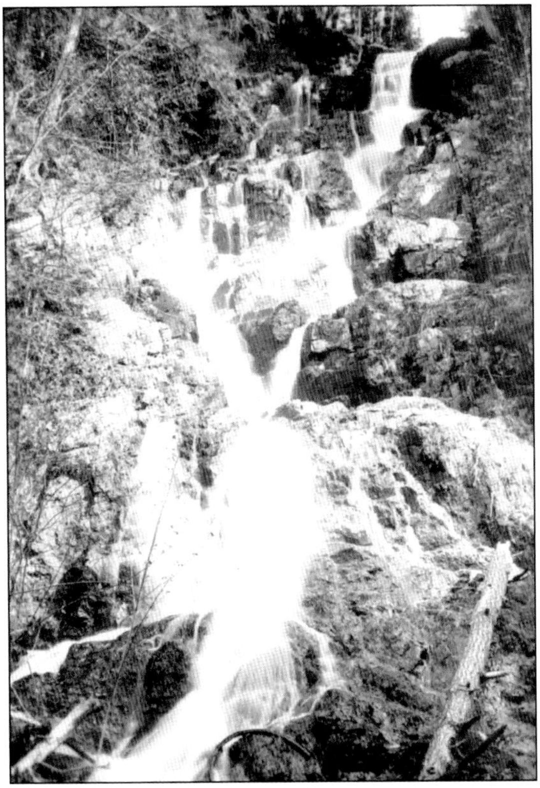

Along with the quiet bay, Port Douglass is also home to Buttermilk Falls, a 168-foot, fast-moving waterfall, which is now privately owned. This area was popular for hikers as well as fishermen. The Hotel Douglass included a trip to the falls, pictured here in 1910, in the itinerary for its guests.

With its ideal location in the middle of a quiet bay on Lake Champlain, the Hotel Douglass was a popular destination. The Hotel Douglass opened in 1901, sporting a tennis court, croquet, fishing, pleasure driving, and a bathing area as its main attractions. Visitors could have all this for $2.50 to $3 a day. This early-1900s photograph captures a panoramic view of the bathing area and boat dock as well as the front and side facade of the hotel.

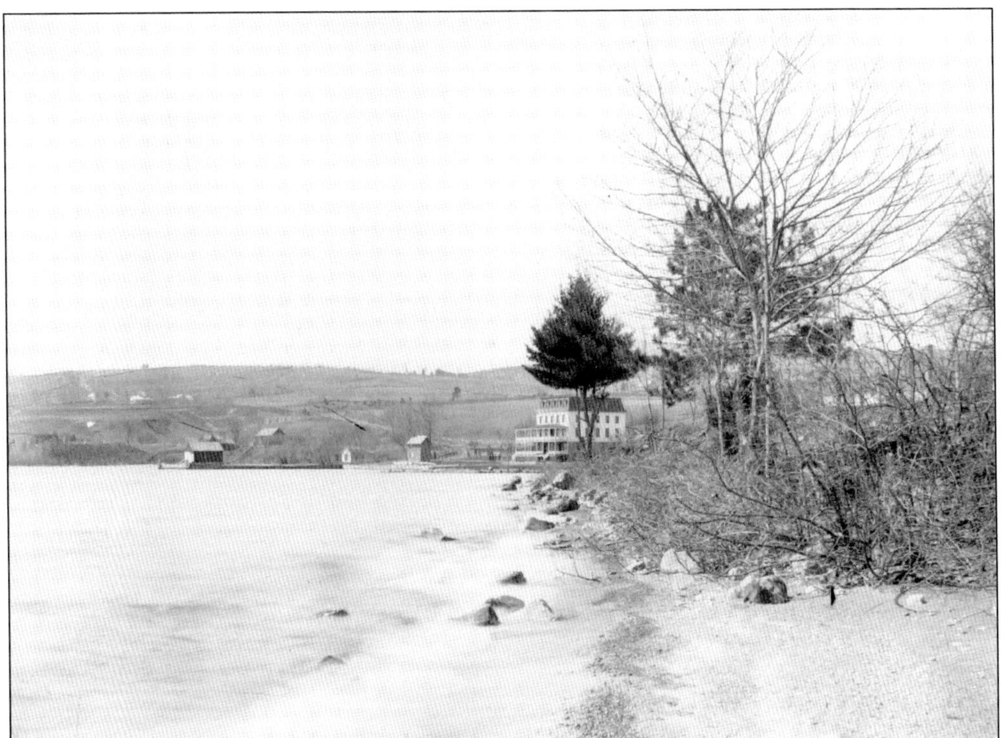

Seven

Augur Lake

Augur Lake is located in the northern part of Essex County, on the outskirts of Chesterfield. The small lake with a depth of 21 feet and a perimeter of just over six miles is nestled in a series of hills and expanses of grass and wooded areas, making it an ideal location for a relaxing hotel. In the 1880s, C.B. White built the Interlaken Hotel on a hillside facing Augur Lake. The region was advertised as reminiscent of Scotland. The hotel, with a capacity of 100 guests, remained in operation into the early 20th century. Today, the area is a popular site for summer rentals as well as fishing, thanks to the wide variety of fish in its waters; however, most fishing is restricted, as the shoreline around the lake is predominantly privately owned.

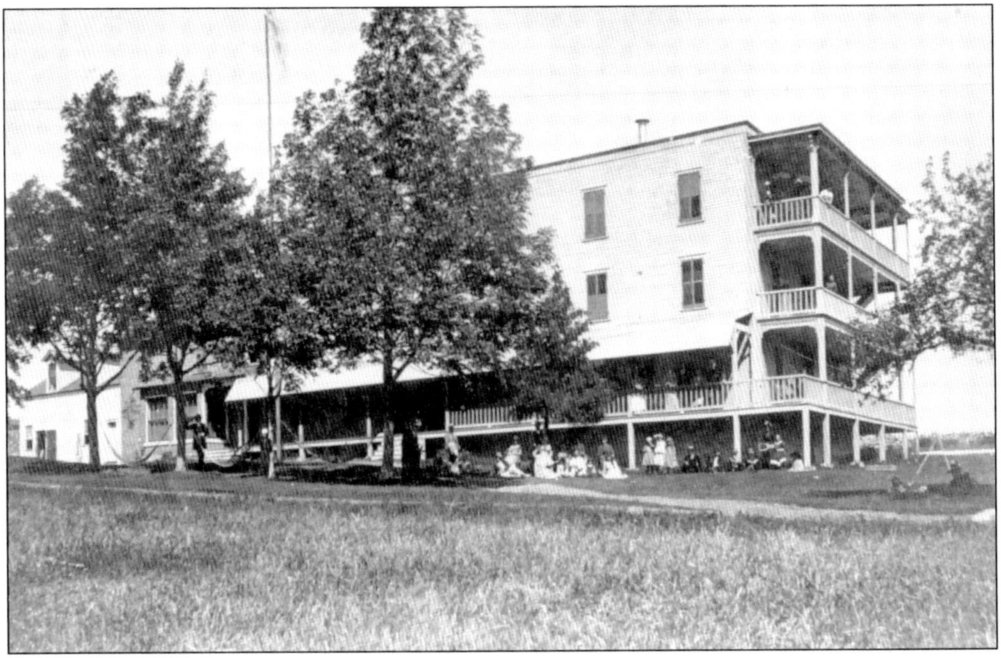

The Interlaken Hotel offered its guests modern conveniences with fresh farm and dairy available, along with an excellent table, livery, wooden drive, and shaded walks. The hotel was open for summer months at a cost of $2.50 a day with weekly rates available. Tourists coming from the Albany region could expect to spend $5 for the trip up to the hotel.

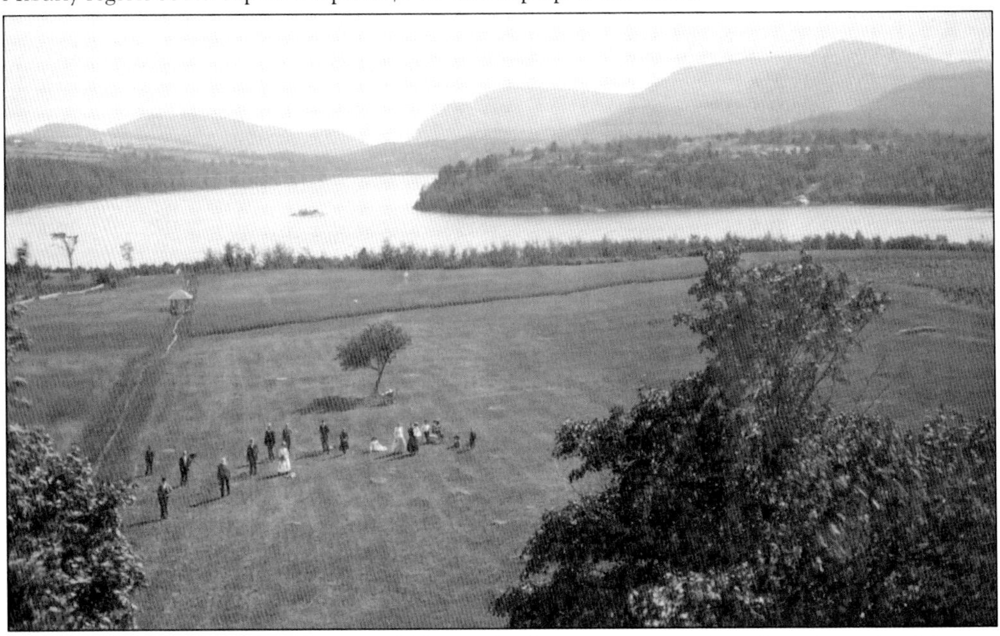

Spanning over 100 miles, the area of Chesterfield encompasses a lot of territory. In this area directly south of Keeseville is the fairly large Augur Lake. The Interlaken Hotel overlooked the lake from a nearby hillside. Nestled in the Adirondacks, Interlaken Hotel offered many outdoor activities, including fishing and boating as well as comfortable lodging in its three-story structure, which featured balconies on all three levels.

Eight

Poke-O-Moonshine

Poke-O-Moonshine, called the Gateway to the Adirondacks due to its northernmost location for visitors entering into the Adirondack Mountains, is a 2,180-foot climb offering amateur climbers a beautiful vista of the surrounding area. This minor peak is located in the township of Chesterfield and is readily accessible from Interstate 87, the Adirondack Northway. Poke-O-Moonshine is home to peregrine falcons, which limits access to the cliffs during mating and breeding seasons.

In 1876, during formal surveying for the state of New York, a high wooden tower was built. In 1912, this was restructured to the current metal fire tower that was used until 1988. In 1995, plans were made to dismantle the tower, but a local organization was formed to preserve and renovate the tower. It still stands today.

The origin of Poke-O-Moonshine's name is unknown, but it is believed to be a variant of the Algonquin words for broken and smooth, *pohqui* and *moosie*, respectively. The mountain is a popular destination for travelers due to the ease of approach as well as the varying difficulty levels of the climb. The trails, which can be fairly easy or rather challenging, all lead to a spectacular view at the top.

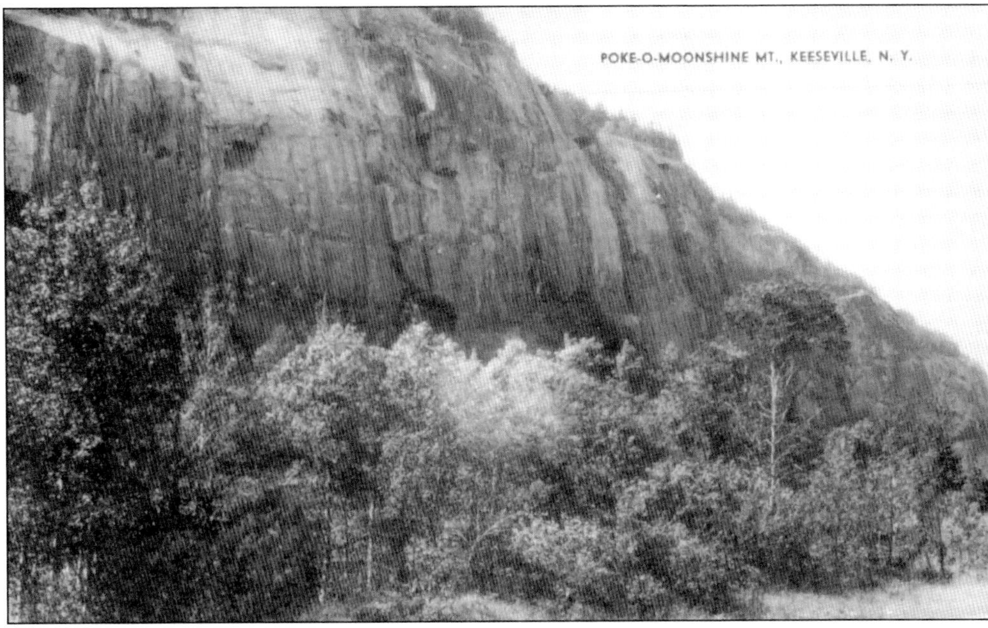

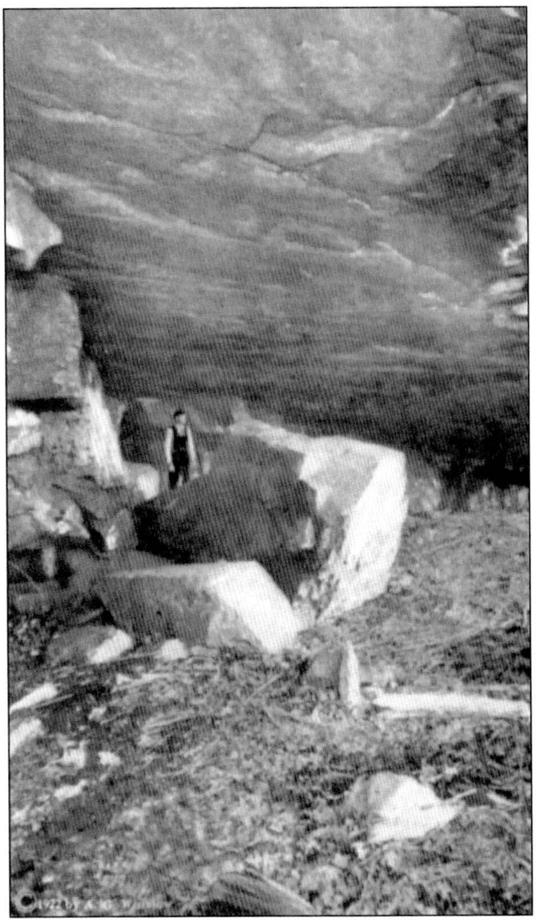

In the 11th century, the Algonquin first settled the area for farming. Poke-O-Moonshine was a popular area for the tribes as it opened access to the mountains to the west and south and the lake to the east.

One of the Adirondacks' best climbing locations, Poke-O-Moonshine is split into three main areas: the Main Wall (the north and east face), the Slab (the rock face seen first when approaching from the south), and the Upper Tiers (the cliffs around the summit). In clear weather, climbers can see as far as Montreal, Canada, from the summit.

Nine

The Keystone Arch Bridge

Nothing is more iconic in the village of Keeseville than the Keystone Arch Bridge, which spans the Ausable River and makes up part of Main Street. Businessmen needed a reliable means to cross the river that could withstand the harsh rains and snows of the North Country. In 1842, master mason Solomon Townsend commenced constructing a keystone bridge across the river. In all, the length of the bridge would be 120 feet. The project would take over one year to complete due to the combative forces of nature. During the spring of 1843, a sudden rain shower added to the already swollen river and caused the partially completed arch and framework to come apart and fall into the river. Purportedly, the crash was heard as far away as Port Kent, two miles from Keeseville. The construction crew muscled on and completed the bridge later that year.

The Keystone Arch Bridge, the iron truss bridge, also called the Upper Bridge (1878), and the suspension bridge (1888), were designated as a National Historic Civil Engineering Landmark in 1987. The bridges sit within a half mile of each other, and each represents a distinct period in the engineering of bridge construction. All three bridges stand to this day. While the iron truss bridge was closed in 2008, in need of repairs before reopening, the Keystone Arch Bridge and suspension bridge are still used every day.

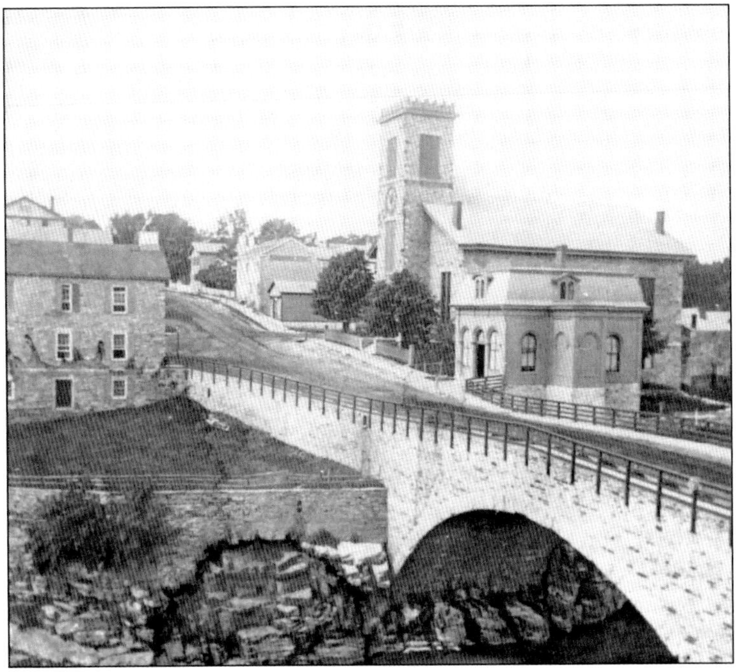

Keeseville has two main thoroughfares; Front Street runs parallel to the Ausable River, and Main Street travels across the river over the Keystone Arch Bridge. This photograph from between 1871 and 1877 highlights the horse nail factory on the left side and the tall Congregational Presbyterian church, now the Masonic hall, on the right.

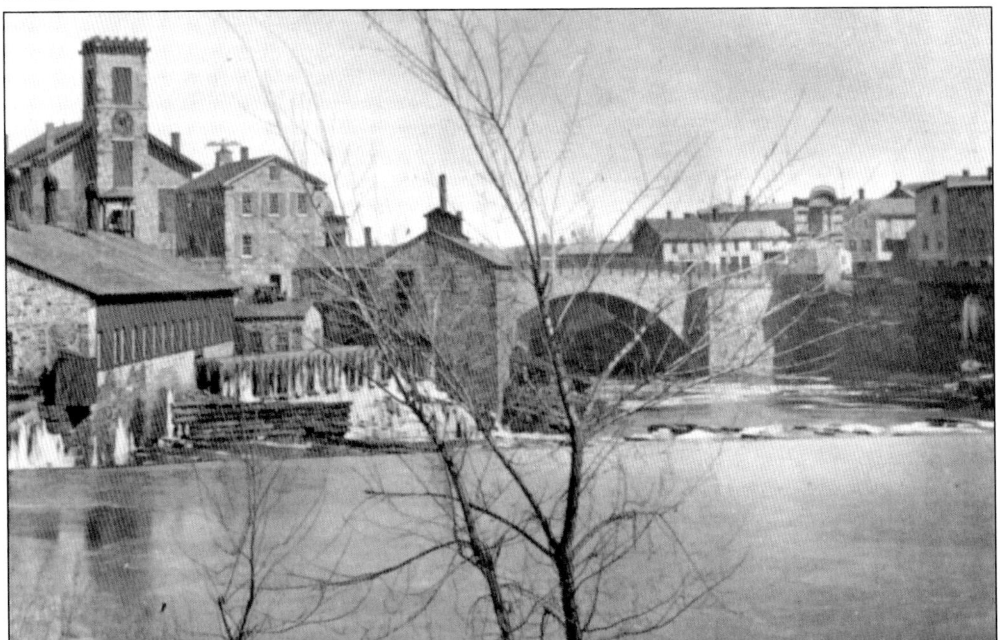

In this pre-1882 photograph, the Congregational Presbyterian church can be seen towering in the background, and the horse nail factory is in the foreground beside the river. In the early 1800s, discussions were carried on between the townships of Ausable and Chesterfield to permanently connect the two across the river. While iron and timber were plentiful, the village elders wanted something more durable to withstand the constant threat of fire as well as the ravages of winter storms, so stone was chosen. In the end, this was a good choice, as it has lasted for well over 100 years.

Bibliography

Brelia, Elizabeth, ed. *Church of the Immaculate Conception Sesquicentennial Issue*. Keeseville, NY: Church of the Immaculate Conception, 1985.

Chamberlin, William P. and Steven Engelhart, eds. *Historic Bridges of Keeseville*. Keeseville, NY: Adirondack Litho, Inc., 1987.

Engelhart, Steven. *Crossing the River: Historic Bridges of the Ausable River.* Keeseville, NY: Adirondack Litho, Inc., 1991.

Meyers, Jeff. *North Country Century*. Plattsburgh, NY: Press-Republican, 1999.

Page, Kyle. "The Peanut Railroad." *North Country Living Magazine* Vol. 3 No. 2 (Summer 2014): 26–28.

Pollard, Dr. Gordon. "Clintonville Iron Industry Chronology & Summary." 2009. Original document on file at the Anderson Falls Heritage Society Museum.

———. "G.W. Baldwin Stereoviews of the Peru Steel & Iron Company Ironworks, Clintonville, New York, 1876." 2009. Original document on file at the Anderson Falls Heritage Society Museum.

Porter, Marjorie Lansing. "History of Keeseville." *The Essex County Republican* (March 31, 1950–April 27, 1951).

Smith, H.P., ed. *History of Essex County*. Syracuse, NY: D. Mason & Co. Publishers, 1885.

Westbrook, Virginia. *A Thoroughly Wide Awake Little Village: A Walking Guide to Keeseville's Historic District*. Burlington, VT: Queen City Printers, 1996.